Women's Work

# Women's Work

## Nationalism and Contemporary African American Women's Novels

COURTNEY THORSSON

University of Virginia Press

CHARLOTTESVILLE AND LONDON

University of Virginia Press

*First published 2013*

9  8  7  6  5  4  3  2  1

LIBRARY OF CONGRESS CATALOGING-IN-PUBLICATION DATA

Thorsson, Courtney, 1978–
 Women's work : nationalism and contemporary African American women's novels /
Courtney Thorsson.
    pages cm
 Includes bibliographical references and index.
 ISBN 978-0-8139-3447-1 (cloth : alk. paper)
 ISBN 978-0-8139-3448-8 (pbk. : alk. paper)
 ISBN 978-0-8139-3449-5 (e-book)
 1. American fiction—African American authors—History and criticism. 2. American
fiction—Women authors—History and criticism. 3. African American women in
literature. 4. National characteristics, American, in literature. 5. African American
women—Employment—In literature. I. Title.
PS374.N4T49 2013
813.009'896073—dc21

                                                                        2012050637

A book in the American Literatures Initiative (ALI), a collaborative
publishing project of NYU Press, Fordham University Press, Rutgers
University Press, Temple University Press, and the University of Virginia
Press. The Initiative is supported by The Andrew W. Mellon Foundation.
For more information, please visit www.americanliteratures.org.

# Contents

# Acknowledgments

I am grateful for the financial, intellectual, and personal support I have had while researching and writing *Women's Work*. At Columbia University, a Marjorie Hope Nicolson Fellowship, William T. Golden Fellowship, and additional support from the English Department launched this project in its earliest stages under the guidance of Farah Jasmine Griffin, Robert G. O'Meally, Brent Hayes Edwards, and Marcellus Blount. Thank you to Marcellus for always keeping me close to the text, to Bob for helping me remember to delight in scholarship and teaching, and to Brent for unfailing intellectual generosity and for always asking productive and thorny questions. Farah, I could not ask for a better mentor; you show me year after year the kind of scholar, writer, and teacher I want to be.

A postdoctoral fellowship in African American literature at Rutgers University provided financial support and intellectual community. Thank you Cheryl Wall, Evie Shockley, Stéphane Robolin, and Carter Mathes for your comments on my work and for inspiring me with yours.

I have been fortunate to find support for my research and a wonderful group of colleagues at the University of Oregon. I am grateful to Lara Bovilsky, Karen Ford, Paul Peppis, David Vázquez, and Harry Wonham for guidance in the final stages of this book; to Mark Whalan for sincere and insightful engagement with my scholarship; and to David Bradley, Allison Carruth, Shari Huhndorf, and Carol Stabile for helping me find my footing, personally and intellectually, in Oregon. Support from the Center for the Study of Women in Society, the English Department, the

Oregon Humanities Center, and the College of Arts and Sciences made the completion and publication of *Women's Work* possible.

Thank you to Cathie Brettschneider, Raennah Mitchell, and Ellen Satrom at the University of Virginia Press for dedicated labor to bring *Women's Work* to print. I am grateful to Tim Roberts at the American Literatures Initiative, Judith Hoover for her careful eye in copyediting this work, and Marilyn Bliss for the index.

Like all scholars, I depend on the generosity and insight of librarians. This project relied on librarians at Columbia's Butler Library; University of Oregon's Knight Library; Emory University's Manuscript, Archives, and Rare Book Library; the Schomburg Center for Research in Black Culture; the Women's Research and Resource Center at Spelman College; and Jim Hatch and Camille Billops, who welcomed me into their home in New York and guided me to archival treasures that have enriched this project and my thinking about African American literature.

Portions of this work have benefited from readers and listeners along the way at Columbia, the City University of New York, Louisiana State University, Pennsylvania State University, the Modern Language Association, and *Callaloo,* where a version of chapter 3, "Dancing Up a Nation: Paule Marshall's Praisesong for the Widow," appeared in 2007. I am grateful to those who have carefully read and responded to my work, including Casey Shoop, Monica Miller, Alvan Ikoku, members of the African Americanist Colloquium at Columbia, and the two insightful readers for the University of Virginia Press. A special thanks goes to Eric Lott, who not only helped me improve this manuscript but also believed I was a scholar long before I did.

Thank you to Jenn Nagai and Duncan Haberly for entertaining years of conversation about this work with no other motivation than love for me. Thanks to Hannah Corbett for letting out a whoop of joy when she realized I was writing about women authors. Thanks to Thora Colot, whose love and encouragement buoy me again and again, and to my mom, Christine Rothman, who inspired much of this book and delights with her whole heart in even my smallest accomplishments.

Emily Lordi and Matt Sandler, I could not ask for better friends, co-conspirators, and partners in intellectual inquiry. Emily, you are a brilliant, patient, and inspiring friend who always makes time not only for reading my writing but also for winding conversations about the big questions of our field, our work, and our lives. Matt, you have put in countless hours making my work and me better. I feel wildly lucky to have a best friend who is also the best reader and thinker I know.

Like everything I do, this book would not be possible without the adventurous, hilarious, ambitious, and kind Peter Colot Thorsson. Peter, your ability to make me laugh and have more fun every single day is amazing. No words could quite express how grateful I am for twenty years of you loving, challenging, and supporting me. Thanks for helping me find my way to this and all my woman's work.

# Introduction

In the last two decades of the twentieth century, Toni Cade Bambara, Paule Marshall, Gloria Naylor, and Ntozake Shange wrote novels that reclaim and revise African American cultural nationalism. Building on and departing from the black arts movement (BAM) of the 1960s and 1970s, their literary fiction defines cultural nationalism as women's work, simultaneously ordinary and extraordinary, in diverse geographical spaces. In decades when literary scholars look increasingly away from the construct of nation, these writers adopt the term *cultural nationalist* to describe themselves and *nation* to hail African America. They employ a practiced cultural nationalism that defines a distinct literary movement in contemporary novels, demanding that scholars address the continued relevance of nation in post–black arts writing. This strand of African American fiction uses scenes of organizing, cooking, dancing, mapping, and inscribing to create a distinct nationalist discourse. A textual-social struggle to envision alternative communities appears in a group of works published in the 1980s and 1990s but depends on long and contested histories of both women's work and African American literature. Although I consider historical context, *Women's Work* focuses primarily on this second category, on the aesthetic history of African American writing that informs and enables the nationalism in these women's novels.

The phrase *women's work* evokes a tangle of associations. It has the pejorative connotation of domestic tasks left to wives whose husbands work in the public sphere. White feminists of the 1960s and 1970s rejected this housewifely role, but the matter was more complicated for African American women, whose long-standing participation in the workforce often prevented them from tending to their own hearths. African American women have a layered history of work as slaves, mothers, wives, clubwomen, teachers, organizers, agricultural and domestic laborers, politicians, and in countless other roles. A feminist shift in the meaning of *women's work* may have signaled the entry of white women into the public sphere in new ways, but African American women had always been there. For these workers, domestic labor had pressed against boundaries between private and public for over two hundred years. Work in white homes stretches well beyond slavery, through post-Emancipation decades, into the 1940s, when women lined "street-corner markets in New York and other large cities—modern versions of slavery's auction block—inviting white women to take their pick from the crowds of Black women seeking work," and continues "as late as 1960 [when] at least one-third of Black women workers remained chained to the same old household jobs" (Davis 90–98).

African American women's work is not always so troubling. Church involvement, community activism, and political organizing are traditional forms of African American women's labor. This role in the community has roots in slavery, as Jacqueline Jones notes: "Beginning in the slave era, the family obligations of wives and mothers overlapped in the area of community welfare, as their desire to nurture their own kin expanded out of the private realm and into public activities that advanced the interests of black people as a group" (3). The public aspect of African American women's work engages both oppression and liberation. Childbearing, for example, has been shaped by slave owners monitoring the growth of their holdings, demands of balancing home and wage-earning work, restricted reproductive rights and forced sterilization, and black power activists calling for women to give birth to the next generation of revolutionaries. On the other hand, women have found community, solidarity, nurturance, and political efficacy working in collectives, from the National Association for the Advancement of Colored People (NAACP) to Marcus Garvey's back-to-Africa movement, the Congress of Racial Equality (CORE), the Student Nonviolent Coordinating Committee (SNCC), and the Black Panther Party (BPP). Work in these collectives, however, yielded some undesirable fruits. While men were often visible leaders, women performed much of the less glamorous work, from publicizing protests and feeding crowds on a march to saving pennies to donate to Garvey's Black Star Line and selling *Panther* newspapers.[1]

Recent historical scholarship sheds light on Anna Julia Cooper's writings; Mary Church Terrell's and Ida B. Wells's public speaking and antilynching campaigns; Septima Clark's, Ruby Doris-Smith Robinson's, and Ella Baker's crucial roles in the NAACP and SNCC; and Fannie Lou Hamer's efforts to register and educate African American voters.[2] Angela Davis places these labors on a historical continuum from the antebellum era to the present: "Proportionately, more Black women have always worked outside the homes than have their white sisters. The enormous space that work occupies in Black women's lives today follows a pattern established during the very earliest days of slavery. . . . It would seem, therefore, that the starting point for any exploration of Black women's lives under slavery would be an appraisal of their role as workers" (5). This "role as workers" remains as important for the study of African American women in contemporary literature as it is, following Davis, for the historical study of lives under slavery. The "enormous space that work occupies in Black women's lives" comes in for close scrutiny and redefinition in novels of the 1980s and 1990s.

*Women's Work* reveals the ways contemporary African American women's novels enter this conversation, using fiction to theorize the public and private work of ordinary women. The relationship between individual and communal identities is a defining theme of African American literature, from Phillis Wheatley voicing a simultaneously African and American identity in verse at the dawn of the U.S. nation-state and Frederick Douglass asking "What, to the Slave, is the Fourth of July?" in the antebellum era to Zora Neale Hurston, Langston Hughes, Richard Wright, Hoyt Fuller, and Larry Neal each insisting across the twentieth century that African American literature is a distinct genre that requires its own writers, readers, editors, and scholars. *Women's Work* is not a cultural history of late twentieth-century African American nationalism but rather a literary study that asks how Bambara's *The Salt Eaters* (1980), Shange's *Sassafrass, Cypress & Indigo* (1982), Marshall's *Praisesong for the Widow* (1983), Naylor's *Mama Day* (1988), and Morrison's *Paradise* (1997) use cultural nationalism in representing the collective identity that shapes much African American literature. I hew to nation, as opposed to collective or community, to describe these novels because that word appears again and again in the works of black women writers. I use cultural nationalism to both articulate an African American nation that is distinct from the nation-state and to place these authors in a literary tradition that includes Wheatley, David Walker, Douglass, Martin Delany, Hurston, and Wright, as well black arts writers.

Bambara, Marshall, Naylor, Shange, and Morrison are all acutely aware of their role as theorists of identity in this literary tradition. These authors study and teach African American literature at colleges and universities; Bambara, Morrison, Naylor, and Shange hold graduate degrees in English or American studies. Their political actions are rooted in literature and the academy. Toni Cade Bambara founded the Search for Education, Elevation, and Knowledge (SEEK) Program to recruit African American and Latino students to New York's City College in the 1960s and served as a faculty mentor to students whose protests led to the rise of black studies. Her work as an editor of *The Black Woman* (1970) and *Tales and Stories for Black Folk* (1971) brought new voices into print.[3] Ntozake Shange asserts that politics ought not be left to politicians and says, "When you take something you believe in and make it affect other people, you're doing a politically significant act" (Blackwell 137). Shange views her literary efforts as politically significant acts, particularly in giving voice to women of color on the page and stage. From her U.S. State Department tour with Langston Hughes in 1965 to currently organizing annual readings by writers of African descent at New York University, Paule Marshall's efforts have brought literatures of the African diaspora to the public. Work with artists organizing for political action characterizes Marshall's career, especially in the 1960s with the Harlem Writers' Guild, the journal *Freedomways*, and the Association of Artists for Freedom.[4] Gloria Naylor is ambivalent about being called a political writer but consistently describes herself as a cultural nationalist who believes "that the Civil Rights Movement did not work" (Ashford 74). Toni Morrison's twenty years as an editor at Random House and her continued visibility as a public intellectual make her an undeniable force on the world literary stage. Morrison's editorial efforts brought Bambara's posthumous novel *Those Bones Are Not My Child* (1995) into print and nurtured two editions of *The Black Book* (1974, 2009), a collection of African American cultural production that she imagined as a kind of family scrapbook. In other words, each of these authors chooses textual work as, in Bambara's words, "a perfectly legitimate way to participate in struggle" (Guy-Sheftall 232).[5]

All of this means two things for the methodology of *Women's Work*: first, these novelists are serious literary scholars and must be treated as such; second, this engagement must happen in their chosen territory of text. In the following chapters, I examine fiction by the authors of the cultural nationalist revision. Closely reading their novels, interviews, and essays, I also engage these authors as literary critics and theorists.

## Novels and Nation

The activism of these authors varies in form and degree; what unites them is their use of the novel in that activism. Though they all write in a number of genres, they each turn to the novel to narrate nation. This turn to fiction represents a significant break with the black arts movement, which privileged poetry and drama as vehicles for nationalist ideology.[6] This shift in genre implicitly critiques the black arts movement, particularly as, throughout the 1980s and 1990s, these authors demonstrate that the novel can do new and nationalist work. They approach the genre in distinct ways: these women authors eschew the individual progress narrative of the *Bildungsroman* and its descendants in favor of nonlinear time and polyvocality; they turn away from the realism of Richard Wright and Ann Petry, engaging instead with the fantastic and conjure of Zora Neale Hurston; they seize on a tradition of formal innovation in African American narrative visible in works by Jean Toomer and Richard Bruce Nugent. They inherit the critique of "masculinist ideologies" deployed in the novels of James Baldwin, Clarence Major, and John Oliver Killens (R. Murray 117). They reject the notion that to be political, literature must be realist and polemic.

The texts I consider here mine a rich African American novelistic tradition but bring to bear the diversity of genre so crucial to African American anthologies from the Harlem Renaissance through Bambara's *The Black Woman*. On the page, this means that the images, recipes, poems, letters, find their way into narrative. Bambara collects the story of John Henry into *The Salt Eaters*, Shange peppers *Sassafrass, Cypress & Indigo* with recipes, Marshall incorporates the poetry of Langston Hughes into *Praisesong for the Widow*, and Naylor opens *Mama Day* with images. The collective and collecting mode of the anthology makes this possible. The multigeneric mode of *The Black Woman* translates to polyvocality, shifting focalization, and formal experimentation in the novels considered here.[7]

These authors make use of possibilities distinct to the novel form as a long narrative read in isolation. Ralph Ellison writes that a "magic thing occurs between the world of the novel and the reader—indeed, between reader and reader in their mutual solitude—which we know as communion" ("Society" 700). The texts I examine each demand such sustained individual work in and beyond the page. Ellison describes the reader as "a most necessary collaborator who must participate in bringing the fiction to life" (701). This readerly labor to work through the text and make use of it in the world is a challenge of the form. Rather than postmodern fragmentation, pastiche, or disjunctive collage, the combination of recipes, images, narrative, and interpolated tales in these novels coalesce to call for community. To read the folktales of both John Henry laying railroad track and Kwan Cheong building a train tunnel in Bambara's *The Salt Eaters*, for example, invites the reader to see the efficacy of cross-ethnic alliances, while Shange's recipes make the reader value diasporic connections and matrilineage by insisting she search for southern and African foodstuffs as well as a mother's handkerchief.

Morrison claims narration as the most effective genre for making these demands, particularly in getting readers to rethink race: "Narration requires the active complicity of a reader willing to step outside established boundaries. And, unlike visual media, narrative has no pictures to ease the difficulty of that step" ("Home" 8–9). Morrison indicates that the depth, breadth, and textuality of novels (as opposed to staged plays, which offer visual components, and poetry, which readers rarely engage for the length of time they give to a novel) make them adept at interrogating "established boundaries" among spaces and identities.

Morrison, Shange, Naylor, Marshall, and Bambara build on the novel's long history of defining nation. Franco Moretti asserts in *Atlas of the European Novel 1800–1900* that nineteenth-century novels were crucial instruments for creating and sustaining the modern nation-state; the genre works alongside the map, census, and museum to codify the nation, as described by Benedict Anderson in *Imagined Communities*. I follow Anderson's definition of nation as an "imagined political community" that is "imagined as both inherently limited and sovereign," as "territorial and social space" (2, 6). While Anderson illuminates the power of imagination in creating culture, I am also interested in the parts of the nation that he does not explore. Avey's nation in Marshall's *Praisesong for the Widow* and Shange's nation in the culinary practices of *Sassafras, Cypress & Indigo* depend not on the print culture and nation-state institutions of Anderson's reading but on the vernacular, embodied practices of dancing and cooking, respectively. The capacious, practiced cultural nation in these novels is thus distinct from the documents and institutions that define a nation-state. Even so, we can see these practices of black cultural nationalism because they appear as text.

Building on Anderson's reading of Jane Austen, Moretti examines the importance of nineteenth-century European novels in creating and defining space, particularly as delineated by national boundaries. He writes, "The nation-state . . . found the novel. And vice versa: the novel found the nation-state. And being the only symbolic form that could represent it, it became an essential component of our modern culture" (17). Moretti argues that the novel functioned as *the* expressive form that could make sense of the nation-state. The novel articulates the nation-state as a group identity, a communal experience of shared cultural and spatial geography. Ellison too claims that the novel is bound up with nationhood, particularly in the United States: "If the novel had not existed at the time the United States started becoming conscious of itself as a nation . . . it would have been necessary for Americans to invent it" as a vehicle for negotiating "class lines so fluid and change so swift and continuous and *intentional*" ("Society" 705). Morrison adds that the African and African American narrative tradition are definitional for the novel, both for its role in nation building (Moretti) and its uses of American Exceptionalism (Ellison). Ellison writes that "one of the enduring functions of the American novel" is "defining the national type as it evolves in the turbulence of change . . . thus, it is bound up with our problem of nationhood" (707–8). In the novels I consider, this claim holds, but the "turbulence of change" becomes a defining feature of black cultural nationhood.[8]

Bambara's vision of a changed future depends on this indeterminacy. Rather than naming a single positive outcome, *The Salt Eaters* holds many possible outcomes in suspension. Bambara redefines nation as a varied, practiced, multifocal entity. The novels of the cultural nationalist revision distribute the power of a collective hailed by "nation." First among these locations for Bambara is the "inner nation" as constitutive of the "outer nation." With each character in *The Salt Eaters* containing his or her own inner nation, it is impossible to settle on a single outcome; each inner nation will be radicalized and in turn reshape an African American cultural nation.

In the space of a nation apart from the nation-state, these texts seize on African American women's work as rich terrain for literary negotiations of raced, gendered, individual, and communal identities. This women's work is both public and private, equally concerned with individual and collective identity, variously incorporates or rejects biological reproduction, and, most important for my purposes, practices a contemporary cultural nationalism.

## Revising and Revitalizing Cultural Nationalism

Cultural nationalism is the belief that people of African descent in the United States constitute a unique and separate culture or, as Ron

Karenga puts it, "Black people in this country make up a cultural nation" (qtd. in Dubey, *Black Women* 14). Amiri Baraka's 1962 essay "'Black' Is a Country" defines cultural nationalism as "the militant espousal of the doctrine of serving one's own people's interests before those of a foreign country, *e.g.* the United States," as part of a "struggle for *independence*" on the part of "the black man" (84). Larry Neal's concluding essay in *Black Fire* (1968) asserts that "the idea that black people are a nation—a separate nation apart from white America"— has existed at least since the late nineteenth century (642). Though the contours of a "cultural nation" vary in each of these visions, they share the emphasis on militancy, racial separatism, manhood, and strained relations with white Americans emblematic of a black nationalist discourse prominent in the 1960s and 1970s and practiced in literature by black arts writers.[9]

Bambara, Marshall, Naylor, Shange, and Morrison define cultural nationalism as a cluster of practices that exceed the brief time period and limited geography of black nationalist movements of the 1960s and 1970s. Their depictions of women's work revisit, revise, and revitalize black cultural nationalism. In their novels, five forms of women's work—organizing, cooking, dancing, mapping, and inscribing—constantly produce a mutable cultural nation. The novels of this literary moment share an underlying assumption that cooking and dancing are far more intellectual and abstract labors than readers might expect, while organizing, mapping, and inscribing are daily practices. For Bambara, organizing happens on the page, in the streets, and in women's bodies. Organizing is direct political action but also gathering women's stories and building one's inner nation. Dancing theorizes African American identity against a diasporic background in Marshall's *Praisesong for the Widow*, and Naylor's title character maps a portable homeland every time she strolls into the graveyard in *Mama Day*. *Women's Work* elevates the seemingly mundane and regularizes the apparently lofty to identify a strand of contemporary African American women's writing concerned with practices of nationalism.

Reading these novels in terms of five forms of women's work disrupts the oral-written binary that has shaped the study of African American literature. Oral and vernacular traditions, especially music, are central to the form and content of African American literature.[10] Working from that assumption rather than seeking to prove it, I offer tools for reading African American literature from its beginnings. Assuming the interdependence and simultaneity of oral and written traditions is useful for reading a number of texts. I am thinking here of Charles Chesnutt's conjure tales, wherein the reader overhears Uncle Julius's spoken tales, reads Chesnutt's ironic portrait of Julius's white listeners, and absorbs the implied critique of Joel Chandler Harris's Uncle Remus tales. Martin Delany's *Blake* (1859–62) also depends on the heard, overheard, and imagined in a way that requires both oral transmission (which imparts the power of conjure to Henry Blake and circulates stories of him as hero) and written transmission (Delany and his protagonist Blake persuade partly through dexterity with the written word and facility with Scripture). We might think too of Zora Neale Hurston's participant-observer position in *Mules and Men* (1935), Jean Toomer's gently critical portrayal of a man imagining the inner of life of a prostitute rather than engaging her in conversation in "Avey" (1923), or Bambara's melding of modes of knowledge from physics to tarot in *The Salt Eaters*. My goal is neither to argue for the validity of oral over written texts, or vice versa, nor to make a case for the presence of vernacular traditions as a measure of a text's authenticity.[11] Rather, I choose organizing, cooking, mapping, dancing, and inscribing to describe women's work partly because these terms do not define that work as strictly oral or written. This cluster of practices draws attention to their differences and interactions. It also allows us to read the work of writing novels in conversation with the fictional women's work in the novels. For example, Morrison's inscription *of Paradise* and fictional acts of inscription *in Paradise* interact in suggestive and dynamic ways. This study pursues the form and content of polyvocal storytelling produced by a variety of women's work. Organizing, cooking, dancing, mapping, and inscribing are useful lenses for looking at the way women's work, including writing novels, constructs individual and communal history.

This cluster of authors writes self-consciously in dialogue with the black arts movement, a group of largely male authors in northern cities in the 1960s and 1970s producing poems and plays for a relatively small audience. It is not entirely surprising that their feminist critique of BAM met some resistance. Literary criticism about African American women's writings published in the 1980s and 1990s deals with the backlash from African American men who objected to the ways men are portrayed in these works. This controversy took shape in the 1970s and 1980s around Shange's *for colored girls who have considered suicide / when the rainbow is enuf* (1975) and Alice Walker's *The Color Purple* (1982).[12] Both Shange's staged play and the movie adaptation of Walker's novel faced protests by African American men.[13] Such critiques did not end in 1980, nor did they exclude Morrison from their venom. Stanley Crouch called *Beloved*

(1987) "protest pulp fiction" meant to "placate sentimental feminist ideology," and the novelist Charles Johnson commented on Morrison's 1993 Nobel Prize by calling her fiction "often offensive, harsh," especially when it came to black men.[14] Freed by the work of feminist scholars such as Deborah McDowell, Cheryl Wall, Barbara Christian, Michael Awkward, and Farah Griffin, I do not have to restage debates here about portrayals of men. Increased attention to novels by African American men, from the inclusion of Colson Whitehead's *John Henry Days* (2001) in the second edition of the *Norton Anthology of African American Literature* (2003) to proliferating scholarship on James Baldwin, also diffuses some of the pressure that gave rise to critiques that, like Ishmael Reed's cutting and insightful satire *Reckless Eyeballing* (1986), carry the scent of sour grapes and overstate the success of African American women novelists in the literary marketplace.[15]

As readers can see now, twenty years on from these debates, literary fiction by contemporary African American women authors not only critiques but also expands the work and territory of the black arts project. As Shange puts it, "I'm the daughter of the black arts movement (even though they didn't know they were going to have a girl!)" (Shange et al., "Artists' Dialogue" 159). This study reconsiders the gender, genre, and geography of African American nationalism, taking Shange's comic disruption seriously and considering literary moves enabled by the black arts movement. The practice of cultural nationalism in this constellation of works is no longer primarily the work of men, appears in novels rather than plays and poems, and claims an expansive literal and figurative geography as its homeland.[16]

In terms of geography, these authors create home, community, and nation without imagining Africa as a monolithic homeland. In his 1925 poem "Heritage," Countee Cullen asked, "What is Africa to Me?"[17] African American authors spent much of the twentieth century offering an astounding variety of answers to this question. My chosen authors offer a version of cultural nationalism that treats Africa as one among many geographical touchstones of African American identity, along with the Sea Islands, the Caribbean, the American South, the kitchen, and the dance floor as spaces that help define collectivity. A troubled relationship rather than direct access to places in and cultures of the African diaspora constitutes a distinctly African American identity practiced in these novels. Rather than locating identity exclusively in geography, I examine how daily, local labor informed by many routes of identification constantly produces an African American nation. *Women's Work* insists that the diasporic is crucial to reading the local but takes the local as its terrain.

The geography of the cultural nation here is not a single land base but a radically imagined alternative space. I use *radical imagination* as defined by Robin Kelley in *Freedom Dreams*: "a collective imagination engaged in actual movement for liberation" (150). Radical imagination is a willingness to dream of and work toward a future of freedom from economic, racial, and gender oppression. For Kelley, imagination becomes radical when it combines the abstract work of dreaming with the concrete work of making a "new world" (2–3). Kelley writes that "progressive social movements," like "great poetry," "transport us to another place, compel us to relive horrors and, more importantly, enable us to imagine a new society" (9). This pairing of theory and practice, of imagining and making a "new society," is at the heart of women's work in the novels I study here. These novels take a future-oriented stance, using radical imagination "to see the future in the present" (9).

"The impulse for territory," Kelley writes, "is not just a matter of land; it is a matter of finding free space" (126). This search for literal and metaphorical territory is definitional for black nationalism. Bambara's *The Salt Eaters* develops a "free space" within Claybourne, Georgia. In the final pages of that novel, Velma Henry comes to see landlessness as a condition of possibility, dispossession as a kind of free space in itself: "Dispossessed, landless, this and that-less and free, therefore, to go anywhere and say anything and be everything if only we'd only know it once and for all" (265). Claybourne, tied to both spiritual and material worlds, is, like Velma, unmoored in ways that invite anything and everything, welcoming radically alternative possibilities for community.

The shared quantity in these works is thus not necessarily a continent, country, or region but rather the faith that something *is* shared. These novels imagine forms of belonging that reenvision spaces and places of community. This may be a defining feature of diaspora. Robin Cohen, in his study of Jewish, African, Palestinian, and Armenian diasporas, asserts that "adherence to a diasporic community is demonstrated by an acceptance of an inescapable link with their past migration history and a sense of co-ethnicity with others of a similar background" (ix). The authors I examine seize on this "inescapable link" as grounds for a nation of placeless people that have cohered into what Cohen calls "nation-peoples" (ix). Though the relationship to a physical homeland differs in each of the diasporas he studies, they share a sense of displacement as affective grounds for collectivity. Rather than focusing exclusively on the trauma and displacement so important in Cohen's analysis, novelists of the cultural nationalist revision draw on connections among African Americans forged by shared history, forced and voluntary migration, and cultural practices to transform the literal geography of nation into a social geography of nation-peoples.[18]

This nation of affect, of shared longing and radical imagining, is particularly African American in the novels of the cultural nationalist revision. Steven Hahn describes a tradition dating from the antebellum period of African Americans striving for "self-governance" both within and against the United States (5). The work of African American activists in the rural South before and after Emancipation defines both the United States and an African American nation apart. Hahn writes, "Their politics and political struggles . . . went into the making of two nations, deeply interconnected and stunningly distinct" (9). From slave insubordination and rebellion to service in the Union Army, participation in Reconstruction politics, and emigration movements in the nineteenth and twentieth centuries, African Americans constantly sought to both redefine Americanness and find power in racial separation, often by organizing politically and building on kinship networks. The United States failed again and again to become a place of justice and equal opportunity. The struggle for a more successful and inclusive American nation persists beyond the scope of Hahn's study and appears in the pages of contemporary African American novels.

The novels at hand utilize a practice of community in which geographical place, alongside shared experience, is one of many factors that define the group. In his essay "Some Questions and Some Answers," Ellison writes, "American Negro culture . . . is not a culture which binds the peoples who are of partially African origin now scattered throughout the world, but an identity of passions. We share a hatred for the alienation forced upon us by Europeans during the process of colonization and empire and we are bound by our common suffering more than by our pigmentation. But even this identification is shared by most non-white peoples, and while it has political value of great potency, its cultural value is almost nil" (263–64). Affect and experience rather than genealogy or geography bind people together. For Ellison, "common suffering" rather than "pigmentation" is the tie that binds.

Ellison locates an alternative nation of affect and experience within the United States. This affect is one of both suffering and longing but also of validation, celebration, and "political value of great potency." Ellison's mode of nationalism marks a shift from "race" to "nation" in mid-twentieth-century black writing: "The use of the term 'nation' by black writers during this period signaled a kind of self-invention and communal imagination that differed from older uses of 'race' and pressed a claim to political sovereignty for blacks in the United States similar to that of colonial subjects throughout the world" (Singh 50). In other words, although the cultural nation was specifically African American, it also depended on a sense of affinity with other colonized peoples around the world. This affinity is possible because *nation* has come to signify shared experience and affect.[19] This radically imagined, politically potent, affective collective is the cultural nation at work in the novels I examine here. Unlike Ellison, contemporary women novelists assign cultural, as well as political, value to this nation grounded in shared experience and affect.

All of the novelists under consideration, while testing the usefulness of the United States as a site of identification, cling to *nation* as a viable term for naming community. As these texts reveal, African American nationalism is more mutable than a narrow look at activism in the 1960s and 1970s suggests. Wahneema Lubiano describes the possibilities and dangers of a nationalist stance in her essay "Black Nationalism and Black Common Sense": "Black nationalism is plural, flexible, and contested. . . . Its most hegemonic appearances and manifestations have been masculinist and homophobic. . . . Its circulation has acted as both a bulwark against racism and as disciplinary activity within the group. I see it as extremely complicated, often reactionary, and dangerously effective in the way that it can and has organized specific groups of black people, under specific circumstances, to ally themselves with harmful and dangerous activities" (232). Cultural nationalism appears variously in contemporary African American women's fiction, functioning as a "bulwark against racism" in Bambara's *The Salt Eaters* but becoming ever more hegemonic in subsequent novels, culminating in Morrison's *Paradise*, where racial separatism operates as "a disciplinary activity" and motivates the type of "harmful and dangerous" behavior Lubiano describes. Marshall, Naylor, and Shange navigate the almost twenty years between these two novels, testing out in practice the "extremely complicated" possibilities and limits of a nationalist stance. The "plural, flexible, and contested" aspects of African American nationalism were present in varying degrees from David Walker and Martin Delany on. The group of authors I consider here is united by a commitment to privileging this legacy of mutability.

Lubiano's cautionary tone is warranted; the novels of the cultural nationalist revision collectively make certain omissions. Each writes against "masculinist" nationalism but puts very little pressure on a "homophobic" one. Largely as a result of work done by literary scholars like Barbara Smith, African American studies increasingly takes heterosexism and homophobia into account. Same-sex relationships are, however, marginal or nonexistent in the works of this movement. This too is a legacy of the black arts and black power era. Though the authors I consider explicitly take up the way feminist movements have excluded women of color, they are less adept at making room for the queer, lesbian, or gay. Gloria Naylor's "The Two" in *The Women of Brewster Place* (1983) stands out as the only depiction of self-identified lesbians in the novels of this moment, and even that portrayal is troubling.[20]

These are the ongoing pitfalls of a nationalist stance. For the purposes of political efficacy and radical imagining, these texts envision a nation that, even in its struggle to honor diversity within unity, erases some differences. The authors of the cultural nationalist revision attend closely to intertwining issues of race and gender but not always to sexual orientation or economic class. This is, in part, because "black nationalism is predicated on the notion of racial solidarity across class lines" (Lubiano 236). The communities in this constellation of novels are always in process, fraught with tension, and practiced under the threat of dissolution and attack. Partly as a result of its tenuous position, the nationalism of these texts revises the sexual and gender politics of other black nationalist projects but does not always provide adequate examinations of class politics or heterosexism.

## Building on Tradition: Novels and *The Black Woman*

In the 1970s, as Madhu Dubey asserts in *Black Women Novelists and the Nationalist Aesthetic*, African American women novelists resisted the equation of nationalism with masculinity by writing novels that depict diverse and complex African American women's subjectivity. The novels of the cultural nationalist revision in the 1980s and 1990s build on the work of their predecessors by articulating subjectivity always in relationship to a community. We can see this shift by looking at the titles of novels in these decades. The 1970s saw the publication of *The Third Life of Grange Copeland, Sula, Eva's Man, Meridian, Corregidora,* and *Song of Solomon*; each of these titles is marked by a single proper name. Titles of many 1980s and 1990s texts suggest a group or an abstract concern: *Sassafrass, Cypress & Indigo, The Color Purple, The Temple of My Familiar, Jazz, Paradise,* and *The Salt Eaters.* This list is admittedly selective, but it is instructive in illustrating the shift from 1970s narratives that sought to give individual subjectivity its due to later works that attempt to recover and revise the nationalist insistence on collectivity, either of a group of women, as in *Sassafrass, Cypress & Indigo*, or a potentially infinite community, as in *The Salt Eaters*.[21]

As Dubey demonstrates, the 1970s were a period of black female revisions of the *Bildungsroman* in reaction to the black aesthetic adherence to a rigid, homogeneous community that limited or excluded women's subjectivity. Dubey argues that although "black feminine identity is invariably located within a communal frame . . . these novels split the black community along gender lines, thus threatening the unified racial community projected in Black Aesthetic theory" (*Black Women* 23). Dubey illustrates that Alice Walker and Gayl Jones write novels in the 1970s that explicitly "strain a nationalist or feminist reading" (2).[22] Jones's early novels *Corregidora* (1975) and *Eva's Man* (1976) use first-person narrators to get at the inner lives of African American, female protagonists. Although these lives have real implications for the public sphere, the self, rather than its place in a collective, is Jones's primary concern. This interest in writing a black feminine subject means that the polyvocality in novels of the cultural nationalist revision differs from its function in Jones's novels. The multiple voices in *Corregidora* are both contained in Ursa's mind and tied primarily to her evolving understanding of self, while the wide range of subjects in Jones's *Mosquito* (2000) are bound by the single voice and point of view of the compelling eponymous narrator. In the case of *Eva's Man*, as Dubey writes, "Eva's unfiltered, insane, first-person narration serves to lock meaning inside the text, and to diminish the text's power to illuminate the reader's world" (*Black Women* 103). The novels of the cultural nationalist revision, on the other hand, employ shifts in point of view and polyvocality to suggest a capacious view of both individual and community with explicit implications for the world beyond the text. The novels I consider in the following chapters build on African American anthologies, critique black arts movement politics, and expand on the work of their immediate 1970s predecessors, such as Jones.[23]

The final paragraphs of Dubey's *Black Women Novelists* point to *Women's Work*. She concludes, "Black women's fiction in the 1980s is engaged with salvaging the values of community, of the oral heritage, and of the historical past in ways that redefine the black nationalist construction of these terms. . . . This revisionist endeavor is surely enabled by the tense dialogue between black nationalist discourse and black women's fiction in the 1970s" (161). I am, in this sense, picking up where Dubey leaves off by examining a cluster of works that employs the terms of this tense dialogue to reclaim and revise African American cultural nationalism.

Freed by the work of 1970s novels, a group of texts at the end of the twentieth century reclaims the potential of community so crucial to black arts writings but continues to explore and expand diverse female characters in relation to a cultural nation and other communities. These works seek to retain the political efficacy of a unified community in the black power mode but incorporate the multivalent and thick female subjectivity of 1970s women's novels. Bambara, Shange, Marshall, Naylor, and Morrison use fiction in the 1980s and 1990s to build on and depart from both a masculinist "logic of communal belonging" and a focus exclusively on the individual subject.

They do so, in part, by utilizing a dual legacy of black arts literature and African American anthologies. Though the cultural nationalist revision flourishes in novels, anthologies are important earlier testing grounds for similar concerns. Bambara's 1970 *The Black Woman: An Anthology* is a particularly important predecessor of the cultural nationalist revision. In a moment when ideological and physical violence against African Americans demanded new ways of imagining liberation, Bambara responded textually. In the wake of urban uprisings, church bombings, government repression, and assassinations of African American leaders, the gains of the civil rights movement seemed marginal at best. By the late 1960s, African Americans were hard-pressed to feel at home in the United States. Though this had long been the case, the violence of these years created a particular kind of urgency. These events left many African American activists disillusioned, unable to imagine any freedom grounded in U.S. citizenship.[24]

Amid the same frustrations that saw the rise of the black arts movement, the many voices in Bambara's *The Black Woman* signal a mode of politics invested in literature as a tool for liberation in local and global contexts.[25] *The Black Woman* opens with poetry by Nikki Giovanni, Kay Lindsey, and Audre Lorde and fiction by Paule Marshall, Alice Walker, and Shirley Williams (Sherley Anne Williams), privileging literature as a key agent in the struggle of African American women to define themselves and their communities. If the anthology is a chorus, the literary voices are the loudest. The black arts movement took as a central tenet that literature should do work in the world. Larry Neal writes, "Poetry is a concrete function, an action. No more abstractions. Poems are physical entities: fists, daggers, airplane poems, and poems that shoot guns" ("The Black Arts Movement" 275). This sense that literature must be a physical entity made the black arts poets Gwendolyn Brooks and Haki Madhubuti (Don Lee) insist on reading their writings aloud amid crowds in bars and on the streets. This practice, if not the violent assertion of literature as fists and daggers, finds an echo in Vertamae Smart Grosvenor's essay "The Kitchen Crisis" in *The Black Woman*. Grosvenor begins with an author's note: "i do not consider myself a writer, i am a rapper, therefore do not read this piece silently. . . . rap it aloud" (149). Like black arts broadsides, the content of *The Black Woman* is meant to circulate in the world. To this end, Bambara insisted that the first edition fit in one's pocket and cost no more than a dollar. Though writers in *The Black Woman* are definitely not about guns and fists (many are self-declared pacifists), black arts literature and Bambara's anthology share ideological and material functions. In *The Black Aesthetic* (1971), Ron Karenga writes that nationalist art must "reflect and support the Black Revolution," "be functional, collective, and committing," and "expose the enemy, praise the people and support the revolution" ("Black Cultural Nationalism" 33–34). Bambara takes up Karenga's command, though "the enemy" she exposes and the "collective" she articulates do not mirror Karenga's. *The Black Woman* frames the labor of redefining community as a textual-social struggle; to "reflect and support the Black Revolution" is undoubtedly one of its goals. The contours of that revolution include many demands that appear nowhere in *The Black Aesthetic* or Neal and Baraka's *Black Fire* (1968). *The Black Woman* offers the feminist revision of BAM that would become central to black women's novels of the 1980s and 1990s.

For example, *The Black Woman* gathers a number of responses to the disparaging portrayal of black women in Daniel Moynihan's 1965 congressional report, officially titled *The Negro Family: The Case for National Action*. The Moynihan Report claims, "The fundamental problem . . . is that of family structure. . . . The Negro family in urban ghettos is crumbling." Moynihan continues with an attempt to rally citizens in support of his project: "A national effort is required that will give unity of purpose to the many activities of the Federal government in this area, directed to a new kind of national goal: the establishment of a stable Negro family structure" (U.S. Department of Labor 2). In this policy document, the government assumes the paternalistic role of managing the "Negro family," partly by pushing African American men into military service.[26] Women come in for the most brutal treatment in the Moynihan Report, which includes a section titled "One-Fourth of Negro Families Are Headed by Females" (9) and calls single or dominant motherhood evidence of a "breakdown" in family structure that has led to welfare dependence (12). The Moynihan Report uses this "breakdown" to characterize African Americans as un-American: "In essence, the Negro community has been forced into a matriarchal structure which, because it is so out of line with the rest of American society, seriously retards the progress of the group as a whole" (29). The Report casts black women as castrating matriarchs, the sole source of any troubles faced by African Americans. They are to be blamed for poverty, crime, and juvenile delinquency. The only solution, as vaguely proposed in the Report, is a "national effort" described thus: "The policy of the United States is to bring the Negro American to full and equal sharing in the responsibilities and reward of citizenship. To this end, the programs of the federal government bearing on this objective shall be designed to have the effect, directly or indirectly, of enhancing the stability of the Negro family" (48). "Citizenship" in the United States thus becomes dependent on three problematic beliefs: first, nonnuclear families are invalid kinship structures; second, black women are a primary cause of many social ills; and third, government ought to exercise a paternal white authority. African American women have been writing back against this form of citizenship since the Moynihan Report was issued in 1965.[27]

*The Black Woman* wages an ideological battle not just with the Moynihan Report but also with black liberation movements that marginalize women's concerns. Joanna Clark calls for "social security and unemployment insurance for every mother" (86). Fran Sanders points to the complicity of African American men in treating African American women as "castrating matriarchs" (88). Kay Lindsey laments that white feminism and black liberation movements have left African American women "on the outside of both political entities" (103).[28] Frances Beale asserts, "To wage a revolution, we need competent teachers, doctors, nurses, electronics experts, chemists, biologists, physicists, political scientists, and so on and so forth" (114). Contributions to *The Black Woman* are intensely practical and wildly diverse. They define liberation as changes in legislation, adequate health care, political involvement, and access to a variety of satisfying work. These simultaneously practical and theoretical concerns are what Bambara means when she calls the volume an attempt to "get basic with each other" (1), to have a conversation that addresses the daily lives of African American women.

Bambara's preface to *The Black Woman* unifies its authors and readers into a community in terms of race and gender but also in terms of this commitment to "get basic with each other." Every author included in the anthology self-identifies with the gender and race designation of the volume's title. The preface, however, frames the volume as defined "by practice." Bambara calls *The Black Woman* a collective "determination to touch and to unify" asserting, "What typifies the current spirit is an embrace, an embrace of the community and a hardheaded attempt to get basic with each other" (1). The goal of the text is clear: *The Black Woman* works to create self-directed conversation and community. This collective will hold on to the "current spirit" of revolution rather than let the powerful activism of the 1960s wane. This community has a bodily presence shaped by love and affection; Bambara emphasizes a loving, physical community with her terms "embrace" and "touch." Her preface makes little explicit reference to the race of the contributors; instead she promises the volume will "embrace the community," a reference to the inclusion of unpublished writers who come from the tradition of activism that she seeks to bring to the page. She promises dialogue about concerns such as poverty, relationships, health care, and consumer culture in order to "find out what liberation for ourselves means, what work it entails, what benefits it will yield" (1). The unifying project is for a "we" to come together, to collaborate and figure out what "liberation for ourselves means."[29]

Within this unifying project there is startling variety, a less noted legacy of the black arts movement. As Phillip Brian Harper asserts, the challenge of a black nationalist project is to "negotiate division within the black population itself" (239). Harper's readings of black arts poetry demonstrate that Amiri Baraka, Sonia Sanchez, Nikki Giovanni, and Haki Madhubuti take up a negotiation of difference. Though we might be dissatisfied with the ways these authors negotiate gender, their work enables Bambara's *The Black Woman* and a number of novels that enter in its wake. Harper writes, "The response of Black Arts nationalism to social division within the black populace is not to strive to overcome it but rather repeatedly to articulate it in the name of black consciousness" (239). The effort "repeatedly to articulate" difference within unity, to constantly practice community on the page, shapes African American literature during and after the black arts movement.[30]

In editing *The Black Woman*, Bambara uses the literary negotiation of difference she inherits from black arts writers to respond to the same alienation from national belonging that motivates black nationalist leaders from David Walker to Stokely Carmichael. She organizes a vision of an African American nation on the page by radically expanding the definition of black women so constricted in the discourses of both legislation and black power rhetoric. The community of the anthology includes voices that vary in terms of economic class, goals, politics, and writing style. The volume brings together poetry, fiction, and nonfiction and texts authored by both groups and individuals. Clark's call for "social security and unemployment insurance for every mother" sits alongside Audre Lorde's poem "Naturally," which asks what "Black is Beautiful" might mean for African American women and Paule Marshall's short story "Reena," which explores a friendship between two women whose lives have taken very different paths. The writings collectively assert that *the black woman* is a multivalent, shifting, complex term.

*The Black Woman* participates in the work of 1970s novels that struggle against narrow portrayals of women. Dubey argues that Morrison's *Sula* (1973) and Alice Walker's *The Third Life of Grange Copeland* (1970) and *Meridian* (1976) resist rigid depictions of black womanhood as a means of writing against the fixity of identity prevalent in many black nationalist ideologies. In Dubey's view, these novels come close to "escaping meaning" in their efforts to portray "the black woman" as a varied entity (*Black Women* 149). Multivalent identity and many sources of knowledge, in other words, threaten to create narratives so diffuse that they erase African American female subjectivity. *The Black Woman*, against Dubey's formulation, is not a postmodern pastiche that borders on meaninglessness but a chorus of voices both united and diverse. The text anthologizes black women as a collective, but that collective depends on discussion and dissent. Contributors to the volume describe African Americans as Romantics (171), Victorians (179), and militants. They depict Africa as both essential and irrelevant to their politics. Bambara asks if the birth control pill is "genocide or liberation" (203), and other contributors offer a variety of viewpoints on reproductive rights. In addition to poems, stories, and essays, *The Black Woman* offers transcripts of discussions, including "Ebony Minds, Black Voices" (227), "Poor Black Women's Study Papers" (239), and a collective "Historical and Critical Essay for Black Women in the Cities, June 1969" (251). These attempts to record conversation on the page bring the discursive model of 1970s consciousness-raising sessions into *The Black Woman*.[31]

The conversational, diverse, and contested mode of *The Black Woman* revisits conventions of African American anthologies. The collection does not announce the presence of an African American literary tradition, as many anthologies do, nor does it follow the practice of Alain Locke's *New Negro* (1925) in asserting the value of African American artistic productions. Bambara takes these as givens, which means she can instead experiment with the possibilities of the anthology form. Brent Edwards writes that James Weldon Johnson's *Book of American Negro Poetry* (1922) "splits its own binding" (50) and remarks on the "mind-boggling breadth" of Nancy Cunard's 1934 *Negro: An Anthology* (310). *The Black Woman*, in this tradition, practices multiplicity.

Pairing the force of BAM with the diversity of anthologies, *The Black Woman* is a happening as well as a text. Theodore O. Mason writes, "*The Norton Anthology of African American Literature* constitutes both text and event" (186). Just as the first edition of the *Norton* (1997) declares a tradition of African American literature, naming the field as a distinct object of study, Bambara's anthology is a declarative event; it insists that "the black woman" is a self-articulated and diverse category joined in a single text for serious study. Like James Weldon Johnson's creation of the term *Aframerican* in his preface to *The Book of American Negro Poetry*, Bambara's use of the capitalized term *The Black Woman* suggests possibilities for a collective identity.[32] The title promises a coherent collective that can be anthologized, but the singular designation *woman* simultaneously insists on individuality. *The Black Woman* unites its authors and readers under a term of identity that bears no explicit allegiance to a single nation-state or location but insists on race, gender, and text as unifying forces that create a cultural nation. Rather than genre, literary recognition, political stance, or methodology, what collectively characterizes the selections in *The Black Woman* is shared women's work to practice collectivity.

Naming a nation is the task of African American anthologies both before and after *The Black Woman*. This nationalist work inspired many anthologies in the 1960s and 1970s; according to Cheryl Clarke, "from 1965 to 1975 more than one hundred anthologies of Afro-American literature were published" (19). Mason insists, "The concept of the nation, and its discursive expression in the realm of the literary, lies at the heart of any consideration of anthologies of African-American literature and their relation to various canons" (192). At a time when the need to articulate nation was particularly pressing in African American literature, *The Black Woman* enters the fray with its own set of terms for the concept of nation. The gender and genres of Bambara's anthology shift the concept of nation onto female ground and move toward fiction as black nationalist literature.[33]

Bambara's volume finds inspiration not only in earlier anthologies and other literary predecessors but also in tactics of community organizing. As an editor, Bambara practices the same women's work on the page that she does in the world. In both arenas, she labors to make space for women's bodies and experiences. She suggests that her anthology has grown almost organically out of community organizing already going on in the world: "Throughout the country in recent years, Black women have been forming work-study groups, discussion clubs, cooperative nurseries, cooperative businesses, consumer education groups, women's workshops on campuses, women's caucuses within existing organizations, Afro-American women's magazines. . . . Unlike the traditional sororities and business clubs, they seem to use the Black Liberation struggle rather than the American Dream as their yardstick, their gauge, their vantage point" (4). Bambara imagines *The Black Woman* as an instance of this mode of organizing "in recent years" in the United States driven by women and informed by "the Black Liberation struggle." She posits organizing a text as close kin to organizing a work-study group for collaborative learning. As this list suggests, "cooperative" women's labor, from nurseries to magazines and political caucuses, is crucial to the vision of community the anthology promises. Lest we miss the preservation of individuality amid all these unifying gestures, Bambara reminds us, "Oddly enough, it is necessary to point out what should be obvious—Black women are individuals too" (5).

*The Black Woman* insists on dissent and complexity. In this anthology and the novels of the cultural nationalist revision, ambiguity and dissent are generative.[34] Conflict and tension haunt the women's coalescences in the works of Bambara, Marshall, Naylor, Shange, and Morrison.[35] Debate and varied goals both define and threaten African American women's collectives from at least the early nineteenth century (White 85). Self-consciousness about such tension is a distinguishing feature of African American women's organizations, from the Washington, D.C., Colored Women's League in the late nineteenth century to bell hooks's contemporary Sisters of the Yam groups.

At the moment of the anthology, "the black woman writer was a much larger category than it is now [in 1999]" (Rowell and Griffin 887). When *The Black Woman* was published in 1970, the sense of being unmoored that later haunts Velma Henry in *The Salt Eaters* is actually a moment of liberation; unfettered by the ideological constraints of any single dominant national movement for civil rights or women's rights or black nationalism, African American women enjoyed an especially ripe moment for self-articulation. Inhabiting and critiquing multiple ideological stances at once, *The Black Woman* resists what Rolland Murray calls "the entrenched opposition between feminism and nationalism"

(115). The anthology and its descendant texts employ a proliferation of voices to occupy and revise both white feminism and black nationalism. The polyvocality of *The Black Woman* is a scenario of possibility, with many voices and eventual outcomes.

The formal, thematic, and political possibilities that motivate *The Black Woman* enable a group of novels that appear in the last two decades of the twentieth century. Bambara, Shange, Marshall, Naylor, and Morrison take up the anthology's definition of the black woman as a multivalent entity constantly engaged in the production of self and community. The unity of the single anthology models the unity of a cultural nation practiced on the pages of the novels considered in this study. In women's work of organizing, cooking, dancing, mapping, and inscribing, a vision emerges of a cultural nation, of "getting basic" to construct a diverse but unified community constantly made in women's work. Echoing the formal experimentation and polyvocality of *The Black Woman*, the novels I consider distribute power among many characters, maintain difference and tension among members of a community, demand participation, and refuse any pat conclusion. The African American nation organized here is one that will embrace and preserve individuality, ambiguity, and difference as well as collectivity.

Bambara recalls that in her labors as a social worker, filmmaker, and community organizer she "became acquainted with folks who demonstrated that their real work was creating value in the neighborhoods— bookstores, communal gardens, think tanks, arts-and-crafts programs, community-organizer training, photography workshops": "Many of them had what I call second sight—the ability to make reasoned calls to the community to create protective spaces wherein people could theorize a practice toward future sovereignty" ("Deep Sight" 174). Bambara makes use of both Du Bois's "double consciousness" (simultaneous knowledge of self-perception and misperception of self by others) and his "second sight" (access to extrasensory knowledge that, according to folk wisdom, is the gift of seventh sons and babies born with a caul). These two terms from Du Bois's *The Souls of Black Folk* (1903) come together in her definition of second sight as the gift of multiple ways of knowing that must be used to build safe "spaces" that allow people to plan "toward future sovereignty." In other words, sovereignty is the goal, it will take many steps to get there, and multiple ways of knowing and working are necessary to attain that goal.

The multiplicity of voices and forms of expression in Bambara's work defies any rigid or monolithic definition of nationalism in favor of various local practices. "Bookstores, communal gardens, think tanks, arts-and-crafts programs," and so on are just the sort of projects that characters in these novels create. *The Salt Eaters* organizes many sources of knowledge to "create protective spaces" that will provide the ground from which to "theorize" how to get from these fruitful forms of women's work to sovereignty. This local organization "toward future sovereignty" describes exactly the practices of cooking, dancing, mapping, and inscribing in the works of Shange, Marshall, Naylor, and Morrison. Each of these authors answers Bambara's "reasoned calls" with a multiplicity of second sight; each uses local rituals to "create protective spaces wherein people could theorize a practice toward future sovereignty."

African American women novelists writing in the 1980s and 1990s practice the formation of a sovereign homeland in spaces as local as the kitchen and as broad as the planet. Bambara, Marshall, Naylor, Shange, and Morrison take advantage of a moment that demands complex allegiances to feminism, black nationalism, and civil rights. In a feminist revision of earlier black nationalism, these authors portray women who organize, cook, dance, map, and inscribe their alternative nation.

## Women's Work

Bambara's *The Salt Eaters* begins a period of African American literature characterized by its future-oriented emphasis on nationalist politics rooted in local women's work for social change. Chapter 1 of *Women's Work*, "Organizing Her Nation" examines how Bambara, a prolific organizer of protests, community centers, and an anthology, uses formal experimentation to write a cultural nation of voices in chorus in the pages of her 1980 novel *The Salt Eaters*. Her text weaves together multiple time frames to narrate the recovery of an ailing civil rights activist, Velma Henry, as a necessary starting point for suturing together an African American community. Organization, formally on the page and thematically in the story, heals fractured individual and communal bodies. Velma's "inner nation" radiates outward in concentric circles of healing to the residents of Claybourne, Georgia, and beyond.

Chapter 2, "Cooking Up a Nation," studies Shange's demands for readerly action in the recipes of *Sassafrass, Cypress & Indigo* (1982). This novel practices a culinary collectivity, expanding the nationalist possibilities of the novel through uses of the recipe form. Didactic, improvisational, and printed explicitly to inspire repeated performance, recipes echo the black arts movement notion that literature should do work in the world.

Cooking in Shange's novel practices a cultural nationalism that, in Bambara's mode, takes landlessness and radical imagination as foundational. The preparation of food following a recipe is ritual repetition, often with improvisation or difference that may signal an annual family gathering, honor the recipe's author, or pass on the work of nurturing from one generation to the next. This is a practice of cultural nationalism because it relies on specific geographic, racial, and gendered markers; in Shange's novel, Indigo performs recipes that call for "facing the direction of your mother's birthplace" (5), and Sassafrass offers her instructions for a meal "that all Carolina would envy" (174). There is a place, race, and gender to these recipes; practicing them is a performance of an African American cultural nation. This collective has its own ways, its foodways. The recipe in Shange's novel is thus an expressive form for a community in practice.

On the islands of Tatem and Carriacou, Marshall's Avey Johnson performs social and sacred dances. These dances practice a cultural nation dependent on diasporic connections in *Praisesong for the Widow* (1983). Chapter 3, "Dancing Up a Nation," argues that Avey dances to achieve self-expression and wholeness by sifting through individual and collective memory to define her distinct African Americanness against a diasporic background. Avey gets a book-length praisesong because she does the work of traveling, literally and figuratively, toward African American collectivity. When she performs her Juba amid the various "nation dances" of diasporic people on Carriacou, she embodies the distinct position of African American culture in relationship to the diaspora.

Chapter 4, "Mapping and Moving Nation" argues that Naylor's *Mama Day* (1988) maps a portable homeland, born in the South but available to African Americans in any geographical space. With its literal map in the front matter and descriptions of both New York and the island Willow Springs, *Mama Day* posits mapping as a means of defining a cultural home for a nation that is not rooted in a single land base. The novel teaches a spatial practice of reading that incorporates characters and readers into a social map. Naylor's Willow Springs proves fertile island ground for women's work to map a broad and flexible cultural nation.

Chapter 5, "Inscribing Community," examines Morrison's *Paradise* (1997) to reflect on the collectivity practiced in this constellation of novels. In *Paradise* markings of text and image both consolidate and disrupt community. Inscriptions, from a letter penned in smeared lipstick to a hidden genealogy and a series of self-portraits, question the form and content of African American history. Inscription is the act of making

textual and nontextual markings that define identity and mark territory. Inscription does not depend on readers to create layered meaning.
Rather, ambiguity permeates composition. Women inscribe texts in
*Paradise*, but their writings are often obscured, hidden, or erased, composed but not read. Such inscriptions become visible in the two isolated
communities of the novel. Morrison uses inscription to take sovereignty
to its limits, critiquing cultural nationalism and questioning the viability
of practicing community.

These women's works are not synonymous. Different labors produce
community in varied ways. Mapping and inscribing generate text, while
dancing and organizing do not necessarily leave textual traces. Cooking, because it can begin with the text of a recipe but also exists in performance, connects the other forms of women's work. The role of the
body is different in each form of work. Bambara's Velma Henry describes
crouching in a bathroom stall, searching for a tampon on a civil rights
march, giving tangible physicality to her political activism. Dancing and
cooking are necessarily physical, as in Marshall's description of a woman
in her sixties giving her body over to dance and Shange's recipes for rituals to celebrate a girl's first period. When Morrison's women lie on a
basement floor and trace their silhouettes to paint self-portraits, inscription too becomes physical labor. Organizing, the key women's work in
*The Salt Eaters*, is explicitly political, but cooking, mapping, dancing,
and inscribing become more visible as agents of sociopolitical change
when we study these women's works as a group. What unites these varied
forms of work is that they all practice an African American nation.

Alongside organizing, cooking, dancing, mapping, and inscribing,
there are two forms of women's work to fashion self and community that
unite the novels under consideration: mothering and archiving. Both are
practices that, though contested and varied, are necessary to make community in the texts of the cultural nationalist revision. From Shange's
Hilda Effania cooking annual Christmas meals for her daughters to
Naylor's Mama Day, nicknamed for the mothering she does in every
sense other than the biological one, mothers of all sorts appear in these
writings. Portraits of motherhood and maternity appear repeatedly in
the novels under consideration. These works acknowledge motherhood
as one among many generative powers of women. Much useful scholarship exists on motherhood, maternity, reproduction, and matrilineage
in African American women's writings.[36] Morrison's Sula Peace rejects
mothering, most explicitly in the line "I don't want to make somebody
else. I want to make myself" (*Sula* 92). Sula articulates "a specifically

feminine newness that cannot be assimilated into Black Aesthetic ideology" (Dubey, *Black Women* 58). Texts of the 1970s like *Sula* and *Corregidora* worked to uncouple African American female identity from reproduction. Authors of the 1980s and 1990s use this ideological loosening to recast motherhood as one, often not primary form of women's work. Partly because mothering is almost always central to discussions of women's work, I am less interested in it here and more concerned with shedding light on the other generative labors performed by women in these novels. The authors of the cultural nationalist revision use fiction to expand the definition of women's work in ways that often make mothering and reproduction less central to the practice of community.

Women's work of unearthing, creating, and practicing an African American archive appears in all the texts in this study as another practice of cultural nationalism. This archive resonates with Albert Murray's "getting place" and Sterling Brown's "folk storehouse," both sources of didactic, musical, and inspirational stories.[37] Zora Neale Hurston too creates an archive with her record of stories, conjure, and aphorisms in *Mules and Men* (1935) and *Tell My Horse* (1938). Gayl Jones establishes oral history as a counterarchive in *Corregidora* (1975). Each of these texts posits a different model for the African American archive. Hurston preserves an archive in written form. For Murray, music and oral transmission carry the archive. Brown imagines the archive as passed on orally but seeks to examine and describe many contents of the folk storehouse in his scholarly writings. Jones depicts generations of women painfully preserving stories of their racial and sexual oppression in lieu of paper documentation that has been burned. As we will see in chapter 2, the archive in Shange's *Sassafrass, Cypress & Indigo* includes recipes for matrilineage and imagined migration. Though the definition of archive is contested territory, these authors agree that the archive travels over time and space. The African American archive traverses the twentieth century through the texts of Hurston, Brown, Murray, Jones, Marshall, and Shange, changing in form and content with each iteration.

In each of these cases, the archive is portable, transmitted across space and generations. The authors considered here make archiving a practice of recovery, documentation, radical imagination, and performance. The archive in these works is not an institution full of papers available to a researcher. Rather, archives can be a space, like Marshall's Ibo Landing, which stores a slave history; a person, like Shange's Indigo, who repeats with difference the healing work and midwifery done by her immediate and atavistic ancestors; a ledger of recipes, like that in Naylor's *Linden*

*Hills*, which documents women attempting to cook their way out of unhappy marriages; or the map, bill of sale, and family tree that open Naylor's *Mama Day*. Archiving in these novels is not a matter of collecting, cataloguing, or even necessarily remembering but of composing and using the past.

Diana Taylor's *The Archive and the Repertoire* is helpful in clarifying the ways the archive works in novels of the cultural nationalist revision. The archive in these texts is practice and performance. Performance, for Taylor, is "a way of knowing" and an embodied "system of learning, storing, and transmitting knowledge" (xvi, 16). Though they sometimes overlap, Taylor asserts that the archive, a collection of written documents, is distinct from the repertoire, a group of performances often revised and always dependent on context and audience. In the novels I consider, the archive borrows from Taylor's repertoire, making embodied practices of "learning, storing, and transmitting knowledge" part of written texts. The performance of a recipe in Shange or a dance in Marshall joins Morrison's written inscriptions in a coherent but diverse archive. In other words, the archive becomes more dynamic and performative, while the repertoire gains the weight and authority of the archive. Taylor asserts, "The repertoire requires presence: people participate in the production and reproduction of knowledge by 'being there,' being part of the transmission" (20). The texts of the cultural nationalist revision bring this dynamic to the archive by representing it as one among many forms of women's work that "requires presence."

Brent Edwards's *The Practice of Diaspora* is crucial to my thinking about how abstract concepts like archive, identity, nation, and diaspora can be practiced. Edwards describes a flexible and multifocal diaspora of people of African descent. Rather than exclusively a function of location, for Edwards diaspora is a function of routes of identification. He uses anthologies, novels, and journals of the interwar period to argue for the possibility of "difference within unity," illustrated by the "articulation" of a joint that requires both connection and break (11). He suspends difference and unity, offering many specific models of texts produced in the connected but broken space of articulation. Cultural nationalism, as one mode of alliance, happens within this space.

This means that diaspora is always in production, always visible as a practice rather than a place. I use *practice* along these lines in *Women's Work* to refer to daily labors of women but also to simultaneously suggest the connotative meaning of practice as conjure or second sight. Practice in each of the novels I consider relies on alternative and spiritual knowledge. In her essay "How She Came By Her Name" (1996), Bambara describes the tension among modes of knowledge that gave rise to *The Salt Eaters*: "I was trying to figure out as a community worker why political folk were so distant from the spiritual community—clairvoyants, mediums, those kind of folks, whom I was always studying with. I wondered what would happen if we could bring them together as Bookman brought them together under Toussaint, as Nan brought them together in Jamaica. Why is there that gap? Why don't we have a bridge language so that clairvoyants can talk to revolutionaries?" (235). *The Salt Eaters* and its contemporaries are a "bridge language." Bambara's novel invokes freedom struggles in Haiti and Jamaica to imagine a unification of clairvoyants and revolutionaries, of supernatural and political knowledge to effect social change. Bambara calls for the strategies of Bookman, a maroon chief who instigated the revolt in northern Haiti that helped bring about the country's independence, and Nan, a rebel leader in Jamaica and the model for the storyteller and survivor of the Middle Passage in Morrison's *Beloved*. These two models rely on the work of men and women, militancy, oral culture, and diasporic resources. These revolutionaries are especially skilled at bringing together "political folk" and "the spiritual community," a melding Bambara insists is absolutely necessary for liberation. When *The Salt Eaters* opens, the healer Minnie Ransom is the clairvoyant, and the protagonist, Velma, is the revolutionary; by novel's end Velma inhabits both roles. The organization of her private self promises political organization no less powerful than that of Bookman, Toussaint, or Nan. *The Salt Eaters* suggests that Velma has a "gift" (293) like Minnie's to see the dead and heal the living. Velma's future work as both seer and political organizer promises to shore up a cultural nation. Practice in this sense encompasses Mama Day's conjure work in Naylor's novel, Connie's and Lone's second sight in Morrison's *Paradise*, and Indigo's powers in Shange's novel. I use *practice* to show that these women's daily labors are bound inextricably with supernatural and spiritual forces.

## Novels as Theory

As a group, these novels render women's labors visible. For Houston Baker, "Afro-American women's expressive production" is a form of "nonmaterial counterintelligence" that operates "at a meta (as opposed to a material) level" (9, 38). I show that meta and material, theorization and labor, are equally constitutive of women's work as Bambara, Shange, Marshall, Naylor, and Morrison imagine it. Sassafrass's curried crabmeat, the steps of Avey Johnson's Juba, and Pat Best's painstaking archival efforts are absolutely material in these novels. The specificity of each of these women's works insists that we not romantically imagine them as part of a homogeneous black female culture. Rather, these are diverse, material practices of a distinct African American cultural nation constantly in the making. Women's work in these novels theorizes African American individual and collective identity as interdependent, constantly repeated with difference, dependent on dissent, and consistently engaged with cultural nationalism.

This group of novels reaches a nonacademic audience and describes daily women's labors in detail.[38] In addition to the women's work depicted, readers encounter women's work performed: that of writing these novels. Each of the texts under consideration contains careful theorization of women's creations, including the novels themselves. This complicates Baker's claim that "there has been a resistance to theory where Afro-American women's literary and cultural studies are concerned—a resistance that has come less from outside scholarly neglect or indifference than from the community of Afro-American women scholars, writers, and critics themselves. In part, this resistance is a warranted suspicion about the intentions of white men, white women, and black women who want 'intellectually' to explain Afro-American womanhood and expressivity" (2). Theory for Baker is an intellectual tool that resides outside of the work of "Afro-American women's literary and cultural studies." A broader notion of theory saturates the fiction of Bambara, Shange, Marshall, Naylor, and Morrison. Not only do their works theorize self and community "intellectually," but each author in this group also writes nonfiction (often literary criticism) and gives interviews in which she theorizes the lineages and meanings of her work. My readings are partly driven by theories in the novels and of the novels offered by their authors. Scholarly discourse is part of the tradition Baker calls "Afro-American women's expressive production" (9). *Women's Work* seeks to acknowledge the importance of novels in that tradition of scholarly discourse, to treat both fiction and nonfiction, both artistic expression and interpretation of that expression as women's work.[39] Theory is not a hermeneutic tool applied to these novels from the outside; it is part of the women's work happening inside these texts.[40]

There are dangers in reading African American women's literary fiction of the late twentieth century as celebrating a vague "Afro-American women's expressive production" rooted in romanticized southern folkways. Not only does this stance elide the intellectual labors of my chosen authors and their contemporaries, but it also perpetuates mystification by limiting women's writings to attempts to "explain Afro-American womanhood and expressivity."[41] The goal of this study is not to "explain Afro-American womanhood and expressivity" but to examine a set of texts that resist this mystification by making women's work legible and visible. In Marshall's *Praisesong*, for example, on the island of Carriacou amid a group of diasporic men and women performing their "nation dances" and "Creole dances," middle-aged Avey Johnson dances a Juba informed by a Ring Shout she saw with her aunt as a girl on the U.S. Sea Island of Tatem. Training, identification, and practice turn her motions not into a vehicle for transmitting vague, gendered wisdom but into a specific, embodied, detailed practice of an African American cultural nation.

In "On the Issue of Roles" (1970), Bambara imagines the individual, the family, and the home as necessary sites of revolution, asserting, "If your house ain't in order, you ain't in order" (135), a serious problem when the individual is "the basic revolutionary unit" (133). The possibilities of women's work on self and in the house hold nothing less than the possibility of revolution, the promise of replacing the current social order with a new vision of community. In various practices of women's work, novels by Bambara, Shange, Marshall, Naylor, and Morrison reclaim and revise cultural nationalism as a set of practices. They make use of long histories of both black nationalism and women's work to imagine new possibilities for collectivity. Morrison says:

> All of us knew in my generation that we always had to work, whether we were married or not. We anticipated it, so we did not have the luxury that I see certain middle class white women have, of whether to work OR to have a house. Work was always going to be part of it. When we feel that work and the house are mutually exclusive, then we have serious emotional or psychological problems, and we feel oppressed. But if we regard it as just one more thing you do, it's an enhancement. Black women are both ship and safe harbor. (R. Lester 49)

In the women's work of organizing, cooking, dancing, mapping, and inscribing, Morrison and her contemporaries insist that "work and the house" are not "mutually exclusive" but mutually constitutive. Recasting women's work as "an enhancement" as well as a necessity resists oppression. This work, whether in kitchens, on political marches, on Caribbean or American shores, at home, or in the streets, is "just one more thing you do," is everyday women's labor to practice individual and collective identity. It relies equally on home and mobility: "black women are both ship and safe harbor," both vehicles for migration and home spaces, where local practices determine global imaginings.

In the last decades of the twentieth century, a group of African American women writers turned to the novel to consider the possibilities of being "both ship and safe harbor," of performing women's work in spaces public and private as a future-oriented practice of cultural nationalism. As Bambara writes in her preface to *The Black Woman*, "This then is a beginning" (6). I turn now to novels of the last two decades of the twentieth century to see what had begun.

# 1 /  Organizing Her Nation: Toni Cade Bambara's *The Salt Eaters*

Toni Cade Bambara's fiction continues the efforts of *The Black Woman* to envision a sovereign cultural nation constantly built by women's work. Her 1980 novel *The Salt Eaters* organizes a collective that is distinctly African American and grounded in the United States. Bambara, a prolific organizer of protests, community centers, anthologies, and artists' groups, uses formal experimentation to write a cultural nation of voices in chorus in the pages of *The Salt Eaters*. This novel claims the recovery of an ailing civil rights activist, Velma Henry, as a necessary starting point for suturing together a community. Organization, formally on the page and thematically in the narrative, heals fractured individual and communal bodies. The novel illuminates the work of practicing cultural nationalism through the story of activist, mother, sister, friend, and wife Velma. Over the course of the novel, Velma repairs her individual "inner nation" (118), which radiates outward to build a cultural nation shared by the residents of Claybourne, Georgia and Bambara's readers.[1] Bambara organizes this nation formally on the pages of the novel through polyvocality, simultaneous temporality, shifts in point of view, and various modes of knowledge. The novel weaves together an astounding variety of characters and possible outcomes into a collective ready to do the work of making social change.

## Concentric Circles of Community

In 1978, following a suicide attempt, Velma comes to the Southwest Community Infirmary in Claybourne. She struggles to get well under the ministrations of Minnie Ransom. To aid in Minnie's efforts, a circle of twelve community members, "the Master's Mind," surrounds Velma and Minnie. The spirit of a dead friend, Old Wife, counsels Minnie during the healing ritual. Dr. Julius Meadows, recently hired at the Infirmary, observes the healing; young, pregnant Nadeen and her boyfriend, Buster, are among those who come to watch Minnie work; activists Ruby and Jan of the Academy of the Seven Arts debate their next steps; women of the Seven Sisters collective sit in the local Avocado Pit Café; Velma's husband, Obie, not knowing of his wife's suicide attempt, seeks to lessen his own pain with a massage; Velma's sister, Palma, arrives in Claybourne (and into the arms of her lover, Marcus) on the suspicion that all is not well; Infirmary administrator and former pimp Doc Serge prepares a lecture to deliver after the healing; bus driver Fred Holt communes with his dead friend Porter; Holt's passengers complain about delays while their driver imagines a series of scenarios, including the bus careening off a bridge and sinking into a marsh, that "might have been" (86–87).

The community of Claybourne overflows; there are far more characters than the reader can easily track. Claybourne is made up of many disparate individuals, each with his or her own complex and fractured internal life. If they cannot become whole on individual and collective terms, terrible alternative realities, from Fred's passengers drowning on the bus (80) to Obie distributing bombs and guns to foment armed revolution (253) and a nuclear disaster (245), threaten to take over. Over the course of *The Salt Eaters*, these characters cohere into a collective determined by Velma's recovery, a community strong enough to choose its own outcome. Bambara connects each person in Claybourne to Velma through textual organization; Velma's story frames the narrative of every other character. Her healing promises to suture this fractured group into a new collective, to organize them into the site of an alternative nation that rejects the oppression, violence, and death that haunt the novel in a series of "might have been[s]."

Worn down by years of activism, Velma is beyond exhaustion. Scattered among various political efforts, she cannot find her place in her late 1970s moment, when no national movement provides a context for her activism. She does not want to return to the marginal position of women in the civil rights movement.[2] One woman's body must be the first site of repair, the first location for healing from the fallout of the gender inequity that saturated earlier black liberation movements. The civil rights movement often put women in subservient roles, and the black power movement subjugated women, as evidenced by Stokely Carmichael's famous assertion that a woman's position in the movement was "prone."[3] Velma acknowledges the racial and gender oppression she has suffered throughout her life but recovers from the state her husband, Obie, describes thus: "It takes something out of you to keep all them dead moments alive" (22). While Obie fails to fully grasp the depth of the wounds created by women's oppression in the civil rights movement, he does show the importance of men to the cultural nation. Obie supports Velma in her journey, exemplified by his insight that many "dead moments" have accumulated, each remaining "alive" for Velma, making continued work for liberation impossible. Bambara says, "I'm mostly future-oriented, but it has to do with memory. . . . My glance is both a back glance as well as a flash forward" (Bonetti, "Bambara"). *The Salt Eaters* exemplifies this stance, being both "future-oriented" in imagining collectivity and connected to memory, insisting that healing toward a new future must make use of the African American past.[4] Instead of living all her past "dead moments" at once, Velma must make them into a usable past for her present and future. The novel follows Velma's mind through her past, making it bear the same weight formally in the narrative as the present. During her healing at the Infirmary, she revisits past hurts in order to give them just the right amount of weight in her present life.

Nation in *The Salt Eaters* inherits the grassroots efforts of the Black Panthers, perhaps best exemplified by the Party's free breakfast program, and the tenet of the black arts movement that creative expression should do work in the world.[5] However, the novel rejects the marginalization of women in both groups. Echoing the work of historians such as Jacqueline Jones, Dianetta Gail Bryan, and Deborah Gray White, the novel organizes a narrative of community in ways that make the details of women's work visible and legible. *The Salt Eaters* witnesses sexism through Velma's recollections of her work in the civil rights movement as "going to jail and being forgotten, forgotten, or at least deprioritized cause bail was not as pressing as the printer's bill . . . being called in on five-minute notice after all the interesting decisions had been made" (25). And this list goes on, piling up throughout the novel, forcing the reader to experience the same cumulative weight of sexism that has made Velma ill. In a postmovement moment of crisis, the novel cries out for new work toward liberation that will not include such a catalogue of sexist acts. In the few hours that pass in *The Salt Eaters*, both Velma and Claybourne take the first steps toward recovery from these decades, finally confronting the cleansing and threatening storm that concludes the novel with Velma, Claybourne, and possibly Bambara's readers ready to face whatever comes next.[6]

"As a cultural worker who belongs to an oppressed people," Bambara says, "my job is to make revolution irresistible" (Bonetti, "Bambara"). Revolution is irresistible in *The Salt Eaters* because it promises not only to record and respond to the exhausting litany of sexist dynamics in earlier black liberation movements but also because revolution promises to heal an individual who has borne this oppression. This revolution comes from a "cultural worker who belongs to an oppressed people," from within obligation and connection to community, rather than from an elevated leader. Velma belongs to her community; if she can recover, so can the community around her. The stakes are massive, but the revolution begins in the very discreet space of Velma's body. She sits in the Infirmary trying to pull together her fractured mind:

> Velma held on to herself. Her pocketbook on the rungs below, the backless stool in the middle of the room, the hospital gown bunched up now in the back—there was nothing but herself and some dim belief in the reliability of stools to hold on to . . . scrambling to piece together key bits of high school physics, freshman philo, and lessons M'Dear Sophie and Mama Mae had tried to impart. The reliability of stools? Solids, liquids, gases, the dance of atoms, the bounce and race of molecules, ethers, electrical charges. The eyes and habits of illusion. Retinal images, bogus images, traveling to the brain. The pupils trying to tell the truth. The eye of the heart. The eye of the head. The eye of the mind. All seeing differently. (6–7)

Velma appears first as a patient, before the reader comes to know her as an activist, mother, wife, and sister. M'Dear Sophie and Mama Mae are Velma's godmother and biological mother, respectively. Stripped of her clothes and her many roles, Velma is "nothing but herself," a daughter and patient in need of care. She has faced the world and, as a result, is fractured and reduced, scrambling to make sense of "herself." Readers meet Velma not as a social force interacting with and reacting to the world but as one woman's body facing the material reality of a backless stool and a hospital gown. Echoing the oscillation among points of view in the novel's omniscient narration, Velma's thoughts begin very small in scope, reaching for a way to understand deceptively simple objects. She thinks of physics and philosophy, moving from common scientific terms for states of matter ("solids, liquids, gases"), to what might be states of mind ("the eyes and habits of illusion"). The eye becomes multivalent, an organ of the heart, the head, and the mind. Mapping the very same movement *The Salt Eaters* makes, this passage begins with a single body "in the middle of the room," shifts attention to "the inner eye," and radiates outward to a broad concern with ways of seeing. Through juxtaposition of the local and specific with the broad and abstract, the novel shows that the physical body of a woman is the first site for melding modes of knowledge (physics and philosophy, balancing on a stool and balancing ways of seeing) to learn how to "tell the truth" with the inner eye. The sight of this inner eye leads to the building of an "inner nation" (118) in Velma and those around her. By the end of *The Salt Eaters*, Velma is no longer a fractured woman perched uncomfortably on a stool but a woman at home in her body and her community. The novel tells the story of Velma making use of "the eye of the heart," "the eye of the mind," and "the eye of the head" to traverse her past and reinhabit her body, to organize the fragments of herself within a new collective context.

The organization of the text, of Velma, and of Claybourne in *The Salt Eaters* is what Farah Griffin calls "textual healing," a literary process of African American women writing "female bodies as sites of healing, pleasure, and resistance," displacing a "legacy of the black body as despised, diseased and ugly" ("Textual Healing" 521).[7] By placing the female body at the center of a potential revolution, *The Salt Eaters* makes it a place "of healing, pleasure, and resistance." "Textual healing" is, like the African American nation, in constant production, always becoming. Describing this work, Griffin asserts, "The healing is never permanent: it requires constant attention and effort. . . . The body can never return to a pre-scarred state. It is not a matter of getting back to a 'truer' self, but instead of claiming the body, scars and all—in a narrative of love and care" (524). Rather than a site of biological reproduction, the female body becomes the first site of healing, "reclaiming," and building a cultural nation. Bambara and her contemporaries use textual healing to move from individual to nation, demanding the reader's "constant attention and effort" to tend her own inner nation. Just as the body must be claimed "scars and all," so the African American nation must be built by claiming its usable past, including the wounds of racial and gendered oppression, into a "narrative of love and care" that can heal and define the communal as well as individual body.

Griffin notes that popular self-help books concerned with healing in the late twentieth century make a clear "movement from individual bodies to psyches to communities" ("Textual Healing" 523).[8] This movement occurs in *The Salt Eaters* as well. The struggle toward wellness begins with Velma's physical self, moves to her psyche or inner nation, and radiates outward to Claybourne and beyond. Through organization of a fragmented narrative, each character's experience and the possibilities that lie on the horizon become concentric circles of textual healing surrounding Velma's individual process. She comes at novel's end back "to the center of the circle" (258), a geometry of infinite horizons.[9]

Velma's work to gather up and organize her scattered self holds the possibility of several outcomes in suspension. This indeterminacy preserves the opportunity for various characters to take part in organizing from a number of locations. Susan Willis notes:

> In all the novel's metaphors for society, the infirmary, the bus, the sidewalk café, Bambara defines focal points in the larger social context that might one day be defined by community. Such a community would not assume race as its primary factor, but would draw on allegiances between racially defined groups and the nascent politics of antinuclear and cultural movements. These will provide the glue that will bring together the community of action. Such a community never comes together during the space of the novel; rather we feel its lack at each of the hectic sites where cacophony prevails. (*Specifying* 132)

"The infirmary, the bus, the sidewalk café" in Claybourne serve as "focal points" drawn together over the course of Velma's recovery. Jan and Ruby in the café are concerned with "antinuclear and cultural movements"; those in the Infirmary are concerned with healing arts; Fred Holt and Minnie Ransom each seek to make sense of the present by communing with a deceased friend. The community formed by Velma's healing promises to gather these varied characters into a "community of action."[10]

Although cross-ethnic alliances are important to Bambara's vision, race remains a "primary factor" in her definition of community. The communities in *The Salt Eaters* and her other writings are made up exclusively of people of color. Although whites are surely a "racially defined group," they are not part of the potential "community of action" in the novel. Inspiring the reader to feel a sense of lack in the absence of a "community of action" is crucial work of *The Salt Eaters*. The novel seeks to heal the lack in Velma, the community, and the African American nation. The possibility that "cacophony" may ultimately "prevail" threatens the nation, threatens to dismantle allegiances. Bambara organizes her text as a means of preserving many voices in "hectic sites" while also unifying those voices into a cultural nation that lies just beyond the wild storm toward the end of *The Salt Eaters*. Bambara unpacks and historicizes a lack of coalition in order to suggest how it might be repaired; she reorganizes social fragmentation into a productive political coherence on the page. This is not an atemporal, romantic vision of African American women as sites of healing. Rather, in the moment after a period of visible national activism, coalescence is desperately needed lest the energy and momentum of the 1960s and 1970s slip away. I read *The Salt Eaters* as the start of a key period of African American literature characterized by its doggedly future-oriented emphasis on nationalist politics rooted in local women's work for social change. The novel asks readers to see the damage done by lack of community in the present and to heal that lack with organized coalescence in the future. Gloria Hull writes, "The Afro-American community is clearly Bambara's main concern. She is asking: Where are we now? Where should we be heading? How do we get there? Above all, she wants black people to 'get it together'" (228). Bambara insists that African Americans, men and women both, organize, "get it together," to build their inner and outer nations.

Reclaiming the female body is the first step in this process. At two moments in *The Salt Eaters*, Velma's menstruation forces her to confront her body, which has taken a backseat to the movement with long hours, "sleep to be snatched" (27), and self-sacrifice. Velma, her sister, Palma, and their friends Jan and Ruby have no space to write their "Statement of Purpose" regarding women's contributions to a local civil rights organization. They make the women's bathroom their office and write the statement there (29). These women activists, literally pushed to the margins of the movement, are stuck in the bathroom. Velma stands at a campaign meeting to read the statement with a "sodden wad of papers between her thighs" (29) to absorb her menstrual flow. It never occurred to the male leaders to put a tampon machine in the building's bathroom, so Velma is forced into discomfort as her body attempts to assert its female presence. She begins to say that the "pattern has to change" in terms of the gendered division of labor, but the men silence her, relegating the women to discounted "input" (31). Velma recalls the women's many objections and concerns, a laundry list of paying for "toll calls, postage or gas," of raising funds, of handling the press, and so on (33–34). The list of women's labors becomes almost unintelligible in its immensity. Velma, sitting in the Infirmary and recollecting the "sodden wad of papers," gets lost in the list of women's work, shifting almost seamlessly to another instance of her menses.

She remembers coping with her period in a gas station bathroom on a civil rights march: "It had been a Gulf station. Of course she remembered that, the boycott had been still in effect and she'd felt funny going in there, even if it was just to use the bathroom. Mounting a raggedy tampon fished from the bottom of her bag, paper unraveled, stuffing coming loose, and in a nasty bathroom with no stall doors, and in a Gulf station too, to add to the outrage. She'd been reeking of wasted blood and rage" (34). During the black-led boycott of Gulf in protest of its operations in Angola, Velma must cross enemy lines to attend to her body. Africa appears only by implication here; a concern with Angola (which goes unnamed) is but a passing hint toward Africa in the context of a very personal moment. *The Salt Eaters* remains nationally bound even as a vague connection to Africa informs Velma's experience. "Mounting a raggedy tampon" "in a nasty bathroom" viscerally asserts the discomfort of the moment. The opening of *The Salt Eaters* suggests that Velma in the Infirmary hospital gown is reduced to total physical exposure for the first time. As this passage reveals, however, she has faced countless such moments. The difference lies in her response. In the Gulf station, she finds no outlet for her anger; she is all "wasted blood and rage." In the Infirmary, recalling this moment, she recovers her "blood and rage" to make them useful. "Mounting a raggedy tampon" becomes part of a coherent life narrative that will strengthen her for the times ahead. Further, this time of "outrage" warns against any political actions that, like the Gulf boycott combined with the march, do not explicitly acknowledge women's most basic needs. This vivid description of a representative moment of Velma's history shows that any political action that cannot account for a woman's body is insufficient. The material reality of gender oppression demands Bambara's painfully detailed description because the movement marginalizes Velma's body. Bambara organizes the past on the page to open up narrative space for this moment. Velma works as an organizer too, revisiting this moment as a way of making space for her body, making space that was denied the woman crouched in "a nasty bathroom with no stall doors."

The Gulf station and campaign meeting are not isolated incidents, but two of many such moments that *The Salt Eaters* recovers in textual space. In these two instances of her period, Velma is forced to push aside her body's needs to participate in the movement. As the need for textual healing attests, the erasure of African American female bodies has a long history. Six decades before Velma appears, Mary Church Terrell, president of the National Association of Colored Women, recalls that menstruating on a segregated train without a bathroom made her consider giving up her work as a lecturer (White 91). *The Salt Eaters* reorganizes a narrative of civil rights to emphasize the stakes of dividing politics from female bodies. The white feminist notion that "the personal is political" does not suffice to heal this breach. *The Salt Eaters* reveals that the personal is always already political but must be public and visible to address both sexism and racism. The novel pushes Velma's personal experience into the public eye. Any failure to consider race and gender together is as divisive a crisis as Velma's division of public from private self. Rupture between private body and public work contributes mightily to the fragmentation of her mind, which leads her to attempt suicide by slitting her wrists and putting her head in an oven. Like the limited notion of women's work in political campaigns as "chickens to fry" and "cakes to box" (27–28), her use of a kitchen appliance as an instrument of death suggests the dangers of misconstruing women's work as strictly domestic. Bambara figures Velma's return to health as "the journey back from the kitchen" (18).

Seeking to understand how a revolutionary could have become so fractured, Bambara turns to the immediate past. Both *The Salt Eaters* and her posthumously published novel *Those Bones Are Not My Child* fictionalize real events of the recent past to make sense of the present. In a moment when several other black women authors in the United States reach to slavery for novelistic material, Bambara looks to recent decades that have shaped her present. In the context of her filmmaking, social work, and political activism, she imagines her writing as women's work to organize "actual experiences" of one's immediate and atavistic past. In terms that echo and revise the goals of black arts writers, she says, "The question is . . . how do you transform actual experiences you have been through, how do you transform people you have encountered in order to make usable whatever lesson it is you've extracted from that experience you want to lift up and share with other people" (Bonetti, "Bambara"). In historicizing the recent past, her novels "transform actual experiences" and make those experiences usable and legible for readers who need practical and spiritual guidance. Publication allows her to share Velma's experience with other people in order to "transform" them. During the post–civil rights era and the Atlanta child murders, treated in her two novels, respectively, the recent past is complex, muddled by mistakes, and complicated by entanglements of class, sex, and race. Bambara writes to make sense of this recent past because the stakes for her are "Where do we go from here?" or "What comes next?" These queries seem especially crucial in the last decades of the twentieth century. In *The Salt Eaters* Minnie Ransom describes this moment of possibility and urgency as the millennium approaches: "Here we are in the last quarter and how we gonna pull it all together and claim the new age in our name?" (46).

The novel looks back from 1980 to understand how Velma, and many African American women, have made sacrifices in the movement, perhaps for only marginal gains. Women's work, from "chickens to fry" to crouching in a gas station bathroom, must be interpreted and historicized for individual and communal African American liberation. On the page and in the world, Bambara labors to make space for women's bodies and experiences. Speaking during the writing of *The Salt Eaters*, she laments, "We did not admit, were not allowed to, could not afford to *admit* pain and suffering and hardship. You're not supposed to do that if you're a black woman" (Guy-Sheftall 247). Velma, forced to the point of such dreaded admission by the depth of her physical and psychic pain, disrupts the strong black woman stereotype that Bambara rightly casts as dangerous. Velma must not only "*admit* pain and suffering and hardship," but must recount it, relive it, and find a place for it in her story in order to reach a new healthiness. She acquires a strength modeled on testifying to reality rather than suppressing suffering.

With a portrait of Velma ill and divided, *The Salt Eaters* "admits pain and suffering and hardship" and envisions a new future. Willis writes, "It seems, reading the novel, that revolution is only pages away. But for all its yearning and insight, the novel fails to culminate in revolution, fails even to suggest how social change might be produced" (*Specifying* 129). Through Velma's transformation, the novel depicts concrete women's work as the first step toward collectivity. The text does thus "suggest how social change might be produced"; witnessing the past to restore a single female body heals the communal body. Just as a local politician's campaign could never get off the ground without the grassroots work of women making cakes, frying chickens, and printing flyers (27–28), Velma's healing relies on the organizing power of women around her, laying on hands, praying, making music, and communing with spirits. Organizing evolves from meaning only political protest to meaning practices of creating a revolution "only pages away." Making room on the page and in the collective consciousness for Velma's body, so marginalized in the Gulf station, is a revolution wrought by textual organization.

The Salt Eaters offers concrete notions of how to bring about this revolution beyond the page. Linda Janet Holmes and Cheryl Wall describe this aspect of the novel as a use of "specific . . . representations of the cultural practices of African Americans" within a text that "maps a larger world." In their introduction to Savoring the Salt, Holmes and Wall note that the novel both "highlights the common values—respect for children, cooperative economics, functional and collective art, and metaphysical beliefs—among traditional communities of color" and "suggests that those values might be the basis for coalitions that would forge a politics for the twenty-first century" (4). The novel's "politics for the twenty-first century" rely on the juxtaposition of local details with global concerns, exemplified in readers' first encounter with Velma, her "pocketbook on the rungs below, the backless stool in the middle of the room, the hospital gown bunched up now in the back" (6), alongside an interest in the global concern of "the eye of the heart. The eye of the head. The eye of the mind" (7). The physical ("the backless stool") and the metaphysical ("The eye of the heart. The eye of the head. The eye of the mind") come together in Bambara's organization of text and community. Bambara says, "One of the calls I'm trying to make in that book is coalition" (Bonetti, "Bambara"). The novel concretely demands coalition, demands collaborative work for social change. In writing a novel that details African American women's oppression in the civil rights movement with often brutal specificity, Bambara asks others to make use of one woman's recovery to activate and organize the revolution that lies on the horizon of The Salt Eaters. Revolution in the novel begins with organizing one woman's experience into a coherent narrative that radiates outward in concentric circles of community.

## Writing the Cultural Nation

Velma's recovery holds the potential to create "radical regeneration of individuals, families, community, the city, and by extension all human beings" (Page, Reclaiming 22) but occurs very locally. Minnie's healing rituals in the Infirmary employ alternative medicine, communication with spirits, and astrology. Melding modes of knowledge is crucial to practicing the cultural nation of The Salt Eaters. A split between ways of knowing causes Velma's illness: "She'd found a home amongst the community workers who called themselves 'political.' And she'd found a home amongst the workers who called themselves 'psychically adept.' But somehow she'd fallen into the chasm that divided the two camps" (147). Velma's search for a home thus depends on the unification of "the two camps," on recognizing that political and psychic women's works are inseparable.[11] This is no easy feat. The novel's opening question comes from Minnie Ransom: "Are you sure, sweetheart, that you want to be well?" (3). Healing depends not just on various modes of knowledge but also on a decision to recover, individually and communally, from oppressions of the past. The chasm must be actively sutured to imagine a new collectivity.

One lesson of *The Salt Eaters* is to balance public work for liberation with personal care and wellness. There is no point in being jailed on a civil rights march if it ultimately limits rather than liberates black women. Bambara posits literature as the place where private and public work can come together, can cohere into a multifocal cultural nation. She says, "The balance between the public and the private utterance is the strength of our literature."[12] She emphasizes this balance by depicting domestic rituals as inseparable from nation. Employing the phrase *inner nation*, so important to the *Salt Eaters*, she says, "The simple act of cornrowing one's hair is radical in a society that defines beauty as blonde tresses blowing in the wind; that staying centered in the best of one's own cultural tradition is hip, is sane, is perfectly fine. . . . We're about building a nation; the inner nation needs building too. I would be writing whether there were a publishing industry or not, whether there were presses or not, whether there were markets or not" (Tate, *Black Women* 18). Bambara connects the private act of "cornrowing one's hair" to the public work of writing for a readership. Both forms of women's work are "radical" and both are "about building a nation." The larger nation imagined in writing depends on the inner nation nurtured by "cornrowing one's hair." Velma, and those around her, must accordingly learn to balance the inner nation with the outer nation, with public action in the community. Because power lies in building one's inner nation, this vision of practiced nationalism radically opens up the notion of who can participate in nationalist work.

Writing, because she would do it "whether there were a publishing industry or not," exemplifies this balance for Bambara. The power of the pen is a practice of the inner nation that becomes visible in the larger cultural nation. Writing, as author and anthologist, is inseparable for Bambara from her work as filmmaker and community activist. This is perhaps best exemplified by *Those Bones Are Not My Child*, which began from her efforts to help solve and stop the abductions and murders of over forty black children in Atlanta in the 1980s. Composed mostly while Bambara lived in Atlanta from endless notes and amounting to almost seven hundred pages even after heavy editing by Toni Morrison, *Those Bones* overflows with the same witnessing and investigation she did in her community. *Those Bones* strives to organize and make sense of the unintelligibly violent and complex Atlanta child murders. The novel describes and enacts organizing; both protagonist Marzala Chandler and novelist Toni Cade Bambara gather and order endless piles of information and disinformation, pursuing every avenue, many of them false leads.[13] The solitary work of writing and the collective work of public action are of a piece for both Bambara and her fictional character. Women's work is both writing alone at home about the murders and mounting a protest against city government's inaction. This duality of the text, as both public and private work, makes it a bridge between the inner and outer nations.

As an object, *The Salt Eaters* is necessarily a means of transmitting the inner nation. Velma's inner nation becomes visible to the reader each time the narration comes from her point of view. As Eleanor Traylor notes, "It is through Velma's consciousness that we hear and observe everything we know about Claybourne; it is Velma's personal transformation that we experience and that figures in the possibility of the community's renewal; it is through Velma's negation and acceptance of the actual and her pursuit of the possible that we learn the identity and enormous re-creative powers of those who have eaten salt together and who have learned to reconcile both the brine and the savor of life" ("Music as Theme" 60). As the "eyes" in the opening pages of the novel suggest, there is no seeing without Velma. Her journey trains those in Claybourne and the reader to align themselves with "Velma's consciousness" to begin "pursuit of the possible."

Traylor identifies community as "those who have eaten salt together," following Bambara's use of a folk myth. The story, told and revisited in many texts, including Julie Dash's film *Daughters of the Dust* (1991) and Morrison's *Song of Solomon* (1977), asserts that eating salt in the New World prevented captured Africans from flying back to Africa. As a character in Bambara's short story "Broken Field Running" puts it, "We could fly. . . . But we ate too much salt. Can't mess with too much salt cause it throws things out of proper balance" (*Sea Birds* 53). *The Salt Eaters* offers a model of how to restore this balance, replacing flight to Africa with "pursuit of the possible" as an alternative ascent that holds out "the possibility of the community's renewal" in the United States. Salt also refers to the ocean, gravesite of many slaves who died during the Middle Passage. Salt evokes "salt of the earth" and sweat too, recalling a history of agricultural labor. These historic resonances are the collective "brine and savor of life" that Traylor describes; they must be reckoned with, used, and "reconciled." The title of *The Salt Eaters*, Bambara says, "goes back to the African flying myth" and "songs about Ezekiel seeing the wheel. . . . As the old folks tell it, we got grounded because we ate too much salt. As some of the old folks say, we got grounded because we opened ourselves up to horror . . . and that created tears and it was that salt that drowned our wings and made us earthbound" (Bonetti, "Bambara"). Consuming salt becomes a way to "eat our own history" and use that history to make new possibilities.[14] All are salt eaters, bound to the New World and unable to fly back to Africa or another homeland. Stuck here in the United States, one must know the wisdom of "eating salt as an antidote," engaging with healing possibilities on this terrain, but not "turn into salt" like Lot's wife or "succumb to the serpent." This motif of salt, snakes, and flight emphasizes that the road to healing is treacherous, dependent on vernacular knowledge, and a marvelous possibility for African Americans, who are indelibly bound to the United States.

This focus on salt eaters marks an important shift from Ralph Ellison's assertions about the form and function of the blues: "The blues is an impulse to keep the painful details and episodes of a brutal experience alive in one's aching consciousness, to finger its jagged grain, and to transcend it, not by the consolation of philosophy, but by squeezing from it a near-tragic, near-comic lyricism. As a form, the blues is an autobiographical chronicle of personal catastrophe expressed lyrically" ("Richard Wright's Blues" 129). With its reference to the Middle Passage and the desire to escape the brutality of slavery by flying back to Africa, the notion of salt eaters does, like Ellison's blues, "finger the jagged grain" of "a brutal experience." Bambara's goal, however, is not primarily to achieve a cathartic "lyricism" or "an autobiographical chronicle" but to use the individual as a model for "fingering the jagged grain" only on the way to collective healing. Ellison posits his model in a 1945 essay on Richard Wright. Thirty-five years later, Bambara replaces the blues mode of Wright's autobiography *Black Boy* with a collective metaphor of salt eaters. The shift from the individual to the group, from the pain of the grain to healing, and perhaps from male to female work, demands a new central metaphor. Deliberately eating salt is a means of "fingering the jagged grain" by tasting tears and the salt of the ocean crossed by millions of slaves. Bambara insists that one must eat just enough of this salt to move forward with knowledge of history. Velma is not Ellison's blues high priestess, exemplified by Bessie Smith; she is an ordinary woman healing as a model for other ordinary people. Whereas Ellison's blues mode culminates in a singular performance of "personal catastrophe," Bambara's salt eaters strive toward a communal performance of healing. Eating salt speaks to painful history but also to making use of folk wisdom, of balancing danger and recovery, of culinary work, and of action as a group. Wright may "finger the jagged grain" to articulate his individual journey, but Bambara's Velma eats salt to begin a collective journey toward African American nationhood.

This journey requires giving women their due in historical narratives. *The Salt Eaters* does this by narrating such moments as a campaign meeting for a local politician, Jay Patterson: "Once again the women took up their pens. They listened to Hampden while calculating: money to be raised, mailing lists to be culled, halls to be booked, flyers to be printed up, hours away from school, home, work, sleep to be snatched. Not that he spoke of these things. . . . The women went on writing: so many receptions to cater, tickets to print, chickens to fry, cakes to box, posters to press, so many gifts to exhort from downtown merchants for raffles" (27–28). Male politicians assume women's labor here without requesting, respecting, or fully comprehending that work. Women are shut out of decision making and theoretical discussion, left instead with "chickens to fry" and "money to be raised." Like "being forgotten or at least deprioritized" (25), moments like these suppress women's intellectual contributions. However, "women took up their pens" and "went on writing" during the campaign meeting. Velma's recollection, or re-experience, of this moment emphasizes that the power of writing rests with women.[15] She controls the moment by narrating it, by inserting women's work into the story of the civil rights movement, and by claiming writing as a key aspect of women's work in that movement.

The power of the pen appears as ritual writing in *The Salt Eaters* in preparations for the annual town festival, a Mardi Gras carnival. Children write "notes to God" on kites released into the air the day before the festival (174). As part of the event, "people were supposed to write down all the things they wanted out of their lives—bad habits, bad debts, bad dreams—and throw them on the fire. . . . One was supposed to draw up a list of dreams and pin it on the Mother Earth float, or stick it in the horn of plenty" (157). These writings function as part of a public ceremony but are simultaneously private because they have no reading audience. These texts are written whether or not there is an outlet for publication. Writing for the festival is multivalent, ritualized, and imagines a changed future. Though these texts have no readers, they are part of a shared ritual intended to actualize dreams and discard the "bad." Ritual acts of writing in Claybourne are thus like *The Salt Eaters*, which melds the private and public and seeks to bring about change. Writing is a powerful resource; those in Claybourne know on some level that text can get rid of "all the things they wanted out of their lives" and perhaps make their dreams come true.

Mothering, like writing, appears in all of the texts of the cultural nationalist revision. In *The Salt Eaters*, Bambara groups mothering with other forms of women's work, making it one form of action toward coalition. She troubles mothering with the revelations that Velma's son, James, is adopted and that Velma has been unable to carry a child to term. Biological motherhood moves aside, making room for other versions of matrilineage. Mothers, when that identity is mutable, have the potential to train their children to fuse together ways of perceiving, to meld knowledge seen by the "eye of the head," the "eye of the mind," and the "eye of the heart." Communal mothering and nonbiological mothers are far more important to healing Velma and Claybourne than biological ones. M'Dear Sophie, helps bring Velma through. Sophie Heywood is a former participant in civil rights protests, "godmother of Velma Henry," and "co-convener of The Master's Mind" (11). Sophie midwifes all stages of Velma's life: "She'd been there at the beginning with her baby-catching hands" (11–12). She often intervenes on Velma's behalf with "the blood mother" (12), Velma's biological mother, Mama Mae, who is barely present in the novel.

Mothering is one among many practices of women's work in *The Salt Eaters*; it sits comfortably beside healing, organizing, writing, and teaching. This is in stark contrast to much African American men's contemporary fiction that lauds a kind of stoic and ever-supportive mother but leaves the work of practicing nation and other communities to men. Ernest Gaines's *A Lesson Before Dying* (1993), for example, insists that men teach mental and spiritual liberation to men.[16] Women in Gaines's novel serve primarily to support and foster this didactic relationship among men. Mothering in Gaines's book, though also nonbiological, occurs in private, domestic settings to prepare men for public work. *The Salt Eaters*, on the other hand, expands the definition of women's work by setting mothering alongside nondomestic labors, again worrying the distinction between public and private. While mothering in the context of black power ideology was the decidedly public work of having babies for the revolution, *The Salt Eaters* divorces mothering from biology. Like many contemporary African American women's novels, *The Salt Eaters* rejects breeding in favor of mothering as a multivalent practice. The novel complicates mothering as a way of rescuing the practice from both Moynihan's portrayal of the castrating black matriarch and what Dubey calls the "black nationalists' womb-centered definition of black women" in the black power era (*Black Women* 19).[17]

The importance of Bambara's own mother to the process of textual healing is clear from the first pages of *The Salt Eaters*. Bambara dedicates the novel to her mother, "who in 1948, having come upon [Bambara] day-dreaming in the middle of the kitchen floor, mopped around [her]." This dedication insists that writing depends on other forms of women's work. Domestic labor supports and surrounds literary creation. Mothering becomes a way of making space for women, here by "mopping around" the writer's territory.

Bambara prefigures the other authors discussed here, each of whom explores alternative or collective ideas of parenting to some degree. This literary progeny is one she would be proud to claim. In an interview with Kalamu ya Salaam she says, "*The Salt Eaters* breaks new ground. For people who live with a comfortable melding of the physical and the meta-physical but don't know how to talk about it yet, and don't know whether they have to find a metaphor for talking about spirit, vibes, for talking about what people call psychic phenomena or whatever, they have called up to say, 'Hey, you handled it in a kind of nonchalant way, I feel better, I'll just go ahead and do it'" (61). The ritualized connection to ancestors in each performance of Shange's recipes, Avey Johnson's dreams of her deceased great-aunt in Marshall's *Praisesong for the Widow*, the conjure work in Naylor's *Mama Day*, and the practice of second sight in Morrison's *Paradise*—these are the fruits of Bambara's "new ground." She consciously mothers and midwifes a "nonchalant" inclusion of "spirit," "vibes," and "psychic phenomena" so crucial to the later novels considered here. *The Salt Eaters* charges other novelists I consider, as well as their readers, to actualize an alternative nation in daily practices as they might occur after the dramatic and ambiguous shift at the conclusion of the novel. The irresistible revolution, the nascent community of action organized in the pages of *The Salt Eaters*, is the first step toward the African American nation that Shange, Marshall, Naylor, and Morrison practice and interrogate in later novels. The writer's mother mopping around her, Velma Henry committing to her political work as well as her adopted son, and Bambara as literary foremother of novels of revolutions wrought by women's work are all valuable versions of mothering in *The Salt Eaters*. Bambara enables her literary descendants to cast multivalent mothering as crucial for social change.

## Fragmentation and Temporality in *The Salt Eaters*

Formal experimentation is a key component of Bambara's legacy. To reflect and cope with a multitude of roles, including motherhood, that have spread Velma so thin, *The Salt Eaters* depicts many temporal and narrative layers bound together by her healing. The first twenty pages of the novel are rooted firmly in the present-day Infirmary, but just a line of white space denotes the transition to "She had on a velour blouse, brown, crocheted. . . . She moved about in the booth, the leather sticky under her knees. . . . She was losing the thread of her story" (20). The backless gown replaced by a velour blouse signals a shift in place and time, but only in details of the subsequent five pages does the new scene emerge as a tense meal with Obie at a local diner in the recent past. As soon as this setting crystallizes in details like "She wiped her finger on the napkin" (24), another line of white space breaks the narrative of marital discord, followed by "'Nice Statement. Strong,' he had said, easing up on her right side when the curator has stepped away to mount another painting" (24). Suddenly the novel, still in its first chapter, has leaped to a moment at least a decade past, when Obie and Velma meet at an art opening. The chapter continues in this way, often dispensing entirely with the use of line spaces to signal temporal shifts. The chapter returns to the diner, moves back in time to the campaign meeting for Patterson, finds its way even further into the past to Velma in the Gulf station bathroom, and then returns for just two sentences to Obie and the diner before concluding in the Infirmary with Minnie encouraging Velma's "growl" (41).

The novel forces the reader to work to make sense of this woman's life, to struggle not to lose "the thread of [Velma's] story." As Velma revisits, reorders, and weaves her life into a coherent narrative, the reader must also piece together this disjunctive first chapter by inhabiting the multitemporal mode that continues throughout the novel. Velma's story organizes several narrative and temporal planes. It is up to the reader to use the "eye of the head," "eye of the mind," and "eye of the heart," all modes of perception grounded in an inner nation, to see coherence in the novel, to see that Velma's healing organizes this seeming narrative disorder.

In the framing story of *The Salt Eaters*, Velma comes through or "crosses over," a phrase associated with "sacred work" as opposed to "making the crossing," which can mean either "being rounded up for the middle passage" or "sending the soul home to the original ancestral place. Africa" (Bambara, "Reading the Signs" 115). In the final chapter of the novel, Minnie Ransom's spirit guide reports, "The Henry gal is coming through" (262), indicating that Velma's passage to strength and wellness is almost complete; Minnie's sacred work has had its effect. The reach of this crossing strains narrative conventions. The implications of Velma's recovery for those beyond the Infirmary, Claybourne, and even the pages of the novel resist the formal constraints of any single point of view or moment in time. Though Velma's healing structures the novel, many other characters take center stage in *The Salt Eaters*. Bambara writes, "My own breakout(s) from the lockup where Black/woman/cultural worker in the binary scheme is a shapeless drama with a cast of thousands that won't adhere to any outline I devise" ("Deep Sight" 164). To break out from any "binary scheme," *The Salt Eaters* refuses a strict outline or linear strategy in favor of textual organization that gives the "cast of thousands" narrative weight. Partly through simultaneous temporality like that of the first chapter, the novel is a polyvocal story with a cast of thousands. Simultaneous temporality and multiple points of view make a formal claim that echoes Bambara's thematic insistence on varied modes of knowledge.

Just as a single time frame or point of view is inadequate for narrating the move from inner to outer nation, so a single way of knowing can never fully account for the cultural nation. Astrology, physics, connection to the loa (spirits or deities), healing rituals, and medical knowledge all play a part in *The Salt Eaters*.[18] In the novel, the Academy of the Seven Arts works to "bridge the gap between our medicine people and our warriors," the Seven Sisters reach across the "Third World gap," and the Infirmary works to "merge the best of so-called traditional medicine with the most humane of so-called modern medicine" (Salaam 61–62). Fragmentation becomes a unified multiplicity, organized into a chorus of voices, coalitions, and modes of knowledge that come to function as a complex, multifocal healing system.

This healing requires Bambara's formal organization of temporal fragmentation. Within the first forty pages of the novel, four moments in time are simultaneous: the healing ritual in the Infirmary, a meeting for Patterson's campaign, Velma sitting in a diner arguing with Obie, and the civil rights march all seem to be occurring at once. The three past scenes (the diner, the march, and the meeting) are those "dead moments" that Velma must relive and reexamine as part of her healing process; she must understand the complex oppression in each of these moments in order to move forward as a cultural worker. In yet another temporal layer, a coming "apocalypse" is signaled by a "sonic boom" (104) in the future that creates ripples of sound in the present. In keeping with much of the African American literary tradition, the past has materiality in the present of *The Salt Eaters*. One of Bambara's innovations is to give the future similar weight. An indeterminate future saturates the present of the novel. A coming breach, a communal mirror of Velma's division of self, threatens to crack open if the disparate people of the novel cannot be stitched together into a community. Minnie suggests that Velma's recovery will be crucial for coping with a possibly apocalyptic future: "Them four horses galloping already, the seven trumpets blasting" (46). Healing and destruction are inevitably intertwined; healing Velma in each of these temporal strands is the only way to head off "them four horses" of the Apocalypse, to make sure that Velma's healing rather than her ruptured consciousness radiates outward to the community. The work at the Infirmary frames both Velma's past and the various events occurring in Claybourne during the healing ritual. When the novel concludes back in the present, we know that Velma has come through, back to a time and place that can make use of the past without being mired in it. Like salt, her dead moments must be used and tasted, but not overindulged.

Minnie's healing organizes Velma's fragmented self into a coherent whole. Minnie transcends the boundary between living and dead, accessing multiple planes of existence in her consultation with the deceased Old Wife. She depends on both Old Wife and the living participants in the Master's Mind group of twelve to bring Velma through. Minnie usually practices a laying on of hands she calls "routine": "She simply placed her left hand on the patient's spine and her right hand on the navel, then clearing the channels, putting herself aside, she became available to a healing force no one had yet, to her satisfaction, captured in a name" (47). Organizing the fractured patient, Minnie's power is outside of language, unable to be "captured in a name," deriving its force from sources other than the pens of Bambara or Velma and her sisters in the movement. Velma's case proves to be anything but routine, however, demanding more time and energy than anyone anticipates.

The spirit guide Old Wife assists Minnie in this difficult process and speaks to the temporal implications of Velma's healing. Old Wife advises Minnie to "thrash out into them waters, churn up all them bones we dropped from the old ships, churn up all that brine from the salty deep where out tears sank" (61).[19] Old Wife, in other words, knows that to "churn up" Velma's hurtful past is to churn up a deeper history of African Americans, that of the Middle Passage.[20] As the stakes of Velma's recovery are communal, so her history is collective. Just as Velma must revisit old wounds to gather up a usable past, so must the community acknowledge and make use of a history of violence and oppression, even though it is a painful struggle to "thrash out into them waters." The work of Griffin's textual healing is not simply passive reading but a willingness to engage the past, "scars and all," on the part of characters, readers, and authors who "thrash out into them waters." For Velma, once Minnie accepts Old Wife's challenge, the signs of healing begin, starting with Velma's wrists, "thick brown wrists no longer banded by narrow red and black bracelets of flaking flesh. Healed" (111). Nadeen, a pregnant observer in the Infirmary, thinks of Minnie's practice as "the real thing" (113), unlike "revival healing" (112). "The real thing" is without fanfare; it occurs as part of ordinary women's work. Velma's healing is successful because it depends on ritual, community, and everyday practice. Women's work of organizing, both revolutionary and ordinary, happens on the page and in the body, in writing and the laying on of hands.

The space of these women's works in *The Salt Eaters* is decidedly southern. In Bambara's novel, the ground of possible recovery, of learning to eat just the right amount of salt, is the South, exemplified by the fictional southern setting of Claybourne, Georgia. Zora Neale Hurston's "muck" in *Their Eyes Were Watching God* (1937) is a prototype for this space of African American cultural nationalism. Willis writes that Hurston's muck is "more south than the rural South," a space that "articulates the recovery of Caribbean culture. . . . The 'muck,' as Hurston portrays it, is a mythic space with just enough reference to migrant agricultural workers to give it credibility" (*Specifying* 48).[21] Southernness in *The Salt Eaters* is not an unequivocally positive trait. Alice Walker's romantic South, where the writer stands "feeling the soil between the toes, smelling the dust thrown up by the rain, loving the earth so much that one longs to taste it and sometimes does" ("The Black Writer" 21), does not quite hold in *The Salt Eaters*. One best not drink the rain or eat the soil in Claybourne; both are likely toxic with waste from the local Transchemical Plant. Bambara troubles the American South as a redemptive space, one of both romantic imagining and brutal specificity. Echoing the earth of Jean Toomer's *Cane* (1923), Claybourne's name suggests red Georgia clay and birth. Southern soil may be stained, as it was for Toomer and

James Baldwin, by the blood of lynching victims. The clay is also a source of the mud that shapes the ancestral "mud mothers" who haunt Velma throughout *The Salt Eaters*. The clay is useful for creative works, though the women at the Academy of the Seven Arts cannot quite balance it on the potter's wheel. Claybourne stands as the most southern of spaces, necessarily imagined in order to work as a mythic space but also material because of the detailed culture therein. Unlike *Cane*, *The Salt Eaters* is no swan song for the South. Bambara uses Claybourne as a birthing ground for a cultural nation that will reach beyond southern borders.

Creating a resonant homeland responds to both the feeling of lack and the irresistible call for revolution at the heart of *The Salt Eaters*. A chapter of the novel focalized through Obie articulates the absence of home that haunts the novel. Obie reflects on efforts to establish a homeland:

> After several tries, they modified the plan: a select few should nab some devalued real estate near the woods and move off for a year and start a brain-trust farm. And finally do what the folks in the nineteenth century had talked about at the Colored People's Conventions, finally do what the African Brotherhood had formed to do in the twenties, finally do what had been a priority item in the early sixties, then pushed aside when the movement was redefined from the outside. . . . But when was there a moment, much less the material resources, to move off for a year? (91–92)

Obie charts decades of African Americans searching for a nation apart, from the nineteenth century on. This long history of seeking a homeland makes up a usable past that Obie struggles to inherit. The tone in this passage is one of deep yearning. Obie feels the sense of lack so crucial to the novel; he longs for a homeland he can fully inhabit. Lamenting that the movement for civil rights "was redefined from the outside," he searches for a new model of activism. His experience, like Velma's, asserts that one must sift through the past and live it in the present to come to a workable plan for change. Men are crucial to the multifocal homeland prepared by *The Salt Eaters*. What Obie comes to realize is that he must begin as Velma does, in Adrienne Rich's words, "not with a continent or a country or a house, but with the geography closest in—the body" (212). Obie comes to the "geography closest in" by recovering from the emotional and physical pain in his own body. Only after a workout, a massage, and a steam bath increase his awareness of his physical self can he see the potential of Claybourne as a homeland. There's no need to "move off" to start a nation apart; the nation apart is already in practice within Claybourne. In the final pages of the novel, Velma comes to see landlessness as a condition of possibility, dispossession as a kind of home in itself: "Dispossessed, landless, this and that-less and free, therefore, to go anywhere and say anything and be everything if only we'd only know it once and for all" (265). Claybourne, tied to both spiritual and material worlds, is, like Velma, unmoored in ways that invite "anything" and "everything," welcoming radically alternative possibilities for community.

## Collectives in *The Salt Eaters*

The Southwest Community Infirmary ("Established 1871, by the Free Coloreds of Claybourne" [120]), the Seven Sisters, and the Academy of the Seven Arts are collectives in Claybourne that draw on various forms of knowledge. The seven sisters of the collective and the seven arts hailed by the name of the Academy draw strength from many sources, including numerology. In scripture, seven is associated with God, who created the world in seven days, and with the seven deadly sins. The term "Lucky 7" appears on everything from New York State Lottery tickets to a chain of convenience stores in Virginia. "The Seven Sisters" is a common name for the stellar constellation known as the Pleiades. In New Orleans "the Seven Sisters" is the name of a brand of bath salts, soaps, and incense used for voodoo-based rituals and a group of houses on Coliseum Street that, according to local legend, were built for seven sisters. Seven is the number associated with the African diasporic goddess Yemoja, who is especially prominent in Yoruban and Brazilian religions. Geographically the reference to seven continents suggests a transnational alliance rooted in the ancient land mass Pangaea. Seven evokes the cyclic time of seven days in the week and the celestial time of seven planetary bodies in early astrology. In tarot card readings, seven indicates balance and wisdom; it insists there is order in the universe even at its most chaotic and is thus an apt sign for Bambara's vision of a cultural nation. This density of meaning permeates every instance of the names of these two collectives in *The Salt Eaters*; organizing even a local group of activists requires multiple modes of knowledge and diverse forms of power.

The Seven Sisters are a nearly successful collective in *The Salt Eaters*. Because the group does not rely on conventional family structures, the Seven Sisters chart an antipatriarchal path for women's work toward social change. The Seven Sisters organize in the late 1970s to recover a moment of the 1960s that Bambara describes as a "missed . . . opportunity to hook up with Puerto Rican women and Chicano women who shared not only a common condition but also . . . a common vision about the future." The Seven Sisters seize on what she calls an "opportunity again in the last quarter of the twentieth century to begin forging these critical ties with other communities" (Guy-Sheftall 238–39).[22] Making plans to help Velma, stop environmental destruction, and teach local classes, the Seven Sisters demonstrate the power of alliances among women of color. These women meet two additional requirements of the imagined alternative nation: they make use of tools as diverse as tarot cards and computers, and they make women central to all work for social change.[23] Even with these strengths, the Seven Sisters leave many resources untapped. They are looking for Velma, their "sister of the yam," but fail to talk to Claybourne residents Jan and Ruby who, sitting just tables away at a café, are also wondering where Velma might be. The Seven Sisters remain unaware of Velma's illness because they are not in touch with happenings at the Infirmary or with Minnie's healing practices. Though they are invested in building a cultural nation, they fail to notice that Velma's inner nation is in crisis.

The Sisters also neglect the loa residing in an old tree behind the Infirmary. By 1978 the loa are "called upon so seldom, they were beginning to believe that their calling in life was to keep a lover from straying, make a neighbor's hair fall out in fistfuls, swat horses into a run just so and guarantee the number for the day. They were weary with so little to perform" (146). These spirits have power to do great work, even bring revolution, but have been left to languish, called upon only for mundane tasks. These "weary" spirits call out to the residents of Claybourne to make better use of the resources at hand. The loa, "weary and impatient with amnesia, neglect, and a bad press" (146), lie in wait as a force to help build an alternative nation. The Seven Sisters are laudable for their multiethnic collectivity and use of arts from the martial to the medical, but they have overlooked older forms of knowledge that must also play a key role in the alternative nation. Coalition in *The Salt Eaters* depends on incorporating the mode of Velma's healing—myth, rootwork, talk, dance, music, connection to ancestors, and reentry into community—into the political work of the Seven Sisters.

Less formal collectives exhibit the collaboration so important to the future imagined in *The Salt Eaters*. On Fred Holt's bus in chapter 3, for example, third-person omniscient narration focalized through the driver breaks repeatedly, his thoughts interrupted constantly by the passengers, making the narrative nearly incoherent for both Fred and the reader:

For years, they hadn't hired colored guys. Now just when he was getting some seniority, they were talking about early retirement.

"Before we sit down to work out the program with the brothers from the Academy, we need to go through these folders. These are skits and poems and some of the posters from International Women's Day."

He hung on to the talk around him lest he overheat too. He felt light and feverish, as though he might float away in delirium any minute, leaving thirty-one passengers stranded. . . . And it had been one crummy lunch. And he was late. And he couldn't afford to blow the extra job, the chartered bus of doctors visiting the Infirmary. . . .

"Mai, change seats with Nilda and help me with this. A piece on John Henry and Kwan Cheong. The Spirit of Iron . . . something like that. We never did work it through."

"The Central and Union Pacific race for profit."

"We could do it as a mime and narrative musical for Sister of the Rice and Sister of the Yam."

"Anything to do with metals should be done by the brothers, I think."

"Unfortunately, they're all Black at the Academy, aren't they? And for the Kwan character—"

"Would you care to expound a bit on that 'unfortunately' before Sister Palma of the Yam and Sister Cecile of the Plantain whip out their switchblade and machete, respectively?"

"You think Velma might join us? Do the music? Palma?"

"John Henry and Kwan Cheong. I'll take notes. Keep talking."

Some notes, the driver, Fred Holt thought. He mopped his face with a handkerchief. He'd like a gander at those notes. (66)

The voices in this passage exemplify the generative dissonance of *The Salt Eaters*. We know the speakers are not Nilda, Mai, Palma, or Cecile because they address or refer to these women, but it is not entirely clear which of the other Seven Sisters are speaking. The reader's disorientation mirrors Fred's uneasiness. As the dialogue between two of the Sisters permeates Fred's internal narrative, the reader must work to knit them together. Fred's physical discomforts (he's "light and feverish" from the heat and sick to his stomach from a "crummy lunch") promise to be mended at the Infirmary, as we learn that is one of his destinations on this day. His personal experiences cannot be separated from the concerns of the Seven Sisters because their dialogue weaves through his thoughts on the page. Thus his oppressive working conditions (that the bus company "hadn't hired colored guys" and now "were talking about early retirement") become inseparable from the labor concerns the women wish to address. John Henry and Kwan Cheong of one sister's planned "Spirit of Iron" work (be it writing, "mime," or "narrative musical") are two folk heroes whose labor made train travel possible, just as Fred's labor enables mobility. John Henry is the "steel driving man" of African American folksong, and Cheong, the hero of a Korean folktale, died in and haunts a tunnel on a route he helped build. In this moment, Fred's bus is stopped in front of train tracks; the train whistle in his ears prompts a journey through memory not unlike Velma's (Mathes, "Scratching" 385). The work of all three men comes together in the claim "The Central and Union Pacific race for profit," implying a critique of the American capitalism once so dependent on those two train lines.

Fred's "crummy lunch," frustration, and need not to "blow the extra job" all become, through this polyvocality, enmeshed in concerns beyond his individual experience. Whether or not he knows it, he is connected to labor issues worldwide, especially in communities of color. The dialogue reveals that the Sisters include a Sister of the Rice and Sister of the Yam, who, like Kwan Cheong and John Henry, are of Asian and African descent. One speaker emphasizes the need for such cross-ethnic collaboration with her lament that the men at the Academy of Seven Arts are "all Black." The other speaker responds heatedly, suggesting that the African American Sister Palma of the Yam and the Caribbean Sister Cecile of the Plantain might respond with violence to any resistance to "all Black" organizations. The tension between defining community as people of color or as people of African descent informs the chorus of voices, spoken and implied, in this passage. However, no one objects to the assertion that "anything to do with metals should be done by the brothers," because the link between iron and the male West African deity Ogun is an unspoken argument for the use of men in this community-consolidating performance.

Oscillation on the page between narration focalized through Fred and dialogue among his passengers (who proliferate throughout the chapter to include a white couple, musicians, and elderly women) intertwines local and global concerns, all of which are tied to Velma, who finally emerges at the end of the dialogue when the women ask Palma whether her sister might "do the music" for "The Spirit of Iron." Velma's story, already well under way by the time we meet Fred and his passengers, frames this bus scene. With her recovery coming in the last pages of the text, her healing bookends the novel, making this formal entanglement of Fred with the Seven Sisters a part of that healing, part of her story. The danger to coherence, suggested by the notion that Palma and Cecile might have a "switchblade and machete, respectively," is constitutive of that coherence. Generative dissonance defines the African American cultural nation constantly organized in *The Salt Eaters*.

It is not crucial that groups like the passengers on Fred's bus, the Seven Sisters, the Academy, or the Infirmary meet a specific metric of success in *The Salt Eaters*. Rather, Bambara, as an organizer, uses the text to coalesce these groups onto the page as models for thinking through the possibilities of coalition. Even failures in each effort are valuable. Bambara explains, "I don't think it's terribly important whether I got it nailed in the book. I explore it, I bring it up, but I don't have anywhere to put it or push it. But I think, if it's done by organizers, then that's the accomplishment" (Salaam 61–62). "The accomplishment" of *The Salt Eaters* is organization on the page, in the body of Velma Henry, and in the community. The novel insists that to organize their cultural nation, the people of Claybourne must claim a local cultural geography that includes such resources as the loa, conjure, and astrology. Carter Mathes writes, "Bambara's writing suggests conceptions of late-twentieth-century racial subjectivity that embrace the seeming chaos of multiplicity and interconnection, not as an erosion of particular identities and locations, but rather as crucial starting points for the realization of the political complexity within them" ("Scratching" 370). The "chaos of multiplicity and interconnection" determine the form of narration that describes Fred's bus and its passengers. This mode of "multiplicity" is diffuse but specific; it depends on "particular identities and locations" as a means to convey thick connections with global implications. The local and specific allows Fred and his passengers to "embrace the seeming chaos of multiplicity and interconnection" and multiple ways of knowing so that they will move forward and head into a healed Claybourne rather than careen off a bridge to their deaths in one of the novel's "might have beens."

## Sounding the "Sonic Boom": Making a Nation

Grappling with political complexity and taking the astrology and presence of spirits seriously are real challenges. There is hope in this enormously difficult work of organizing a collective struggle through the recent past and toward a new future. This struggle belongs to the reader as well. Reviewers and scholars comment on the difficulty of *The Salt Eaters*, citing especially its nonlinear structure and shifts in point of view.[24] The challenge of holding in one's mind the tangle of past, present, and future in the novel forces the reader to experience "all those dead moments" that are as large in Velma's mind as they are on the page, interrupting the present-tense narrative for the reader just as they interrupt Velma's present-tense life. Cheryl Wall, expanding this notion of difficulty, writes, "The novel's challenges are not only formal. Readers' response to *The Salt Eaters* depends in part on their willingness to take seriously a wide variety of spiritual beliefs and practices that the novel argues are fundamental to social and political transformation" ("Toni's Obligato" 30–31). The work of reading is difficult in texts as formally innovative as Bambara's. In order to "unravel the political ends of Bambara's literary project," a reader must use a "nonlinear, multisensory reading practice" (Mathes, "Scratching" 375). More than being a difficult read, the novel is, as both Mathes and Wall suggest, difficult work. It demands not just comprehension but also alteration from its reader, who must expand her inner nation to include "a wide variety of spiritual beliefs and practices" in its topography. *The Salt Eaters* asks the reader to accept astrology, tarot, rootwork, and connection to the deceased so that she may inhabit the outermost of the concentric circles emanating from Velma's healing. The novel invites us, like characters in its pages, to take on difficulty, to participate in the struggle toward building an inner and outer nation using the tools the novel offers.

Whether or not the reader takes up this struggle, Velma's inner nation does radiate outward to change people in Claybourne. Gloria Hull notes that healing extends to the community: "Like Velma, all of the major figures who need it undergo a healing change" (219). Hull observes these changes: "Nadeen becomes a woman, Fred sees Porter in the streets, Meadows vows to give the Hippocratic oath some real meaning in his life" (224). Nadeen, a pregnant young woman watching the healing process in the Infirmary, "knew she was not the stupid girl her teachers thought she was, or the silly child the nurses thought she was. . . . She was a woman. Or at least, she wrinkled her nose to herself at too big a jump, she was womanish" (105–6). Standing close during Velma's healing, Nadeen is among the first to experience a shift in consciousness. She feels "a barrier falling away between childhood and adulthood" under the influence of "the sonic boom echoing back from a blasting event to occur several years hence" (104). Seemingly as a result of future change, Nadeen comes to see herself as a woman or "womanish," the latter term indicating transition and process rather than static achievement of a new mature status. She is both the girl who "wrinkled her nose" at the big idea of being an adult and a woman feeling power gathering in her.[25] Nadeen's realization that she is womanish suggests that, like Velma, she is in the process of claiming a multivalent, powerful, African American, female identity. Soon to give birth to a new citizen of a healed community, Nadeen is crucial for the alternative nation.

Velma's healing emanates to men as well. Dr. Julius Meadows, a physician returned to the South to work at the Infirmary, exemplifies a shift in consciousness and practice. From the beginning of Velma's healing, Meadows thinks of medicine in terms beyond his training. For example, he speculates that Velma looks catatonic and wonders "where catatonia was, if it might be in the woods behind the Infirmary" (57). His capacity to imagine the alternative space of catatonia and to consider Velma's healing as an out-of-body experience suggests that he has a role to play in envisioning healing as a multivalent process. Meadows exemplifies the split between modes of knowledge that *The Salt Eaters* seeks to mend. He wanders around Claybourne struggling with the gap between the "country mind" of his youth and the "city mind" of his adulthood. His divided mind mirrors the break between camps of workers that Bambara seeks to repair in the novel. After Meadows explores the town and interacts with its residents, "his city and his country mind drew together to ponder it all" (126). Like Nadeen becoming womanish, Meadows is evolving. He comes to read the "industrial arrogance and heedless technology" of the Claybourne Transchemical and nuclear power plants as "first and foremost a medical issue, a health issue, his domain" (281). The southern space of Claybourne and the communal ritual of Velma's healing make it possible for Meadows to meld country and city ways of knowing and thus enter the community he has decided to serve.[26] He experiences the resonating force of Velma's healing as a shift in his thinking, a "conversion" (282). Just as Obie helps Velma recover from a life of "keeping all those dead moments alive," Meadows is a man who, carrying the transformative lessons of a woman healer and a woman healed, will effect change in the uncertain future on the horizon of *The Salt Eaters*.

Nadeen's boyfriend, Buster, reveals that Meadows is not the only man bound to reap some recovery from witnessing Velma's healing. Buster sees fragmentation all over Velma's face, which he imagines with a domestic simile as "cracked and crazed like the soup tureen in his aunt's china cabinet" (58). Buster identifies with this fragmentation: "And for a second there, he'd have been willing to swear that he saw two faces at once on Mrs. Henry. Like an artsy photograph or like when he took his glasses off too fast. Or like he felt sometimes walking with a bump, his night face sinking down behind the day one and him touching himself to be sure he was there" (58). As a witness, father-to-be, student, and reporter, Buster too feels divided. Division in this scene, though, breaks into a binary; like Meadows's country and city minds, Buster has a "night face" and a "day one." Velma appears to him as having "two faces at once," but her identity emerges as more layered over the course of *The Salt Eaters*. If she can bring together all of her faces as adoptive mother, wife, spokesperson, sister, lover, corporate spy, and (if the promise of the novel is fulfilled) healer in Minnie's footsteps, surely Buster and Meadows can unite their binary selves. Velma's recovery models this work of unification among selves, labors, and modes of knowledge. As witnesses to her fusion, a coming event in direct opposition to the dangers of nuclear fission, Nadeen, Meadows, and Buster can partake of a healing rather than destructive form of radiation. Velma replaces emanations of nuclear fallout with emissions of recovery.

Radiating shifts of consciousness outward, Velma's body, like Claybourne, is a generative site for the broader cultural geography of *The Salt Eaters*. Her body instantiates a recovery promised for the South and the African American nation. Political and social change begins with Rich's "geography closest in—the body." Rich asserts that women must inhabit their bodies as means of "locating the grounds from which to speak with authority *as* women. Not to transcend this body, but to reclaim it" (213). As Minnie says, echoing Rich, "The source of health is never outside" (120). Velma accordingly must choose to get well, to return to her body in the physical world. Rather than allow all those dead moments to drive her to suicide again, she must recast the past as preparation for a better future. Her choice to heal, to answer yes to Minnie's opening question, "Are you sure, sweetheart, that you want to be well?," inquires the same of other individuals, communities, and the African American nation. Velma's body, the "geography closest in," becomes a ground zero, displacing the Claybourne Transchemical Plant, a nuclear power plant, and potential apocalypse as possible first sites of radical change. The sonic boom sounding back in time from the last pages of *The Salt Eaters* is not necessarily radiation or destruction but quite possibly the emanations of Velma's recovery (104).[27]

The change in weather at the end of *The Salt Eaters* is an ambiguous force that promises both destruction and rebirth. The waiter and journalist Campbell thinks, "Whatever cataclysmic event it might turn out to be . . . it couldn't simply be a storm with such frightening thunder as was cracking the air as if the very world were splitting apart" (245). The gathering storm is threatening, a struggle like Velma's healing, that the residents of Claybourne and the reader must work through to prepare for whatever comes next. Uprisings in nature issue a call to echo the change in weather with a change in the world. In fact none of the oppressive conditions that have brought Velma and Claybourne to the moment of the novel has changed when Velma emerges healed.[28] The end of *The Salt Eaters* indicates that Velma's healing is an act of preparation. In the final chapter, during the storm, the narrator notes, "Velma would remember it as the moment she started back toward life. . . . And years hence she would laugh remembering she'd thought *that* was an ordeal. She didn't know the half of it. Of what awaited her in years to come" (278). All the work to be well, to heal Velma and the community, is only a first step toward continued struggle for liberation "in years to come." The labor of healing and the shift signaled by the storm opens up an unknown future, one in which Minnie may train Velma to use her own gift and become a healer (293).[29] The ambiguous future is valuable because its uncertainty leaves room for community to be radically reimagined. The reader knows only that it will be a period of further cultural work, one in which the loa will come back into use: "one" (Velma, the reader, anyone in Claybourne) will "lure the saving spirits out to talk and be needed finally" (246). Neither armed revolt, death by drowning, nor nuclear disaster need be the "cataclysmic event" to come. The *Oxford English Dictionary* defines *cataclysm* as "a political or social upheaval which sweeps away the old order of things"; this is just the revolution promised by the circles of transformation that begin with Velma. *The Salt Eaters* employs the conditional case in its final pages to illuminate the possibilities ahead. In this new future, spirits could rejoin the community and "would open up and welcome one in before the end, welcome one in time to wrench time from its track so another script could play itself out" (247). Velma's recovery invites one to "wrench time from its track," averting the terrible events in the incessant conditional of what "might have been" in favor of "another script." Velma, Claybourne, and Bambara's descendants must turn the conditional into the actual. It is up to novelists writing in the wake of this healing event to inhabit this space to write "another script" for an African American cultural nation. Bambara prepares this ground. The labor of putting together a text, a community, a body, a nation is the women's work of organizing. Bambara's organizing enables the work ahead: that of cooking, dancing, mapping, and inscribing nation and other communities in the space born of *The Salt Eaters*. If the storm is to promise rebirth rather than destruction, Claybourne and the reader must, like Velma, answer yes to the query "Are you sure, sweetheart, that you want to be well?" The authors I examine in the remaining chapters answer Minnie with a resounding yes and take up the hard work of practicing a cultural nation.

# 2 / Cooking Up a Nation: Ntozake Shange's *Sassafrass, Cypress & Indigo*

Ntozake Shange's *Sassafrass, Cypress & Indigo* (1982) overflows with the creative output of Hilda Effania and her three daughters. The novel uses recipes to define cooking as a practice of an African American cultural nation. For several female characters in late twentieth-century novels by African American women, recipes are one fruitful space of self-expression. They are a form of what Alice Walker calls "our mothers' gardens"; recipes can document a woman's life and artistry. In *Sassafrass, Cypress & Indigo*, printed recipes, the Sea Islands setting, and the character Indigo each serves as cultural archives necessary for the preservation and practice of an African American cultural nation. Recipes in particular celebrate women's bodies, invite participation, pass on personal and familial history, and make imagined travel possible. Shange explores the potential of the recipe as a form that moves from the private space of text to a collective performance of community.

In Shange's writings, the recipe expands the possibilities of the novel form, breaking conventions of narrative. Like the works of Bambara, Marshall, Naylor, and Morrison, Shange's writings are driven by an investment in the possibility of local, often domestic practices to inform and create coalitions. The recipe exemplifies highly local, everyday women's work to practice a cultural nation. In an interview for *Ms* magazine reprinted in the second edition of *Nappy Edges* (1991), Shange says, "i am really committed to pulling the so-called personal outta the realm of non-art. that's why i have dreams & recipes, great descriptions of kitchens & handiwork in *sassafrass, cypress, & indigo*" (21). The recipe proves especially effective at moving women's work "outta the realm of non-art" by making that work legible, reproducible, and public in the pages of a novel.[1] In other words, it is less important to Shange's cultural nationalist aesthetic that the "personal is political" than that recipes demonstrate the power of women's work in shaping the public sphere. Cooking describes more than shopping for groceries and preparing food. Cooking refers to a set of practices, to foodways of fashioning self and community. This work, always in progress, cannot be pinned wholly to the page. Recipes are didactic and seminarrative; they proceed through linear time and are produced explicitly for infinite repetition and variation beyond the page. Shange inserts recipes in her novel to represent in text the shifting, ongoing, work of creating self and community.[2]

## The Recipe as Ritual

In one key possibility created by recipes breaking into novels, the culinary form becomes not a prescription for domestic labor confined to one kitchen but a ritual for travel to places on and off the map. The first recipe in *Sassafrass, Cypress & Indigo* is for a "moon journey." Narration stops, several lines of white space appear, and Indigo's recipe emerges:

> *Find an oval stone that's very smooth. Wash it in rosewater, 2 times. Lay it out to dry in the night air where no one goes. When dry, hold stone tightly in the right hand, caress entire face with the left hand. Repeat the same action with the stone in the left hand. Without halting the movement, clasp left stone-filled hand with the right. Walk to a tree that houses a spirit-friend. Sit under the tree facing the direction of your mother's birthplace. Hold your hands between your bosom, tight. Take 5 quick breaths and 3 slow ones. Close your eyes. You are on your way.* (5)

The moon, evocative of women's menstrual cycles, appears often in Shange's prose and poetry, in this case as a destination. Just two years after Bambara's Velma Henry struggles to make room for her menses in a narrative of black liberation and healing, Shange writes of Indigo as a young woman with rituals for celebrating her cycle. In the same italicized format Shange uses for culinary recipes in the novel, Indigo prescribes deep care for the body, insisting that a woman "caress entire face" as part of this ritual. When this recipe is performed, "You are on your way," but there are few details of the experience on the moon. The destination promises to be a homeland, but its contours are not entirely clear. In *Sassafrass, Cypress & Indigo*, the moon is journey's end for some African Americans, especially women. Indigo's Aunt Haydee, a midwife on the Georgia Sea Island Difuskie, tells of the moon as a place of "marvelous parties" (6). Shange's narration insists that women "sidle up to lunar hills every month" (6) as their menses bring them close to this alternative space. Allegiance to the imagined space of the moon demonstrates that ties to any single land base or community are inadequate markers of identity. Though Indigo's is a family of southerners, they have a foot in the space of the moon as well.

Indigo's recipe calls for "a tree that houses a spirit-friend," making use of the same loa that Bambara's Seven Sisters in *The Salt Eaters* leave to languish. Knowledge of one's maternal line, of the "mother's birthplace," is essential to this ritual. The practice occurs in a female body, signaled by "between your bosom." If every girl had Indigo's recipes, there might never be another illness like Velma's. Regularly using her maternal and spiritual resources in this ritual, Indigo experiences none of the fracture that threatens to dismantle Velma. Across Shange's canon such rituals create a cultural community that can restore multiplicity to African American women as a diverse group. This is not an amorphous idea of collectivity, but a set of practices. With ingredients relatively easy to find ("an oval stone," "night air," and one's own body), this recipe is meant to be followed. Just in case the reader does not know "the direction of [her] mother's birthplace," Shange offers "ALTERNATIVE MODES OF MOON JOURNEYS" (5), dependent instead on the more easily obtained "handkerchief handled by some other woman in [the] family" (5) as the ingredient symbolizing matrilineage. The didactic form of the recipe and the options for variations on the ritual insist that the reader perform the text.

All Shange's works maintain this concern with guiding African American girls toward womanhood, most famously the choreopoem *for colored girls who have considered suicide / when the rainbow is enuf* (1975).[3] She addresses black girls in the introduction to her 1972 volume of poetry *Nappy Edges*, lamenting, "if you are 14, female & black in the u.s.a. / you have one solitary voice though you number 3 million / no nuance exists for you / you have been sequestered in the monolith" (3). Indigo dramatically expands the possibilities of being "14, female & black in the u.s.a." by using recipes as practices of multivalent identity. The "monolith" that threatens diverse identity is not only a homogeneous notion of Africanness or blackness but also a restrictive reading of black girlhood. "Sequestered in the monolith," young African American women suffocate under a limited horizon of possibilities. Indigo and her recipes are meant to liberate them from the monolith, to pull them out from under the dominating force of a "solitary voice." Accordingly Indigo finds many ways to express and celebrate being young, female, and African American in all its complexity and variation.

As a young woman of "nuance" and possibility, Indigo does not limit her arts to imaginative travel but also expresses herself by making dolls and playing the fiddle. Her dolls, like her moon journeys, depend on both black matrilineage and figurative black female mobility, with an added emphasis on the African diaspora:

> Indigo had made every kind of friend she wanted. African dolls filled with cotton root bark, so they'd have no more slave children. Jamaican dolls in red turbans, bodies formed with comfrey leaves because they'd had to work on Caribbean and American plantations and their bodies must ache and be sore. Then there were the mammy dolls that Indigo labored over for months. They were almost four feet high, with big gold earrings made from dried sunflowers, and tits of uncleaned cotton. They smelled of fennel, peach leaves, wild ginger, wild yams. (6)

Indigo's dolls represent various locations in the diaspora. The dolls document history, make transnational connections, heal bodies (exemplified by the use of comfrey leaves to soothe aches), and take control of reproduction with "cotton root bark so they'd have no more slave children." Her power to right wrongs like the birth of children into slavery and to foster physical recovery foreshadows her later work as a healer and midwife on Difuskie; she is powerful even in her childhood play. Though this passage is not set off from the narrative or italicized, it suggests the recipe format by listing the ingredients for her creations. Her "mammy dolls" even smell of foodstuffs: "fennel, peach leaves, wild ginger, wild yams." Like moon journeys, Indigo's dolls become a site for celebrating the female body, here through the inclusion of "tits of uncleaned cotton" and later when, after getting her first period, she fashions velvet pads for each doll's underwear as though they too are menstruating (19). Indigo marks the occasion of her menses with a ritual "As told by Indigo to her dolls" for "MARVELOUS MENSTRUATING MOMENTS" (19). She not only makes room for honoring her own body but tries to pass on this reverent stance "to her dolls" and implicitly to the reader, asking both to enact "union with [their] magic" (19). These instructions, like the explicitly culinary portions of the novel, are set apart, italicized, and under a capitalized title. Though some ingredients, such as "white water lilies," may be difficult to obtain, others, such as clean sheets, baths, and strawberries, are more readily available for the reader who might perform these rituals (19–20).

Through the formal conventions of recipes (didactic tone, narrativity, linearity, reproducibility) *Sassafrass, Cypress & Indigo* invites the reader to perform the text; moon journeys and celebrations of menses function like traditional culinary recipes. The text of a recipe strains against the page, printed explicitly so that it can be performed in the world. In conversation with Claudia Tate, Bambara uses food terminology to describe her vision of "ways to link up our warriors and our medicine people." She describes this desire to "link up" as writing "in hopes that sisters of the yam, the rice, the corn, the plantain, might find the work to be too thin a soup and get on out there and cook it right" (Tate 25). Recipes inhabit the space created by such a "link[ing] up"; recipes reach toward action, struggling to leap off the page to "get on out there." Shange too speaks of a desire to write in a way that acts upon the world, describing her distinct punctuation and capitalization as born from "the idea that letters dance," so that "reading becomes not just a passive act and more than an intellectual activity, but demands rigorous participation" (Tate 163).

Shange's use of the recipe breaks new textual ground, using the form to capitalize on the narrativity of a novel while subverting linear time by presenting acts of cooking meant to be repeated outside the text in "rigorous participation." Patricia E. Clark asserts, "The language of a food recipe is not merely a set of instructions, but also contains the imperative meaning through its secondary, 'unspoken,' aim—the consumption or the taking in of a dish—by way of a detour through its primary aim, the creation of a dish" (153). While recipes proceed narratively through the linear time of creating a dish, the form also suggests cyclic time (each performance of the recipe is a repetition with difference) and monumental time (following a recipe for Easter ham, birthday cake, or a Christmas goose marks an event). Collective consumption of the product of the text refuses the isolation usually associated with the reading and writing of novels even as the seminarrative form demonstrates the kinship between recipes and fiction. The "secondary 'unspoken' aim" (eating) refuses to be pinned down in print or oral narrative; the unspoken outcome exists only in action, in the world of the reader outside the page, who, in "the creation of a dish," may achieve the goal of sharing and consuming it as well. Shange uses the tactics of the cookbook to make the novel more collective, improvisational, and demanding of reader participation. Clark notes that *Sassafrass, Cypress & Indigo* "invites the reader to participate, to use the recipes to create her own versions, adding to the repertoire of knowledge cataloged in the novel" (156). This knowledge includes the many modes of creation, including writing letters, weaving tapestries, making dolls, dancing, fiddling, and bringing babies into the world.

Including so many acts of creation in her novel, Shange sets writing on equal ground with other women's work. There is no distinction between the value of the author and the value of the cook; both are necessary cultural workers. *Sassafrass, Cypress & Indigo* calls for reader participation, for more cooks in the kitchen. Shange, following Amiri Baraka, Gwendolyn Brooks, and other black arts poets, insists on the life of a poem outside the page; she asserts, "A poem shd happen to you" (*Nappy Edges* 24), and she extends this urgency to her prose, using the demand for a life beyond the page inherent in recipes as a strategy for all of her writing.

Further pressing against generic boundaries, Shange refuses a binary opposition of written and oral; she calls upon her skills as poet, playwright, and novelist to pin to the page a set of recipes mostly passed on orally or by example. Accordingly her culinary text is performative and reflects oral culture. On the level of the sentence, her poetry and prose employ unique spelling, punctuation, and capitalization, sometimes reflective of speech. Tejumola Olaniyan terms this tactic "anticonventional punctuation and orthography."[4] On the level of complete works, novel and cookbook cannot be untangled; performance, oral narrative, and written novel entwine. The generic experimentation that marks Shange's theater pieces appears in *Sassafrass, Cypress & Indigo* as well. In addition to recipes, we get Hilda Effania's letters, which frame her daughter's stories. These letters, along with enclosed recipes, punctuate narratives of the women's lives. Each of Hilda's missives gets its own chapter in this form, which Doris Witt aptly terms a "recipistolary novel." For Witt, Shange's "appropriation of the genre of the novel" is radical because the text "requires not simply to be read or spoken (or even viewed in a theatre); it demands instead that we perform and consume it—that we cook and eat its recipes as an integral part of our experience of the work" (11). *Sassafrass, Cypress & Indigo* is a radical "appropriation" of an elevated art form (the novel) to demand action.

Demonstrating the flexibility of the recipe, Shange uses the form to situate cuisine and conjure together. Indigo offers explicit conjure recipes in the first section of the book, such as "IF YOUR BELOVED HAS EYES FOR ANOTHER" (15) and "TO RID ONESELF OF THE SCENT

OF EVIL" (30), the latter with the tag of authorship "by Indigo." Recipes for food appear later, in the sections that focus on Indigo's two older sisters. By making rituals for self-care, conjure, and food of equal textual weight and similar appearance, Shange forces the dynamism of the culinary recipe to saturate her other recipes. In other words, by using almost the same format for "Cypress' Curried Crabmeat" (111) and "EMERGENCY CARE OF WOUNDS THAT CANNOT BE SEEN" (50), Shange suggests that the reader can practice conjure and healing rituals as she would follow a recipe for food.[5]

## Shange's Culinary Critique of the Black Arts Movement

Cooking is not exclusively a practice of healing, sustenance, and liberation; it can also record pain and oppression. Indigo's sister Sassafrass,[6] for example, finds pleasure in cooking for her lover, but this creativity occurs within the confines of a patriarchal and abusive relationship. Sassafrass makes her lover, Mitch, a meal of "Sassafrass' Rice Casserole #36," "Sassafrass' Favorite Spinach for Mitch #10," "Sassafrass: The Only Way to Broil Fish: Mackerel," and "Red Sauce: Sassafrass' Variation Du-Wop '59" (83–84). Each recipe includes her name so that, like the recipes "by Indigo," these instructions bear a mark of individuality and female ownership. "Variation Du-Wop" asserts that cooking is akin to making music. Like reading a musical composition, following a recipe demands improvisation; it requires both a unique skill set and variation. A musician is "really cookin'" when he knows a piece of music so well he can take it beyond notation and into varied, exciting, "hot" performances. Like a musical composition, recipes have a single author but can be performed in infinite varied repetitions by many others if they acquire the requisite skill. The single authorship indicated by "Sassafrass' Rice Casserole" or "by Indigo" serves as an invitation to collaboration with a culinary soloist.

Even the liberatory creativity of these recipes, along with their possibilities for community formation, is bound inside Sassafrass's relationship with Mitch, where she is often "stuck in the kitchen" (82) and worries that "if she prepared this scrumptious meal there wouldn't be hardly enough food left to finish off the week" (83). While Mitch spares no expense on his oil paints, Sassafrass is caught between managing economic realities and striving to be the artistic woman he demands. He is "into her being perfect today" (83) but hardly reciprocates her efforts to make room for his music and painting. Adding insult to injury, he forces her to serve her gorgeous meal to his friends Otis and Howard. Their visit is marked by a break in narrative titled "THE REVUE" (87).

This section of the novel offers an explicit critique of black arts and black power gender dynamics. "THE REVUE" is a misogynist dramatic dialogue, a brief interpolated play in the novel. "Ebony Cunt," Otis's poem within the "THE REVUE," asserts the right of black men to rape black women. Performed with jazz accompaniment, Otis's poem signifies on black arts poetry by men. Though she often mentions the influence of Baraka and Ishmael Reed on her work,[7] Shange here calls out the sexism and violence in these men's literary tradition. "Deeply informed by black American vernacular practices, Black Arts Movement poetics, and the militant reverence for the new music and its exponents" (Clarke 95), Shange also comments on sexism in BAM. Acknowledging the poets who inspire her but taking a new direction, she exhorts, "The same rhetoric that is used to establish the Black Aesthetic, we must use to establish a women's aesthetic" (Blackwell 136).

In *Sassafrass, Cypress & Indigo* this break comes to a head in Shange's satiric, angry depiction of black arts performance. A poem inside a play inside a novel, "Ebony Cunt" goes so far as to claim the Middle Passage as a means of transporting sex to black men. In the voice of an African American man, Otis's poem addresses its title character: "15 millions of your shinin' blk bodies crossed the sea to bring all that good slick pussy to me" (88). Sassafrass responds with profanity and anger, telling Mitch, Otis, and Howard, "Don't you ever sit in my house and ask me to celebrate my inherent right to be raped" (89). Though her resistance is immediate and vocal, it is also constrained, appearing as scripted stage dialogue within "THE REVUE." Her response in fact follows the stage direction "Sassafrass (standing still)" (89). Formally, "THE REVUE" is the context for her words.[8]

This reflects Shange's relationship to the black arts movement, whose scripts surrounded her at times. From within at least some of its ideologies, like Sassafrass from within "THE REVUE," Shange critiques BAM. Of the authors considered here, she is the most explicit in responding to the masculinist cultural nationalism that informs black arts politics. Much of Sassafrass's story first appears in Shange's 1976 novella *Sassafrass*, published by Shameless Hussy Press.[9] *Sassafrass, Cypress & Indigo*, though published in the 1980s, has roots in the 1970s. *Sassafrass* appears almost in its entirety in the later novel. It converses with and critiques versions of black nationalism that put women largely in positions of servitude. By 1998, with her cookbook *If I Can Cook / You Know God*

*Can*, Shange writes herself beyond this necessity, but her earlier work is a more direct response to black arts discourse. Nowhere is this more evident than in *Sassafrass*.

In the novel, Sassafrass calls the men "muthafuckas" (89) and speaks her rage in the context of a misogynist discourse; Shange's expression from within a black arts context is also often surprising, humorous, and a welcome disruption. She describes her departure from her black arts predecessors in culinary terms: "I have to feed the people but when I feed the people I can't give them rations, I have to give them a meal that's nurtured with love and that has particular spices for particular tastes" (Shange et al., "Artists' Dialogue" 159). She both claims her black arts legacy and revises it. Her work is not the bare minimum for survival; it is not rations, but a meal. This distinction suggests that a narrow, masculinist nationalism can produce the necessary rations of physical survival but not the meal of sustaining community that accommodates diversity within its ranks. Unlike the vision of Mitch and his friends, Shange's cultural nationalism is infused with individual "particular tastes," love and nurturance, as well as the terms of domestic production of a meal that promises a level of sensory pleasure clearly at play in Sassafrass's kitchen. Using food preparation as a metaphor for writing, Shange implicitly reiterates the assertion of *Sassafrass, Cypress & Indigo* that the two forms of women's work, writing and cooking, are of equal value, regardless of the number of people who consume the final product.

Though influenced by black arts poetry and black nationalist politics of the 1960s and 1970s, Shange diverges from these discourses explicitly when it comes to food. Sassafrass responds vehemently to the misogynist discourse of Mitch and his friends, and the novel takes up this conversation through recipes. The culinary territory of black power revolved mostly around soul food. Witt describes this stance: "The rise of Black Power contributed to the celebration of foods previously stigmatized because of their association with the slave diet—fried chicken and collard greens certainly among them." Witt charts the process in which "soul food cooking was related to the concurrent vilification of African American women as castrating matriarchs" (6).[10] Sassafrass, a sexy, feminine artist, bears no obvious marks of a stereotypical mammy, Sapphire, or "castrating matriarch" laboring in the kitchen. She takes joy in food preparation, making a group of dishes that, though certainly soulful, are not soul food like the items Witt lists. This sensual culinary pleasure, along with Sassafrass's ownership of her recipes, is marred by its circumscription within a patriarchal interaction between Sassafrass and the men around her. The differences between black power and black feminism as well as between 1960s black nationalism and contemporary African American visions of community are central to this exchange. Sassafrass negotiates this tension with kitchen practices. Her culinary arts reflect and revise the nationalist expressions of Mitch's horn playing, the offensive "Ebony Cunt," and the limited script of "THE REVUE." Shange displays a sexist dynamic but also shows Sassafrass navigating that dynamic by working outside and beyond the dramatic structure of "THE REVUE." Beyond the reach of that narrow script, Sassafrass writes her own poetry, finding refuge in her weaving, "the only tradition Sassafrass inherited that gave her a sense of womanhood that was rich and sensuous, not tired and stingy" (92), and uses her culinary arts as one creative labor among others rather than an act of service for men.

An abundance of creative production in *Sassafrass, Cypress & Indigo*—from dolls to recipes, music, tapestries, poems, and dances—demonstrates how fruitful women's cooperation can be, particularly in fostering a "rich and sensuous" "sense of womanhood." Sassafrass turns to the art of weaving, learned from her mother, to find a healing outlet. By novel's end, we hope she will pass on this family tradition to her newborn daughter. In Shange's novel, the collaboration of four women, Hilda Effania and her three daughters, is powerful enough to suggest a broader community.

Not all women's collectives fare so well. Just as the multiethnic coalition of the Seven Sisters in Bambara's *The Salt Eaters* has conflicts and failings, a women's collective of dancers, the New York group Azure Bosom, fails in *Sassafrass, Cypress & Indigo* to serve as a home for Hilda Effania's middle child, Cypress. At first, Cypress delights in being surrounded by women, living with them, ensconced in photos and paintings of women such that "Cypress saw herself everywhere she looked" (139). This gendered separatism initially serves as a breath of fresh air. The spectrum of possibility for love among women is nurturing, but the practices in this "woman-being space" (140) eventually devolve into bitter complaints against men and jealous rivalries for women lovers. In a heterosexist turn of the plot, Cypress heals from heartbreak after a lesbian affair with fellow dancer Idrina only by falling in love with a man, Leroy. She expresses her contentment, her sense of being at home in New York, by bringing the South to her, cooking "a meal that all Carolina would envy" (174). Though southern culinary standards are the ones she cares about, Cypress's creation roots her decidedly in New York as well. Accordingly she titles her recipes "CYPRESS'S MEAL FOR MANHATTAN NIGHTS" (174).

Once again, cooking proves both pleasurable and problematic. Cypress, like her sister Sassafrass, finds expression in preparing food for a man. There are no scenes in the novel of Cypress feeding her female lover, though she cooks for and hosts mixed-gender groups of friends. While the reader can hardly resist the love between Cypress and Leroy as perhaps the only successful romance in the novel, we must recognize the patriarchal and heterosexist dynamics even in this fulfilling relationship. Cypress creates this luxurious meal just after she has assured Leroy that she now loves Idrina "like one of [her] sisters," and he, despite his best intentions, tries to "fuck" Cypress "into loving" him completely, so that she'll never "leave [him] for that bitch" (174). The gender separatism of Azure Bosom and Hilda Effania's household allows Cypress to be a woman among women. This is absolutely necessary to the possibility of her sustaining and loving relationship with Leroy. That relationship also depends on the novel's foreclosure of any future lesbian relationships. The specter of same-sex romantic love from the Azure Bosom days folds into the dynamics of Hilda Effania's home; Cypress will think of her former lover only as a sister. This familial affection diffuses all same-sex erotic possibility in the violent moment of Leroy wanting to fuck away any lingering romantic interest in women, leaving room in Cypress's heart and body only for him. Though Leroy effectively eliminates the "woman-being space" of Azure Bosom from Cypress's future, he partly redeems himself by celebrating Hilda Effania's Charleston home, insisting that he and Cypress get married there.

Hilda Effania's home is the foundation that teaches her three daughters to emerge from underfoot in their mother's kitchen to reign kitchens, literal and metaphorical, of their own. The most satisfying women's work in *Sassafrass, Cypress & Indigo* is accordingly not the dances of Azure Bosom that celebrate the vulva and ovaries but the local, ordinary, and less obviously performative work of cooking. The best of women's work in Shange's novel is not the explicitly public, staged, and declared feminist performances of Azure Bosom, but the "so-called personal" domestic work moved "outta the realm of non-art" by a family of women.

In the mode of cultural nationalism in all the novels under consideration, individual women's work in *Sassafrass, Cypress & Indigo* forges community using collective pasts and futures. Hilda Effania and her daughters create a successful "woman-being space" partly through a connection to history. The refrain "the slaves who were ourselves" saturates the novel in ways both subtle and overt. Indigo's dolls, music, and midwifery; Sassafrass's tapestries and culinary creations; Cypress's dance and woven dance notations; Hilda Effania's weavings, cooking, and letters all document, honor, and build from "the slaves who were ourselves." The past tense here indicates that slavery is an inherited and meaningful but not ongoing condition for these women. Rather, women's work broadly defined, with some acknowledged roots in slave labor, is the foundation of an alternative cultural nation because it both expresses lineage and looks forward, adopting Bambara's future-oriented stance as necessary for sovereignty. Just as Sassafrass learns weaving from her mother but remakes it as fine art rather than functional craft, taking it "outta the realm of non-art," and Cypress uses her mother's southern cooking as a springboard to create her own Manhattan recipes, the women of Shange's novel inherit a legacy of African American enslavement but use it to inform present and future liberation through artistic creation.

## Kitchens, the South, and Other Nationalist Spaces

The mother's home in Charleston is the first site for training Sassafrass, Cypress, and Indigo in the ways of this daily labor toward a mutable community. Houston Baker writes of the domestic aesthetic in Hilda Effania's home:

> Hilda Effania's work is precapitalist productivity. It is precisely "outside" the mainstream economics. . . . Her weaving is a redaction, in fact, of the codes of slave production. . . . There are also other acts of subversion, such as Hilda's recipes. These recipes are recurrent items in the narrative.
>
> They are wisdom transmitted from generations past; they are, also, present instruction for nourishment. . . . Designed for a nurturance that can only be "activated" by the recipient, her texts are phenomenological. They are altars in themselves, transforming the raw into the culturally cooked—into home cooking.
>
> Weaving, conjuring, recipes, letters are all products of Hilda Effania's domestic space. In her quarter of Charleston, *making* is always in progress. Beyond its subsistence function, this making seeks to transform the lives of black women. (182–86)

Baker's reading attends to the way Shange uses recipes as calls to action and as "subversion." He is right that this "making seeks to transform the lives of black women," but his reading romanticizes this making as "altars" and vague "transmitted wisdom." His celebration of culinary arts as an aspect of "Afro-American women's expressive production" does not fully consider that such expression often occurs within a troubling gender dynamic, as between Sassafrass and Mitch. Reading recipes as abstract altars and romanticized "precapitalist productivity" runs the risk of erasing specificity. The recipes Baker has in mind do transform "the raw into the culturally cooked," in a riff on Claude Lévi-Strauss, but they also literally describe how to transform the raw into the edible cooked, which is at least as important in *Sassafrass, Cypress & Indigo*. The value of the recipe is that it renders the labor of cooking (planning, shopping, measuring, sifting, mixing, baking, serving, and so on) entirely visible and largely transparent. The danger in divorcing the recipe's "subsistence function" from its social power is to erase the actual, detailed, specific work of women that saturates Shange's writing at every turn.

This women's work takes place largely in southern spaces. "A southern home," Baker asserts, "is coextensive with all of the narrative's aesthetic events" (199). The South in Shange's texts is multivalent, both geographic and cultural and able to travel to and influence other spaces. Southernness migrates with Hilda Effania's daughters to California and New York. The Sea Islands and the adjacent Atlantic Ocean in the South serve as archival spaces. They are not a set of documents, but sites of cultural transmission, particularly as Indigo's training ground for midwifery. In specifying Difuskie, which, unlike Paule Marshall's Tatem or Gloria Naylor's Willow Springs, is a real Sea Island on maps of the United States, Shange partly escapes the danger of romanticizing the region as a site of direct African cultural retention and primitivist fascination for residents of the mainland. The adjacent Atlantic Ocean becomes a flexible route of identification. Because it is neither a homeland of actual people nor tethered firmly to a single nation-state, use of the ocean spares *Sassafrass, Cypress & Indigo* the cultural tourism that, as I discuss in chapter 3, shapes Marshall's overwater journeys in *Praisesong for the Widow*.

In Shange's novel, the ocean as cultural repository helps make sense of the absent father Albert. Sassafrass recalls, "daddy was a seaman / a ship's carpenter. he was always goin' round the world / that's what mama said / & he died in the ocean offa zanzibar / that's what mama said the ship just caught fire and went down to the bottom of the ocean / that's why she & sassafrass & cypress & indigo wd toss nickels & food & wine in the sea down the coast / so daddy wd have all he needed to live a good life in the other world" (108). The ocean gravesite of slaves who died during the Middle Passage, so potent in much contemporary African American literature, serves as a resting place for Albert. His death is mythic, like the tale of flying Africans, made stronger with each telling; Shange emphasizes the storytelling mode with repetition of "that's what mama said." His passage to "the other world" is a spectacular one that strains belief: a vision of a ship ablaze on the ocean. Sassafrass and her sisters come to doubt their mother's story of their father's death more and more as they grow up. Cypress resolves, "One time there just was no more daddy but what you could remember, what you would make up in yourself that would be like him" (187). Hanging on to "what you could make up in yourself that would be like him," the daughters never abandon the sense of magic in the tale of their father's death. They use storytelling as a way to "be like him," magical Geechees.

The ritual of placing "nickels & food & wine in the sea" leads Sassafrass to access her own southern magic when, as a girl hanging around the Charleston docks, where such gifts are launched into the ocean, she insists, "i'ma be a cunjah." The dock workers reply "you awready a geechee / how much more magic you want?" (109). They recognize her power and magic rooted in her connection to the African American Geechee culture of the Sea Islands.[11] She inhabits this legacy by novel's end, becoming a priestess in a community in "the lush backwoods of Louisiana," where "ordinary folks seeking another life had made home" (214). Amid creative people who worship the deity Shango in a southern space, Sassafrass becomes a vessel for Oshun, an orisha who, in Yoruban and Cuban religious practice, represents love, maternity, and intimacy.

Like Obie in *The Salt Eaters*, Sassafrass's cultural nationalism leads her to radically imagine a separatist, southern community. Unlike Obie, Sassafrass fulfills her imaginings by finding her way to an alternative homeland. Such radical imagining proves harder to access the further she is physically from the South. In practices of creative expression, however, she can access this power, as she does all the way from California (another coastal space) when, listening to Mitch and his band, "she was just dancing and falling back to the South" (129). Music made on the domestic instruments of an ironing board and a washboard (129) brings Sassafrass "back to the South," putting a feminine cast on both the journey back and the music previously claimed for rigid masculinity by Mitch and his compatriots in "THE REVUE." Shange's notion of the South is accessible from a distance, a practice rather than a place. Sassafrass ultimately must return to the geographical South to assume her role as priestess. Inhabited by Oshun, she finds the power to reject the abusive Mitch and return to her southern maternal home in Charleston to birth her child with Indigo's aid.[12]

Indigo, the youngest child, whose experiences open and close Shange's novel, is marked by the refrain "the South in her" (4, 8, 14, 28, 29). She remains rooted in the South, moving from Charleston to the Sea Islands, where she becomes a midwife. With "the South in her" Indigo becomes more southern than the place around her; she, rather than a land mass, embodies the intense and metaphorical southernness of Zora Neale Hurston's muck or Naylor's Willow Springs. A healer and midwife rooted in the Sea Islands, Indigo embodies southern African American history from her initiation early in the novel to the Junior Geechee Captains to her claiming of her ancestor Blue Sunday at the close of the novel (222).[13] She becomes a practitioner of the embodied archive. She can dance on the shores of the island with "the slaves who were ourselves" (224) because she is so entangled with her cultural history that she not only inherits it but makes it. Indigo emerges as the site and continuation both of her family's tradition and of a broader cultural nationalism. She is more than a doll maker, conjurer, and fiddler named for a dye used in traditional West African cloth and her mother's weaving. The blue of her name is the color associated with the Yoruban mother goddess Yemoja, who appears in numerous African diasporic religions as the patron deity of women, especially pregnant ones. Indigo fulfills the promise of her name, performing as a midwife in the broadest sense, literally bringing babies into the world and figuratively ushering in an increased consciousness of a history that celebrates "the slaves who were ourselves," "the South in her," the legend of flying Africans, and the liberating ancestor Blue Sunday. Yemoja is also the patron saint of fishermen and shipwrecked sailors in Brazilian culture; like Blue Sunday, Yemoja is connected to water. Indigo's name reveals her as the repository of all these inheritances. She holds her community's connection to a lineage of female power derived from both a vast multivalent motherhood and the ocean where her father and millions of slaves lie. She is thus an embodiment of the many modes of knowledge Bambara calls for in *The Salt Eaters*. Indigo is the nationalist culture worker Velma Henry plans to be.

The connection to ocean spaces and diasporic spiritual practices demonstrates that, rich as it is, the U.S. South alone cannot wholly stand as the site of identity for the women of *Sassafrass, Cypress & Indigo*. Each of the daughters has roots in various spaces and systems of knowledge; these women practice nation as a diversity of allegiances rather than a homogeneous, static community. The novel uses the recipe form to shift routes of identity from literal space into practice. The community defined in this novel is one of participants practicing a cultural nation in wildly varied ways. Indigo comes to inhabit the words that open the novel. She is the "woman who knows her magic. . . . With a moon falling from her mouth, roses between her legs and tiaras of Spanish moss, the woman is a consort of the spirits" (3). Her mother gradually perceives her daughter's importance to the cultural nation: "Hilda Effania knew that Indigo had an interest in folklore. Hilda Effania had no idea that Indigo was the folks" (224). Indigo takes on the work of Blue Sunday. She performs an archive, recording and transmitting the diasporic spiritual and matrilineal history of "the folks." She midwifes and celebrates female bodies and varied creative output, becoming the heroine of the novel. The key figure of Shange's African American community in practice is not a man lecturing from a podium, blowing a horn, or shouting out his poetry, but a young woman helping other women give birth.

Concerns with mothering pervade Shange's canon. Like cooking, motherhood redefines women's work in terms of both the individual woman and an African American nation. In *Sassafrass, Cypress & Indigo*, Hilda Effania, the immediate maternal relative, plays the crucial role of guiding her daughters toward creative expression. Mothering in Shange's work becomes, in the context of many women's arts, far less literal. Shange repeatedly pulls the reader back from any romanticized notion of a black mother. Her poem "Oh, I'm 10 Months Pregnant" in *A Daughter's Geography* oscillates between the physical and literal details of pregnancy like "the urine test & the internal exam" and a more figurative entanglement of birthing babies with birthing poems: "the baby doesnt know / she's not another poem" (31). Shange positions writing and giving birth as equally difficult and deeply connected forms of women's work. She insists on difference between the two in "Oh, I'm 10 Months Pregnant" by pointing repeatedly to the baby's agency. The speaker says that the child "believes the uterine cave is a metaphor" (31), using both humor and insistence on the baby's agency to undercut any vision of childbirth as abstractly sacred and "spiritual." The speaker of the poem worries, "This baby wants to jump out of my mouth" (31) because it thinks it is a poem to be heard. "10 Months" achieves humor through imagery and a mildly self-deprecating tone. Motherhood becomes an individual physical experience, something to laugh about, one form of women's many labors, and collaboration between mother and child.

"10 Months" and the portrayals of maternity in Shange's prose snatch motherhood back from the patriarchal conscription Witt describes thus: "By presenting the wombs of African American women as a battleground for phallus-driven interracial politics, men such as H. Rap Brown [and other black male nationalists] transformed long-standing investments in the myth of black female dominance into an opportunity for the public staging of fears about the future of whiteness, blackness, and the beleaguered manhood of both" (95). In reclaiming motherhood as undeniably physical in "10 Months" Shange recovers maternity from the romanticization, patriarchy, and political abstraction that Witt describes. Across her canon, Shange presents motherhood as an infinitely varied, ordinary practice of mostly pleasurable work done by both parent and child. Though the child in Shange's works is almost always a girl, the parent or guide is sometimes male; this particular work toward sovereignty is open to both genders.[14] As is true for many of the authors considered here, motherhood for Shange is serious collaborative work akin to writing. However, Shange approaches parenting with more humor and play, making the work of mothering like cooking: fun, improvisational, performed by women and men to make something that was not there before.

More broadly, Shange's canon strives to mother female readers.[15] Her works *Daddy Says* (2003) and *i live in music* (1994) are explicitly for young readers, but her writing for adults also seeks to teach and guide women. Indigo's recipes for celebrating her female body are a handbook for the reader; the novel yearns to both heal the female reader's younger self and suggest tools for mothering strong, secure, embodied women. Shange, with Indigo's doll making in mind, says of her imagined audience:

> I collect dolls and the reason I collect dolls is because there's a person in me who's still a little girl and she loves them. I also collect dolls because I want to give the person in me who's a little girl the things that I should have had and never got. The reason that *For Colored Girls* is entitled *For Colored Girls* is that that's who it was for. I wanted them to have information that I did not have. I wanted them to know what it was truthfully like to be a grown woman. I didn't know. All I had was a whole bunch of mythologies—tales and outright lies. I want a twelve-year-old girl to reach out for and get some information that isn't just contraceptive information but emotional information. . . . If there is an audience for whom I write, it's the little girls who are coming of age. I want them to know that they are not alone and that we adult women thought and continue to think about them. (Tate 161–62)

The labor of motherhood becomes not only birthing and raising a child but also writing a text that displaces "tales and outright lies" to convey the practical guidance needed to navigate one's "coming of age." Text can also guide readers of both sexes to be better mothers. Shange says, "I'd like Black people to think about whimsical and courageous little girls as ordinary. That's important" (Gomez 9). Brave, smart, and compassionate, Indigo is a model of the type of girlhood Shange wants "Black people" to expect from their children. Indigo's recipes for self-care are racialized lessons in parenting. *Sassafrass, Cypress & Indigo* mothers the reader, offering a set of guideposts and a demonstration that "adult women thought and continue to think about" these "whimsical and courageous little girls." Finally, Shange's writings insist that girls like Indigo are entirely "ordinary" if we only understand that every little girl is marvelous in her own way.

## *Sassafrass, Cypress & Indigo* and Other Cookbooks

*Sassafrass, Cypress & Indigo* engages traditions of African American literature and a tradition of African American cookbooks. Cookbooks appear as complex archives of African American women's lives not only in fiction like Naylor's *Linden Hills* but also in a rich cookbook tradition increasingly uncovered in contemporary scholarship on African American foodways.[16] Vertamae Grosvenor's *Vibration Cooking or the Travel Notes of a Geechee Girl* (1970) is a model for Shange. *Vibration Cooking* blends genres, weaving narrative and imperative into a gumbo of memoir, travelogue, social commentary, and cookbook. Though a long history of African American foodways writing precedes both Grosvenor and Shange, Grosvenor shifts foodways literature toward genre experimentation, black liberation politics, and transatlantic reach, all of which set the stage for *Sassafrass, Cypress & Indigo* and Shange's 1998 work *If I Can Cook / You Know God Can*.[17] Laying claim to the tasks of gathering and preparing food, these cookbook authors place culinary arts in the same sphere as organizing, writing, dancing, mapping, and inscribing. The meaning of women's work shifts from a term for women relegated to domestic labor in the private sphere to a term for women's daily rituals that coalesce and determine communities, from family to nation.

Published when the Black Panther Party was at its most visible, *Vibration* evidences the same 1970s militancy, racial separatism, and troubling gender politics that Shange resists in *Sassafrass, Cypress & Indigo*. The recipe form in Shange's work copes with gendered legacies of the 1970s that Grosvenor elides. Recipes for honoring one's "marvelous menstruating moments" and taking moon journeys are relatively accessible in *Sassafrass, Cypress & Indigo*. Though published in the early 1980s,

*Sassafrass, Cypress & Indigo* is in many ways a 1970s novel, engaged in the same work of claiming diversity and power for African American women done by Bambara's *The Black Woman*. Decades later, *If I Can Cook* inhabits the space cleared by *Vibration Cooking*, *The Black Woman*, and Shange's own *Sassafrass, Cypress & Indigo*, using the recipe to destabilize identities it earlier bolstered, to practice a mutable community. *Vibration Cooking* bequeaths the recipe as an agent of change to *Sassafrass, Cypress & Indigo*, while *If I Can Cook*, the more obvious progeny of Grosvenor's line, uses recipes in increasingly metaphorical, abstract, and sometimes inaccessible ways.[18]

Witt asserts that *Vibration Cooking* posits a "protodiasporic model of selfhood" created to "negotiate a position between black nationalist and white feminist discourses" (15). *If I Can Cook* falls in this lineage with its assertion of a migratory, culinary black subjectivity. Far less invested in a discursive exchange with white feminism than Grosvenor's cookbook, *If I Can Cook* exemplifies the consistent focus in all Shange's writing almost exclusively on communities of color. In the tradition of Zora Neale Hurston, Shange chooses to celebrate and explore manifestations of blackness, though she never elides contexts of racial oppression as Hurston sometimes does. As a result of similar commitments, Grosvenor takes pains to recover the terms *nation* and *soul food* in *Vibration Cooking*, giving rise to a potentially reductive concept of African American identity. Experimenting with the possibilities of the recipe form in *Sassafrass, Cypress & Indigo* and expanding them in *If I Can Cook*, Shange claims and revises the tradition of culinary writing she inherits from Grosvenor.

By treating culinary improvisation as a learned and shifting practice, Shange insists on maintaining a broad and diverse notion of diasporic identity. If *Vibration Cooking* is protodiasporic, *If I Can Cook* is diasporic precisely because it maintains difference within unity, perhaps exemplified most visibly by Shange's consistent attention to South America. In portraying cooking as mobility, Shange moves away from nostalgia to Bambara's future-oriented stance, where food becomes not just about archiving black history or bringing together community but also about expanding the borders of that community by radically imagining a changed future where foodways rather than traditional maps chart a cultural nation.

*If I Can Cook* culminates in an assertion that this culinary work toward liberation, this home in food, revises a nationalist project. "Virtual Realities, Real People, Real Foods," the final chapter of Shange's cookbook, opens with a quotation from Homi Bhabha's *Nation and Narration*: "A nation is a soul, a spiritual principle" (87). For Shange, real, material food and people are the stuff of a virtual, imagined, and spiritual community, whether or not *nation* remains a relevant term. Bhabha's elusive "soul" becomes concrete in the kitchens of *Sassafrass, Cypress & Indigo* and *If I Can Cook*. Shange writes, "We remain a concept of sorts without the substratum of soil. . . . We've had to circumvent the realities of place and language to re-create a 'where' for our people. I am referring here to the tens of thousands of African-Americans who are committed to an 'other' way of life besides the American way" (*If I Can Cook* 87). Nation becomes cultural; the nation is people without soil. The "where" that can be home for this "we" is the space of the kitchen and the recipe. This landless community is African American but decidedly opposed to the American way. Rather, this collective has its own ways, its foodways. The recipe is an alternative way, an expressive form for practicing a diverse community in progress. The recipe gives form, material existence, and performance possibilities to a "spiritual principle."

Shange uses first-person plural, the "we" of this spiritual principle of collectivity, more and more frequently over the course of *If I Can Cook*, emphasizing the audience's increased solidarity as they progress collectively through the book with lines like "We already learned how to do this" (36) and "how we play the dozens" (38). This solidarity among people of color of both genders is the goal of her text. Like the characters in *Sassafrass, Cypress & Indigo*, she seeks out detailed healing rituals for people of African descent in the New World. Cooking is one such ritual. The voice of *If I Can Cook* searches for her nation, for a space of collective identification. In a 1989 lecture at San Francisco State University Shange said of her formal experimentation, "I'm trying to make a land for us, where we can live" (*Lecture and Conversation with Angela Davis*). The recipe form is both a map toward community and a home in culinary practice. Lest the reader have missed these stakes of *If I Can Cook*, Shange concludes in homage to spiritual, literary, and culinary traditions of African America, "We've found bounty in the foods the gods set before us, strength in the souls of black folks, delight in the *guile* (smell) of our sweating bodies, and beauty in Jean Toomer's image of a November cotton flower. What and how we cook is the ultimate implication of who we are. That's why I know my God can cook—I'm not foolish enough to say I can do something the gods can't do. So if I can cook, you know God can" (103). Cooking as a practice of the soul and a spiritual principle takes definite shape here; culinary rituals ("What and how we cook") become a site of collective identity ("the ultimate implication of who we are"). The promise of the title is fulfilled; "what and how we cook" can bring us close to the gods or God. This is not a melting pot but a gumbo in which, in a single spoonful, we can savor each distinct ingredient and notice what is missing. In the final lines of Shange's cookbook, we get a taste of monotheism and polytheism, of Toomer's *Cane* and Du Bois's *The Souls of Black Folks*, of sweat and laughter. *If I Can Cook* offers a guide to the difficult and divine work of cooking up a cultural nation.

As for each of the novels in the cultural nationalist revision, the difficulty of this work lies partly in its demands on the reader. Bambara's organizing of the fractured individual prepares Velma Henry to organize the communal body to act for social change. As I discuss in the next chapter, a cultural nation coalesces through dance in Marshall's *Praisesong*, partly because she smoothes over obstacles to transnational connections. Naylor's cultural nation too coheres with relative ease, as we will see in chapter 4. This is due in part to the ways class and gender conflicts take a backseat to an impulse to unify. Tension and fracture come to the fore in Shange's recipes, which explicitly take up gender conflict and the challenges of cooking up a nation on a budget. All of these novels are concerned with negotiating the relationship of the individual to her community, a relationship that becomes increasingly troubled across these works. Marshall's, Naylor's, and Morrison's novels continue the cultural nationalist revision partly by illustrating the difficulty of simultaneously fashioning self and community. In Marshall's *Praisesong*, only after over sixty years of life, in her widowhood, does the protagonist Avey Johnson find a way to dance up her nation.

Dancing Up a Nation: Paule Marshall's
  *Praisesong for the Widow*

Bambara's Velma Henry journeys through time from the very local space of a "backless stool" in an Infirmary to organize herself and her community toward wellness. Shange's women traverse kitchens and the moon as they cook up a nation. Paule Marshall's Avey Johnson gets a book-length praisesong because she travels, both literally and figuratively, toward African American cultural nationalism. In Marshall's novel *Praisesong for the Widow* (1983), Avey sifts through her individual and collective past, achieves diasporic consciousness, and, ultimately, dances as a practice of nation. Her journey, like Velma's, is women's work to "be well."[1] Avey's migrations bring her to a cultural nation informed by the African diaspora and articulated in dance. Dances on the South Carolina Sea Island of Tatem, in the living room of a Brooklyn apartment, and on the Caribbean island of Carriacou perform self and community as identities that exist only in relation to one another.

## Meanings of Dance in *Praisesong*

The nation practiced in dance unfolds in four sections in *Praisesong*: "Runagate," "Sleeper's Wake," "Lavé Tête," and "The Beg Pardon."[2] In these sections, Avey, an African American widow from New York, feels uneasy while on her annual Caribbean cruise with friends. She leaves the ship suddenly, intending to catch a flight back to her comfortable suburban home. Instead she spends time in Grenada and joins an excursion of "out-islanders" (75) to their nearby homeland, the island of Carriacou, where she observes and ultimately joins the annual Big Drum Dance. This is the last of three scenes of dance that span her life: Avey in childhood observing her great aunt Cuney shuffling a Ring Shout on the Sea Island of Tatem, Avey dancing with her husband, Jay, in the living room of their first apartment, and the Big Drum Dance on Carriacou. In Marshall's 1959 novel *Brown Girl, Brownstones*, the first book of a loose trilogy that *Praisesong* concludes, Selina Boyce dances her black, female *Bildungsroman*. In her afterword to *Brown Girl*, Mary Helen Washington writes, "When Selina dances at the end of the novel we see her way of being in the world. . . . She dances memory and passion, expressing her own individuality, her reflections of other people, and the needs of us all caught in the cycle of life and death" (322). Dance in *Praisesong* reaches beyond individuality to a collective, embodied articulation of diasporic consciousness. Every moment of physicality in *Praisesong*, from Avey's seasickness to sex with her husband to her actual performances of dance steps, is a kind of dance if we understand it in this way.

Zora Neale Hurston's depiction of African Americans practicing self and nation informs my reading of dance in *Praisesong*. Hurston signals the important work done by storytellers in *Mules and Men* by noting that they are "lying up a nation" (19). In her fiction and anthropological writings, men telling tales on a storefront porch in an all-black town are nation builders. Her phrase "lying up a nation" depicts lying or storytelling as a practice that articulates a cultural nation of African Americans within the United States. *Lying* points to both the artifice of storytelling and to resting, suggesting performances that create safe spaces of repose. Examining Hurston's writings, Susan Willis describes the collective activity of a "lying contest": "Telling stories like these affirms the group more than its individual members. It allows each participant to experience the force of cohesion. . . . The stories . . . affirm race, but they do not transcend racial prejudice. . . . The stories Hurston records . . . position themselves on the brink of formulating an alternative vision" (*Specifying* 45). Dance in *Praisesong* follows Hurston's storytelling by forming a community defined by race, cultural practice, and "an alternative vision." Dance, as Marshall portrays it, is a practice with kinship to Hurston's lying, though with the key difference that Marshall's arts are practiced largely by women, while the bulk of Hurston's storytellers are men.

In the vein of storytelling, several scholars emphasize the role of griot suggested by Avey's full name, Avatara.[3] The OED defines a griot as "a member of a class of traveling poets, musicians, and entertainers in North and West Africa, whose duties include the recitation of tribal and family histories; an oral folk-historian or village story-teller, a praise-singer." Avey, however, plays a particularly African American role. Though her work as a storyteller resonates with that of the African griot, she does not simply replicate his labors. Avatara signals *avatar*, which the OED defines as "the descent of a deity to earth in incarnate form" or "manifestation in human form."[4] In the action of the novel, Avey's role as a griot is less central than her role as a "manifestation" or model of diasporic consciousness. Marshall narrates Avey dancing her nation in a diasporic context; she does not actually depict Avey passing on oral history to her descendants. It is important that Avey decides to spread the foundational cultural narrative of Ibo Landing, one version of the often told and revised tale of the flying Africans discussed in chapter 1.[5] Women's work in *Praisesong* is not storytelling but dancing a nation that makes use of this story. If Avey is a potential griot, surely Marshall earns this title as well. Avey's future work promises to reshape this role for an American context; Marshall's work as a griot occurs in the pages of the novel. Although the novel concludes with Avey as a potential griot, I focus on dancing as the key form of women's work in *Praisesong* because Avey rejects the griot's role of storing and passing on cultural narratives until the very end of the novel. This potential practice of cultural nationalism, storytelling, is one we do not see in the novel. Avey's work of dancing is a precursor to her potential work as a teller of cultural narratives.

Dance becomes a "radical art" in Robin Kelley's terms: "The most radical art is not protest art but works that take us to another place, envision a different way of seeing, perhaps a different way of feeling" (11). Avey Johnson literally and figuratively moves to "another place" and finds "a different way of seeing" and "feeling" when she dances up her nation in the island spaces and water crossings of *Praisesong for the Widow*. Her performance transports readers to an island homeland and invites "a different way of seeing" with what Kelley would call radical imagination and Bambara would call the "eye of the head," "eye of the mind," and "eye of the heart." Avey's dance, like Hurston's storytelling, is performed for self and others; it is collaborative, reliant on both precursors and innovation, and takes place in specific settings among groups of people of African descent. Like Hurston's lies, Bambara's organizing, and Shange's cooking, Avey's dances are vernacular strategies for performing an alternative vision of community, for practicing a different way of feeling.

Avey's different way of seeing and feeling is a nascent cultural nationalism dependent on diasporic consciousness. Marshall portrays diasporic consciousness as a useful mind-set for African Americans consolidating their nation apart within the United States. This is not so much a full and complex engagement with a transnational community as an instrumental use of transnational movement. The nation Marshall charts is both imagined and real, determined by geography and a shared culture. Transnational travel and dance are crucial practices of Avey's nation. I use *dance* to refer to such practices as they articulate the nation in opposition to the nation-state; in *Praisesong* dance refers to choreographed and improvisational movement set to music but also to other physical, embodied experiences like travel and sex.

Through physical and mental travel, Avey's dances emerge as a practice of cultural nationalism. In the first section of *Praisesong*, Avey's "Runagate" takes her physically away from a Caribbean cruise and mentally back to her childhood. She recalls a Ring Shout on Tatem:

> The old woman [Avey's aunt Cuney] (she had been young then) had been caught "crossing her feet" in a Ring Shout being held there and had been ordered out of the circle. But she had refused to leave, denying at first that she had been dancing, then claiming it had been the Spirit moving powerfully in her which had caused her to forget and cross her feet. . . . Some nights, though, when they held the Shouts she would go stand, unreconciled but nostalgic, on the darkened road across from the church, taking Avey with her in August. Through the open door the handful of elderly men and women still left, and who still held to the old ways, could be seen slowly circling the room in a loose ring.
> They were propelling themselves forward at a curious gliding shuffle which did not permit the soles of the heavy work shoes they had on to ever once lift from the floor. . . . They sang . . . used their hands as tambourines, slapped their knees and thighs and chest in dazzling syncopated rhythm. They worked their shoulders; even succeeded at times in giving a mean roll of their aged hips. . . . Arms shot up, hands arched back like wings. (33–34)

This passage reveals a great deal about the function of dance in *Praisesong*. Dance is powerfully evocative of memory, both for Avey recalling this moment long after it occurs and for Aunt Cuney, looking on her former community with "nostalgia." "Caught 'crossing her feet,'" Cuney has also crossed the line between sacred ritual and secular dance. Breaking the codes of the Ring Shout by stepping over the fine line between circular shuffle and dance, Cuney is pushed out of her religious community. Dance is ritualistic, repeated as indicated by Cuney's "taking

Avey with her if it was August" and thus during Avey's annual visit. This ritual preserves an endangered way of life; the Ring Shout participants are those "who still held on to the old ways." In this case, it is a working-class practice (and for Avey a site of identification with working-class people), as suggested by the "heavy work shoes" of these Christians, who are indeed dancing although they would not use that term. Though no feet cross, this dance is boldly physical and loud, with hands serving as "racing tambourines and syncopated rhythms pounded out on the body. For young Avey, watching rapt, "it felt like dancing in her blood" (35). She quietly emulates the churchgoers' songs and movements in the shadows, where she stands watching this ritual. An outsider in a community where she has family ties, Avey does not participate in this dance. Years later, when she, like these dancers, is somewhat aged, she takes part in a secular ritual that looks a lot like the sacred ring shout: the Big Drum Dance. The Big Drum Dance in the final section of the novel marks Avey's entry into her cultural nation. This dance locates individuality within collectivity. Avey's individuality increasingly serves to consolidate the unity of African Americans rather than of all people of African descent. Her journey reveals that her individuality is distinctly African American and can be articulated only in relationship to a diasporic group of dancers.

Marshall asserts, "Black people in this country [the United States] really do constitute a nation apart" (Bröck 205). This chapter examines the formation and contours of that nation as Marshall imagines it in *Praisesong*. Her protagonist serves as a model for others. The novel is a guide, a how-to manual for making a cultural nation. bell hooks writes of *Praisesong*, "The novel really offers a map, charts a journey where people who have lost their way might come back to themselves" (*Yearning* 225). Like Velma Henry's work in *The Salt Eaters*, Avey's travels are a model for others rather than only one individual's journey. Building on Bambara's and Shange's practice of community as women's work, Marshall moves toward an African American cultural nationalism rooted in diasporic consciousness.[6] For Marshall this is a return to the U.S. South. Avey's dance toward individual and collective self-discovery depends on exchange with the African diaspora but culminates in the practice of a particularly African American cultural nationalism.

## "Manageable Landscapes": Islands and Waters

Dance as practice of community in *Praisesong* first takes place on the Sea Islands. Off the coast of the southern United States, partly unmapped, inhabited largely by people of African descent, and both connected to and separate from the United States, these islands are rich ground for imagining an alternative nation, as Indigo's work on the Sea Island of Difuskie in Shange's *Sassafrass, Cypress & Indigo* suggests. The Sea Islands occupy a special place in African American fiction as a site of identification. West African, especially Congolese and Angolan practices of language, agriculture, dance, and storytelling persist in the culture of the Sea Islands alongside the development of resorts and golf courses on some of the larger islands. The islands are thus able to hold in suspension the double consciousness of Americanness and African Americanness. Their natural beauty and retention of African cultural practices make the Sea Islands a site of fascination for linguists, anthropologists, and travelers. African American authors are not immune to the draw of the Sea Islands as both imagined and real. They appear as a central site of identity in the fiction and nonfiction writings of Marshall, Naylor, Shange, Julie Dash, Vertamae Grosvenor, and Jacqueline Jones, among others. Naylor defines this space in her fictionalized memoir *1996* (2005):

> It was while I was doing research for my third novel, *Mama Day*, that I discovered St. Helena Island. It is one of the barrier islands that sits off the coast from North Carolina to Florida. Collectively, these are called the Sea Islands, and they hold a different topography from the rest of the South. They were home to the Gullah people, who were brought there as slaves. Since they were separated from the mainland during slavery days, they developed a distinct language and culture of their own. Originally fishermen, farmers, and basket weavers, the Gullah are a dark skinned and regal people, who are trying to hang on to their culture as their young cross the bridges to resettle around the United States. The young people leave and the developers come. They are drawn by the warm winters, the live oaks dripping with Spanish moss, the palmettos fringing the salt marshes that extend for miles, weaving in and out of strips of land that lie below a blue and welcoming sky. You feel more like you're in the Caribbean than in America. There is a stillness about the place. The sandy soil under your feet, the gentle marsh breezes coming from the east, all seem to speak of eternity. (9–10)

Echoes of Jean Toomer's swan song for the rural South in *Cane* reverberate in Naylor's lament that "young people leave and the developers come."[7] Even so, this thick, sensory southern space of "warm winters" and "live oaks dripping with Spanish moss" remains a touchstone for

Naylor's vision of an African American community, largely because it is connected to the Caribbean and exhibits "distinct culture [Geechee] and language [Gullah]." Fishermen and farmers labor for sustenance and engage daily with the land and sea. Basket weavers form a distinct lineage of artistry reliant on the local sea grasses.[8] Naylor's narrator experiences time as "eternity" and "stillness" rather than linear progress. This romantic vision of the Sea Islands and their dynamic relationship to Africa, the Caribbean, the United States, and the South shape the radical imagining of the South and of the African American nation in the works considered here.

By writing an African-informed space as a seat of power specifically useful for black American women, these authors are able to get away from problematic, essentialist uses of Africa. They treat the U.S. South with the romantic gaze that other authors reserve for Africa. Marshall and Naylor do not escape problematic, romantic portrayals of the South. Rather, these authors struggle to simultaneously hang on to the cultural weight of southern spaces, evoke the African cultural retentions of Sea Islands, and also break with strict narratives of reverse migration to romanticized southern folkways like that in Alice Walker's "The Black Writer and the Southern Experience." The Sea Islands thus serve several literary and ideological functions: they insist on diasporic connections without romanticizing an imagined African homeland; they literalize double consciousness by being both American and not; and they invite a kind of shuttling between real and radically imagined spaces. The Sea Islands embody black feminism's both/and ideology.

Marshall uses the Sea Islands to write a dynamic relationship among spaces of the diaspora in *Praisesong*. Carriacou's connection to neighboring Grenada echoes the exchange between the fictional island of Tatem and the United States. Residents of both small islands live and work among the population of a larger nation-state without total allegiance to the mainland. Marshall is part of a long tradition in African American literature of exploring a relationship to Africa that is politically effective in the United States.[9] Gay Wilentz counts Marshall, along with Walker and Morrison, among African American contemporary women authors "who portray their African heritage as an alternative to mainstream America" (xvi). This need for an "alternative," still imagined in relationship to America, motivates the nation Avey dances in *Praisesong for the Widow*. Shut out from power by institutional racism in the United States, the sexism of early black nationalism, and the racism of white feminism, an alternative is necessary for African American women. The collective that Bambara organizes in 1970 on the pages of *The Black Woman* anthology and again in 1980 in *The Salt Eaters* is such an "alternative to mainstream America," an African American cultural nation practiced in women's work.

As they practice this alternative nation *Praisesong* and the other texts examined here are invested in diversity among African Americans. These novels are concerned with Africa and the Caribbean primarily as those places inform African American identity.[10] Diasporic consciousness, awareness of diasporic locations even as a tourist, creates an island space in *Praisesong* in which various nations can communicate if they claim their individuality. Accordingly members of the excursion to Carriacou represent various African nations, each with its own dance that, like the Tatem Ring Shout, occurs as collective performance in an island space. While the relative geographic proximity of Carriacou to Africa is significant, the figurative proximity of Carriacou and Tatem, a Sea Island, is at least as important to Marshall's diasporic sensibility. Her use of a Caribbean or African imaginary serves to inform a nascent African American cultural nationalism. Avey's cultural tourism ironically creates the diasporic consciousness that allows for a marginal internationalism. Marshall's use of an idea of African diasporic culture is at times problematically romantic, but her use of islands simultaneously dismantles any stereotype of Africa as a timeless monolith. If the site of Avey's growing diasporic awareness need not be Africa, authors need not portray Africa as a homogeneous space that offers the only alternative to Americanness. Marshall and her contemporaries use the Sea Islands as a bridge, a space from which to do this work of claiming and redefining Americanness without reliance on a romanticized Africa.

Marshall's allegiance to a nation of islands and waters rather than to a single continent is clear in much of her fiction. In *The Chosen Place, the Timeless People* (1969), her invented Bournehills is the island closest to Africa of all those in the West Indies.[11] Her novels are full of islands: Barbados in *Brown Girl, Brownstones*; Bournehills in *The Chosen Place*; Tatem and Carriacou in *Praisesong*; and Triunion in *Daughters* (1991). Her notion of an island homeland both draws on existing spaces and needs new ones. Just as her characters draw on the past and innovate new routes of identification, so their author relies on both real and fictional islands to construct her map of homeland.

Marshall describes the usefulness of islands in a passage that could easily refer to the Sea Islands, though she is discussing the West Indies:

> There was always the sense that the West Indies was in some way important to my understanding my self. So when I started to write, there was always that presence of the islands that sense that that was part of the South. Then, too, there was the practical, technical aspect to it. I found that because the islands were small, they permitted me to deal with a manageable landscape. I could use that to say what I wanted to about the larger landscapes, the metropoles, and so I found them technically to my advantage. (Pettis, "Interview" 119)

Marshall indicates her reliance on an idea of the South that is linked to a "sense" of island spaces. The South in this passage encompasses both the West Indies that Marshall specifies and the southern space in the United States that includes Tatem. Her use of small land masses, "manageable landscapes," to write about "larger landscapes" parallels the work she does in using an individual, Avey, to write about community. *Praisesong* uses the local to speak to the global; this is Marshall's "technically" effective way to specify steps toward cultural nationalism.

Tatem is the manageable landscape of an island-informed, flexible South that Avey plans to return to at the end of the novel. This places Marshall squarely in a tradition of late twentieth-century African American women's fiction that validates a return to the American South as a restorative, romantic homecoming to a southern space, often figured in agricultural terms.[12] Shange partakes of this tradition by narrating Sassafras's return to her southern home and by describing Indigo as having "the South in her." This trend of reverse migration creates a particular tension: uses of the South in contemporary African American women's writings both problematically border on romanticization and, wonderfully, recast a connection to southern soil as liberating, rewriting that land as a cultural wellspring rather than only the site of slavery. The novels in this study engage with a complex notion of the American South, each author finding her own way to negotiate this tension.

The farther Avey strays from Tatem, her literal and metaphorical South, the farther she is from a sense of community and home. Marshall introduces Avey in this state of unease, figuratively homeless, long after her last visit to Tatem. According to Lebert Joseph, whom she meets in Grenada, Avey is one of the "people who can't call their nation." Joseph leads her from Grenada to Carriacou as part of an annual excursion for the Big Drum Dance. On Carriacou, Avey learns to answer the question that haunts the novel: "What's your nation?" (167). Until she claims

Tatem, site of Ring Shout and Juba, in the American South and rich with matrilineal culture, she cannot answer this query. When she recognizes Tatem as her nation, she can dance the Juba and become part of a diasporic ritual on Carriacou precisely because she has learned to claim her distinctly African American cultural nation. The question "What's your nation?" relies on an international collective. In other words, the question is relevant only if people from varied nations are at the Big Drum Dance. African America becomes one among many diasporic nations that meet in this dance.

When readers meet her, however, Avey has miles to go before she can claim her nation. Carriacou and the cleansing journey to the island are, like childhood boat rides on New York's Hudson River and visits to Tatem, important sites of identification for her. These journeys host her sense of community and connection to others. Water crossings and island geography, both exceeding national boundaries, help define home for Avey. Marshall's map in *Praisesong* is a collection of islands: Martinique on the cruise Avey abandons; Grenada as the first site of her escape; Carriacou, where she joins the Big Drum Dance; Tatem, the place of her childhood summers watching the Ring Shout; and Manhattan, where she spends the early years of her marriage. Avey's travels map nation in a reworking of the term that disassociates it from the state. African America is defined instead by movement among the islands and waters of the African diaspora. Carriacou, like many of the Sea Islands, is a place "they don' even bother putting on the map" (77). By being unmarked, known only to those who call it home, Carriacou becomes a free space, outside documentation, and not on the map of any nation. Benedict Anderson reads maps as colonizing documents, asserting in *Imagined Communities* that census, map, and museum are institutions that "profoundly shaped the way in which the colonial state imagined its dominion—the nature of the human beings it ruled, the geography of its domain, and the legitimacy of its ancestry" (164). Carriacou and Tatem refuse the "extremely clear place" (166) and "totalizing classification" (173) assigned to locations and identities by maps and census data. The undocumented nature of these islands creates a productive ambiguity. Marshall seizes on this indeterminacy to articulate a supple map in *Praisesong*. For Anderson, the colonizing process begins with mapping, followed by taking a census and, finally, building a museum. One function of the museum, according to Anderson, is to drain the sacredness from ritual objects and practices. By being unmapped, islands in *Praisesong* resist a theft of meaning that would reduce the usefulness of the Big Drum Dance as a practice of diaspora. Avey dances Carriacou, Tatem, and Manhattan onto the same space, the same map.[13] Marshall's collection of islands remakes national boundaries to form a culturally rather than institutionally determined homeland.

## "They Never Heard of the Mind-Body Split"

Examining the relationship of mind to body is one key step in practicing this cultural homeland. Barbara Christian writes, "The recurrent motif throughout the novel, that the body might be in one place and the mind in another, is characterized not as fragmentation but as a source of wisdom, stemming from a history that forced displacement of blacks in the West" ("Ritualistic Process" 75).[14] Barbara Waxman reads dance in *Praisesong* as a complex, multivalent ritual that can "heal the mind body split" (91). In the tradition of Audre Lorde's "Uses of the Erotic," she asserts, "Eroticism, resistance to sexual oppression, and self-proclamation, as well as communal unification and spiritual rejuvenation, then, are some of the pleasures of dance" (92). Both Christian and Waxman rightly call attention to the shifting relationship between Avey's mind and body. Avey can sort through her past only by mentally leaving her body on several occasions in the novel. As Christian notes of the section titled "Sleeper's Wake," "The action takes place entirely in Avey's mind while her limp body is stranded in a Grenadian hotel" ("Ritualistic Process" 77). For Marshall, this division is freeing but also always temporary or even false. In her essay "From the Poets in the Kitchen," Marshall reads the Barbadian women's term for one another, *soully-gal*, as evidence that the soul or spirit and the body are of a piece, always spoken together. These women, whose talk shaped Marshall's consciousness and writing, "had never heard of the mind-body split" (29). Avey's departure from her body is accordingly a wandering that ultimately reconnects her spirit to her physical self.

With her mind free to travel, Avey recalls her life, including sacred moments like childhood boat rides on the Hudson River, visits to Tatem, and dancing in the living room with her husband, Jay. Her mental distance from her body helps her recall physicality as a crucial part of her past, especially the romance of her first married years. A temporary separation of her mind from her body is an important tool that allows her to sift through her history to gather up a usable past.[15] Key to this usable past is a reunification with the erotic, which Lorde broadly defines as self-fashioning and creative expression. This process of reclaiming the erotic begins for Avey with recalling a sensation of threads (190) that connected her in girlhood to all the others riding on boats up the Hudson River. She thinks back as well to dancing with and making love to her husband.[16] Their sexual encounters turn her into an African goddess: "Erzulie . . . Yemoja . . . Oya" (127). Marshall elides the difference and specificity of each of these deities in order to suggest a cohesive notion of African goddess that shapes Avey's African Americanness.

Avey must revisit and reclaim her erotic self to become an effective avatar of an alternative nation. Roseanne Hoefel describes this dynamic: "When the body ceases to be treated and carried as a temple, it is no longer an accessible conduit for the musical emanations of the ancestors" (141). Having recalled what it felt like to be a goddess, "an accessible conduit" while crossing water, making love, and dancing, Avey can begin to recover that embodied, ecstatic state. Both modes of connection, threads and making love, are informed by an idea of Africa, the sexual interaction more obviously by Avey's role as West African goddess and the threads less overtly. These threads of connection are vague, neither matrilineal nor atavistic nor geographically bound, giving Marshall the freedom to emphasize connection for its own sake without specifying any other point in this web beyond Avey. Marshall describes this sense of connection: "That was part of my awareness as a child, that there was this larger world of darker peoples across the Atlantic. And so these were the strands that I see as informing my perception of the world . . . for me, Africa is a part of that way of seeing the world. It's a way of my more closely defining myself" (Bonetti, "Marshall"). While the tie to ancestors is very private in her marriage, the threads of connection become increasingly public as Avey assumes the role of conduit for a shared past. Both public and private notions of connection are shaped by a "perception of the world" in terms of a "larger world of darker peoples across the Atlantic," very much including an idea of Africa.

Through separation from and reunification with her body, Avey establishes a self built on small rituals of her history, practices of connections informed by Africa and threads, beginning with the connection between her and Jay. Having found her powerful, erotic self in her individual past, she is ready to access a collective past. Ibo Landing on Tatem is a crucial space of a collective past in *Praisesong*; it is a site of travel across water, ritualized in tellings and retellings of local history. Enslaved West Africans, Ibos, stood on the landing, looked into their future, and, rejecting the abuses that awaited them in the New World, turned around and walked across the ocean, returning to Africa. Susan Rogers reads faith in the Ibos' story as essential to a politics of liberation. She asserts that Aunt Cuney holds "a literal belief in the Ibos' story, the belief that it is possible to defy the body's limitations and, in so doing, to escape the bonds of enslavement" (80). For Rogers, Avey's adulthood dream of fighting with Cuney signifies, in part, a struggle over whether to believe the story of Ibo Landing. Avey's return to Tatem, promised at the close of the novel, will consolidate her inheritance of possibility and power from this story, which she finally accepts as true.[17] Because the Ibos are reacting to the horrors of slavery, their story implicitly documents the violence of racial oppression in the United States and performs an archive with each telling of the story. Expecting Avey to retell the story of Ibo Landing, Cuney "had entrusted her with a mission she couldn't even name yet had felt duty-bound to fulfill" (42). Avey must undergo many water crossings, including from Manhattan to Brooklyn, annual Caribbean cruises, and finally on the small boat from Grenada to Carriacou, to name and find this "mission": recognizing her nation as African America and sharing this recognition with others. *Praisesong*, however, narrates only the first half of this mission.

In *Praisesong* Avey discovers and performs diasporic consciousness. This journey to a distinctly African American cultural nationalism shapes her whole life. When her husband recites Langston Hughes's poem "The Negro Speaks of Rivers," Jay voices not the lines of this poem that refer to the Mississippi River or New Orleans but those that mention the Euphrates, the Congo, and the Nile (125). In eliding those lines that refer to American spaces and emphasizing those that speak of African rivers, Marshall uses Hughes as a means of Africanizing the small, domestic ritual of poetry recitation in Jay and Avey's Harlem home.[18] In this model of connection to an imagined African heritage, Marshall increases the specificity of homeland that Hughes's poem begins to attain. She confines the wide reach of the poem to the "manageable landscape" of an apartment. Within the walls of their New York home, Avey and Jay have traversed the African diaspora to define their African Americanness. Avey's later journey to the Caribbean performs this function in literal travel.

Whether journeying metaphorically with Hughes across the rivers of the African diaspora or literally to the Caribbean, Avey travels toward a nascent cultural nationalism dependent on a degree of erasure of geographic particularities. Like the use of islands as manageable landscapes to speak of an expansive geography, the small ritual of poetry recitation allows her to recognize her connection to a broad community. When the couple stops reciting African American poetry, playing blues and jazz records, and dancing in the living room, they lose the "small rituals that had once shaped their lives" (137) and allowed them to imagine themselves in relationship to what Marshall calls "a larger world of darker peoples across the Atlantic." In the novel's second section, "Sleeper's Wake," Avey reexperiences her past and realizes that the man she fell in love with died long before Jay passed away. The days of dance and poetry and Sunday morning coffee cake spoke of "an ethos they had in common" and "reached back beyond her life and beyond Jay's to join them to the vast unknown lineage that had made their being possible" (137). This atavistic past, "the vast unknown lineage," gains the force of specificity not through imagining Africa but in local rituals in the small space of their apartment. Avey realizes that the seemingly insignificant "small rites" (137) of her early marriage were crucial to a sense of self as connected to an imagined larger community.

Jay's capitalist labor in the public sphere increasingly undermines his ability to participate in Avey's cultural nation. In Marshall's fiction, as in Naylor's novels, striving for the American Dream of home ownership and middle-class economic status almost always means a loss of identity, especially for men. The power of domestic ritual is, however, clearly accessible to men in *Praisesong*. Dorothy Denniston points out that when Jay stops the fastidious maintenance of his mustache in the early years of his marriage to Avey, he ceases to tend his "private self" (135). He neglects what Bambara would call his "inner nation." Jay changes his outward appearance to signal an investment of his energies in the public sphere of work, a decision that costs the Johnsons the sense of connection embedded in their rituals at home.

Early moments of connection between Avey and Jay are communal in the sense of metaphorically traversing transatlantic space in Hughes's poem "The Negro Speaks of Rivers" and individual in the sense that this participation takes place in the very intimate context of their marriage. The two modes are inseparable in *Praisesong*. Jane Olmsted writes, "The loss of a loving ritual represents a separation from lineage that depends on memories and stories of subsequent generations" (261). The "loving rituals" of dancing in the living room and reciting poetry are just as important to participation in "lineage" as Avey's later, more public participation in the Big Drum Dance on Carriacou. These domestic rituals shape her idea of home and eventually inform her idea of nation. Jay's distance from domestic ritual as he strives for economic gain leaves both spouses estranged from their cultural nation. Olmstead refers to "generations" because, although Avey has missed the opportunity with her own daughter, her grandchildren will act as culture bearers if Avey can recover and pass on the private and public rituals that create nation in this novel.

Echoing the power resonant in Avey and Jay's home, Marshall describes the force of women's creative expression in local, domestic contexts in her essay "From the Poets in the Kitchen": "I grew up among poets. Now they didn't look like poets—whatever that breed is supposed to look like. Nothing about them suggested that poetry was their calling. They were just a group of ordinary housewives and mothers, my mother included. . . . They talked—endlessly, passionately, poetically, and with impressive range. No subject was beyond them" (24). Marshall hears one form of what Walker calls "our mothers' gardens" in this "talk." As Avey comes to realize in *Praisesong*, local domestic rituals make the home a base of power, often shaped by women.[19] In a kitchen that ought to remind readers of Shange's kitchens in *Sassafrass, Cypress & Indigo*, Marshall's women discuss everything from the economy to their husbands to Marcus Garvey, who was "their God" (25). Garvey's appearance signals the collective power of the "poets in the kitchen." Marshall suggests that Garvey's best hope for achieving his goal of taking many African Americans to Africa may have been the support of such women. Garvey's black nationalism shaped the way her mother's generation imagined community: "Their embracing of the movement, their support of Garvey suggested something to me when I thought about it years later, which has been very important to my writing. Not only did it say that they had a political perspective, but they also saw themselves in terms of the larger world of darker people" (Bröck 197). Garvey matters to Marshall's mother and her friends because he articulates a working-class diasporic sensibility that invites a connection to Africa and a collective past. Talk in the kitchen is a practice of cultural nationalism. As Marshall puts it in an earlier essay, these women's conversations "declared that they retained and always would a strong sense of their special and unique Black identity" ("Shaping" 104). Talk is a way for these women to establish and consolidate a shared identity.

Marshall's mother and her friends, all Barbadian immigrants and "ordinary housewives and mothers," share experiences of immigration to an urban center, interest in Garvey's nationalism, and the daily challenges of performing domestic work in their own homes and the homes of employers in the mid-twentieth century. As in *Praisesong*, local rituals are a powerful force for imagining community and nation, particularly as a collaborative, artistic enterprise. Marshall asserts, "Talk functioned as an outlet for the tremendous creative energy they possessed. They were women in whom the need for self-expression was strong, and since language was the only vehicle readily available to them they made of it an art form that—in keeping with the African tradition in which life and art are one—was an integral part of their lives. And their talk was a refuge" ("From the Poets in the Kitchen" 26). The talk is a "refuge," indicating that this conversation creates a much-needed safe space. In this essay, the kitchen becomes not the site of domestic labor but a home for creative expression, a place Marshall calls "the wordshop of the kitchen" (30). The "poets in the kitchen" thus gave Marshall a model for local rituals that express identity "in terms of the larger world of darker people." Her vision depends on a monolithic idea of an "African tradition in which life and art are one." Although that principle is true for some African cultures, the notion of an "African tradition" here is useful precisely because Marshall disconnects it from a specific, material, geographically located history. Talk as a local practice of community depends on a kind of global thinking that abstracts Africa's many nations, cultures, and languages. This broad idea of an African tradition allows talk to take place as an art form in a small and defined space, in the "the wordshop of the kitchen."

An individual identity defined by a relationship to "the larger world of darker people" is precisely what I mean by "diasporic consciousness." Both phrases signal a collective identity of people of African descent in the United States who depend on varying degrees of knowledge of and encounter with the Caribbean or Africa to define that collective identity. This is important for Marshall's fiction because, as she suggests in her emphasis on women's talk, awareness of her identity "in terms of the larger world of darker people" taught her to recognize and represent rituals that, like the talk of the "poets in the kitchen," constantly practice community. While Barbados, the site of emigration for Marshall's family, is crucial for her work as a unique, specific, geographical homeland, her fiction is broadly concerned with an awareness of this "larger world of darker people" for which Barbados, like Carriacou, is one of several markers. This invites readings of *Praisesong* like that offered by Eugenia Collier: "*Praisesong for the Widow* . . . links the Black individual with Black people worldwide, showing a vast multitude of people sharing a common past and, by necessity, a common future, in which the individual is made whole only by awareness and acceptance of this massive community. Here is the closing of the circle, the healing of the centuries-old hurt" (296).[20] Like most Marshall scholars, Collier shies away from recognizing that in positing "Black people worldwide" as a "massive community," Marshall risks treating the Caribbean with the same primitivism that some African American authors have used to imagine Africa. The political utility of imagining diasporic connections is always in tension with the danger of using the Caribbean, or the African diaspora, as a catchall notion of "Black people worldwide." This tension appears as Marshall oscillates in interviews between "people" and "peoples" when referring to "the larger world of darker people." The singular elides specificity in favor of a totalizing unity, but the plural invites a specificity that may distract from the unity necessary to the cultural nationalism of *Praisesong*.

Marshall negotiates this tension by imagining affectively important spaces and giving them intense specificity, even when, like Tatem, they are fictional. The U.S. South is perhaps more romantic and imaginary than either the Caribbean or Africa in *Praisesong*. As Marshall's 2009 memoir *Triangular Road* reveals, her first trip "below the Mason-Dixon line" was in 1983, the year *Praisesong* was published (40, 51). She had more experience with Grenada and Carriacou, having traveled to both and witnessed one incarnation of the Big Drum Dance firsthand (140–47). While her insistence on a kind of intrinsic connection among people of African descent problematically erases cultural distinctions, class differences, and geography, she makes a productive move in locating her imaginary alternative space in the United States, moving the site of "Black people worldwide" away from the monolithic notion of Africa that informed U.S. Afrocentrism at the time of *Praisesong*'s publication in the early 1980s.

Both talk and dance are rituals for expressing what Marshall, borrowing from Baraka, calls "that nigger feeling."[21] As Marshall writes in 1973, "It was this nigger feeling—Afro-Caribbean perhaps, in particulars, but solidly Black at its base—which informed what the women at this kitchen table had to say" ("Shaping" 105). The important term for identity in her construction is not geography but race. Like Africa, the Caribbean matters, but the kitchen is the key space defined by a common racial identity. Race, for Marshall, depends on shared experiences, reclamation of a disparaging racial epithet (nigger), and an affective connection (feeling).

The kitchen practices of black nationalism so crucial to Shange's writing appear most explicitly in Marshall's first novel, *Brown Girl, Brownstones* but are important to her later fiction as well. Talk in the kitchen models the creation of a diasporic community, "Afro-Caribbean perhaps, in particulars, but solidly Black at its base," that expands well beyond Brooklyn kitchens. The "particulars" make sense only in relation to an idea of a universal blackness. This models the useful if sometimes problematic difference within unity of the Big Drum Dance, which I discuss in detail later in this chapter. Christian puts it thus: "*Praisesong for the Widow* explores the cultural continuity of peoples of African descent, from South to North America, as a stance from which to delineate the values of the New World" ("Ritualistic Process" 74). Crucially Marshall models this "stance" as a base of power that does not lie exclusively with a homogenized or romanticized Africa. Africa is one of several important geographical touchstones, including the kitchen, that host the collective culture she articulates in *Praisesong*.

## Passage to Carriacou

Avey Johnson's journey is a literal and figurative movement toward an alternative homeland. Marshall's notion of useful rituals for building this homeland draws on Christian Scripture. The second section of *Praisesong* is titled "Sleeper's Wake," suggesting Ephesians 5:13–14, which reads, in part, "Wake up, O sleeper, rise from the dead, and Christ will shine on you."[22] Avey finds such a light by recalling a sermon from her youth that included the congregation responding with the lyrics of "This Little Light o' Mine." Cheryl Wall writes, "The subject of the sermon is resurrection, the theme is redemption, and the aim is catharsis" (*Worrying* 202). Marshall employs these Christian processes and other rituals from the African diaspora in order to let Avey's light shine as a beacon to guide others through a similar journey. To chart this course of "resurrection," "redemption," and "catharsis," Avey must run away from the cruise, wake to the value of her practiced African American culture, and be cleansed to reembrace that culture. The cleansing occurs in the section of the novel titled "Lavé Tête," the term for a Yoruban ceremonial head washing. Just as Marshall uses dance to blur the lines between secular and sacred, so she uses ritual to bring together Western and African spiritual traditions.

Purged and baptized, Avey is reborn as a member of the annual excursion to Carriacou. The cleansing finds her shedding the proper, suit-wearing, middle-class self who sacrificed her happy marriage to a capitalist American dream and allows her to return to her younger self, formed on Tatem with Aunt Cuney. This process, though individual, relies on collective cultural memory. Travel across water holds collective history, as evidenced by Avey's visions on the boat ride to Carriacou. During this difficult journey, she momentarily sees "other bodies lying crowded with her in the hot, airless dark. A multitude it felt like lay packed around her in the filth and stench of themselves, just as she was" (209). There is no mistaking this moment; Avey experiences an echo of the Middle Passage. Her homeland includes bodies of water, which can hold a history, here the violence of slavery, that nation often cannot account for or suppresses. The water between Grenada and Carriacou, like the water surrounding Ibo Landing and Tatem, is an archive of racial violence.

Avey must pass through individual and collective histories, reliving the past to make use of it. Like Velma Henry's "coming through," this passage is part of a quest to fashion self and community. Missy Dehn Kubitschek asserts that Avey's break with materialism and her connection to a collective past rely almost entirely on women. Citing in particular the bathing ritual that Rosalie Parvay, Lebert Joseph's daughter, performs on Avey, Kubitschek writes, "Although Lebert/Legba secures Avey's presence on Carriacou, the characters who enable her to retain her sense of worth through her purging ordeal, and to participate in the fete, are women." Building on her reading of Lebert Joseph as an incarnation of the dually gendered West African deity Legba, Kubitschek continues, "Even Lebert becomes female during the dance. Clearly, female forces serve as midwives for Avey's rebirth into her true self, Avatara" (52). In Marshall's fiction, women are far more likely than men to connect to ancestors. While gender does determine many details of Avey's journey, Marshall does not indicate that the diasporic consciousness of *Praisesong* is available exclusively to women. Rather, she portrays Jay and Avey's marriage as one in which Jay participated in rituals of cultural nationalism before losing sight of this goal in pursuit of material gain. Lebert Joseph not only leads Avey to the Big Drum Dance but also instructs her on the process of nation reclamation, insisting throughout the novel that Avey has a nation, even if she has yet to recognize it. Avey plans to pass her diasporic consciousness, represented in part by the story of Ibo Landing, to her grandsons, suggesting that men too can practice this nation.

While the gender of Marshall's diasporic consciousness may be flexible, its cultural and economic boundaries are more rigid. Avey's process of attaining an identity in terms of "the larger world of darker people" relies on class mobility and cultural tourism. She practices her nation not among the working-class Ring Shout dancers of Tatem, nor fully in her working- and later middle-class New York homes, but as part of a vacation. Travel on a tiny boat to Carriacou occurs only after her journey on a cruise ship, an annual luxury that marks the hard-won middle-class status of Avey and her friends. The same economic striving that alienates Jay from his cultural nation enables Avey's journey to hers. Her journey depends on only partial rejection of her middle-class American existence. Marshall calls Avey "an unapologetic bourgeoise" (*Triangular Road* 147). Her protagonist must both use and obscure her improved economic status to participate in diasporic ritual.

Only by revisiting and claiming her past, in all its class complexity, can Avey achieve the wholeness Marshall depicts in the Big Drum Dance. Avey's vomiting on the boat to Carriacou and her subsequent bath on the island purge some trappings of middle-class American life (most explicitly the waste of overeating mediocre food on the cruise ship), but she also reclaims the joy of the early years of her marriage and her childhood summers on Tatem. These memories of a woman who will return to her comfortable life in the United States shape the nation she dances on Carriacou. Avey asks herself, "Hadn't there been a tub like it out in back of the house in Tatem? . . . One the same size even, and with the same three or four grooves by way of decoration running around the top" (221), emphasizing the link between Tatem and Carriacou and showing that even a bathtub can be a home space. Both the tub and the islands cleanse and transform their inhabitants, making the journeying protagonist feel at home.[23]

The bathtub marks rural locations and a humble class status. Tatem and Carriacou share not just dances and island topography, but poverty as well. Used in the absence of running water, the metal tub is a far cry from the comforts of Avey's prized White Plains house. This bath is both tourism and homecoming, dependent on the luxury of a vacation at sea and a return to familial ways. Avey's dancing on Carriacou works this way as well; her participation in the Big Drum Dance is both tourism and return. Her quest begins when, in girlhood, she witnesses Aunt Cuney "caught 'crossing her feet' in a Ring Shout" on Tatem. When Avey reenacts the movements of the Ring Shout years later, "arms shot up, hands arched like wings" (33), in her sixties, thousands of miles away, she effectively restores not just her place in a community but Aunt Cuney's as well. The sense of renewal on Carriacou is less a rejection of the past than a selective reclamation of the usable aspects of that past. The bridge between past and present formed by Tatem leads to Carriacou. The final section of *Praisesong*, titled "The Beg Pardon" for the first of the ritual dances that make up the Big Drum Dance, is the culmination of Avey's journey to a self and nation informed by both islands but rooted in Tatem because that island is a site of Avey's lived past.

The dancers on Carriacou use both past and present in the Beg Pardon, which first asks ancestors to forgive the transgressions of the dancers. Next come "nation dances," in which a "lone voice" calls the dancers with "the power of a field holler." They respond by "saluting their nations" and "summoning the Old Parents" (238). After each group "dances their nation," the "Creole dances" start up, and all comers are welcome to join in (241). In her study, *The Big Drum Ritual of Carriacou*, Lorna McDaniel explains that in these ritual dances "dancers perform singly in the Nation dances," representing the Cromanti, Ibo, Manding, and other African nations. From its inception in the eighteenth century, the Big Drum Dance defines nation as more about "a linguistic/ethnic group" than "a geographic region" (24–25).[24] Prior to Avey's arrival, this practice of diaspora in *Praisesong* has already defined nation for its own purposes as cultural, dependent on repeated ritual, and meaningful in the context of other distinct national groups. Collaboration among nations can occur only because each participant has both claimed a particular nation and acknowledged separation from it. The dance on Carriacou performs past and present, convergence and divergence.

McDaniel asserts that the lyrics she heard sung in the nation dances as performed in the 1980s conceive of nation as metaphorical, "varied," and sharing an investment in "social, spiritual, living, and ancestral systems of kinship" (36). The simultaneity of living and ancestral systems speaks to the use of past and present so important to Avey's diasporic practice. Marshall figures the spiritual and the social as inseparable by depicting Juba (social) and Ring Shout (spiritual) as nearly identical. Avey's participation is possible once the Creole dances begin, signifying that creolization is crucial to this vision of nation. The Creole dances employ solos, partner dancing, group performance, and the flared skirt that Avey associates with Juba. As one of the Creole dances and a version of the Ring Shout that Avey observed as a child on Tatem, Juba brings the past into the present as she first recognizes and then participates in its steps. Wall notes, "The references to juba suggest again how the two elders in *Praisesong* stand in for each other: it is as though Cuney has played the music for the solo part of Avey's journey. Lebert Joseph urges Avey to continue her journey by joining the community at the Big Drum" (*Worrying* 200). Wall's focus on elders reveals the figurative proximity of Tatem and Carriacou: both are sites where an elder guides dance as a diasporic ritual. Avey participates only on Carriacou, demonstrating that she has become one of the elders. This incorporation of the outsider is part of the practice of the Big Drum Dance. In *Praisesong* and McDaniel's depiction, as the Creole dances expand to become more inclusive more dancers enter the circle and the drumming increases in tempo. Other musicians join in, welcomed by the collective spirit, and one musician plays a goatskin drum to create the sound of unity, a "single, dark, plangent note . . . like that from the deep bowing of a cello," which "sounded like the distillation of a thousand sorrow songs" (*Praisesong* 244). In evoking African American slavery with "sorrow songs," Marshall indicates that the Creole dances encompass the African diaspora in the New World. This single note sounds out a collective history: "The theme of separation and loss the note embodied, the unacknowledged longing it conveyed summed up feelings that were beyond words, feelings and a host of subliminal memories that over the years had proven more durable and trustworthy than the history with its trauma and pain out of which they had come. . . . Its source had to be the heart, the bruised still-bleeding innermost chamber of the collective heart" (245).

Finally, just pages before *Praisesong* ends, Marshall can write of a "collective heart" without relying on a problematic notion of access to an imagined Africa or vague deep memory. This is so because she has carefully guided Avey through the process of using individual history and experiences as a means of accessing "subliminal memories." The "longing" and "feelings," not an imagined Africanness, are the shared culture here. While acknowledging Africa in the Creole dances, Marshall is not arguing for a long-held set of African practices but for a shared culture of yearning, of longing for the very connection that these dances provide. The need and search for common ground, for an atavistic past, for culture lost, is itself common ground. Defining commonality this way, Marshall follows Ellison, whose book of essays *Shadow and Act* is one of her most treasured resources.[25]

In the mode of Ellison's nation of shared experience and Kelley's radical black imagination, Avey makes use of longing to practice her nation. The memory that sates shared longing is not of others' experiences but of one's own life. Avey remembers Juba from Tatem and performs it on Carriacou, emphasizing that diasporic connection is more an affirmation of self than a literal journey. This validation is possible because her performance is not of general, imagined, African-inspired rituals but of the very specific story of Ibo Landing and the tradition of the Ring Shout, both practices located in the southern United States. The cultural heritage that connects Avey to her nation is one informed by an American past. The dance on Carriacou is a ritual for consolidating her cultural nationalism and celebrating her personal history. In recognizing Juba as a form of the same Ring Shout Aunt Cuney was cast out of, Avey refuses to separate sacred and social dance. As dancing in the living room with Jay is a sacred ritual, so the Ring Shout is among the secular dances on Carriacou. Avey's individual experience becomes visible and worth celebrating when Marshall sets it against a diasporic background. Avey's nascent cultural nationalism, her urge to celebrate her African Americanness, can emerge only within this migratory, island context.

Christian illuminates the working of the Big Drum Dance not just to signal Avey's journey to a spiritual home but also to articulate a broader black diasporic collectivity: "It is also a ceremony that combines rituals from several black societies: the Ring Dances of Tatum [*sic*], the Bojangles of New York, the voodoo drums of Haiti, the rhythms of various African peoples brought to the New World. . . . It is also the embodiment of the history and culture of New World Blacks. Avey hears the note that distinguishes Afro-American blues, spirituals and jazz, Afro-Caribbean Calypso and Reggae, Brazilian music" ("Ritualistic Process" 82). The Big Drum Dance is a performance of diaspora. Avey's diffuse but culturally bound diasporic nation of islands and water is made visible in this "embodiment of the history and culture of New World Blacks." This is possible only because Avey has taken the individual journey necessary to articulate her cultural homeland. She models the formation of a nation defined by difference thrown into relief by unity; her experience as a unique individual is legible only in relationship to collectivity. McDaniel notes that "the Big Drum differs from all other African-based rituals in that its program is united, but at the same time it resists complete musical and national integration" because each nation both participates in the collective and remains distinct (50). Diasporic space, as Avey discovers, is flexible, constantly constructed in repeated ritual practices, reliant on individual and collective pasts, and defined in both unifying and individuating terms.

Marshall's definition of diaspora posits the Caribbean as more important to the formation of Avey's consciousness "in terms of the larger world of darker people" than as a unique complex space. She offers a guidebook for how to develop a diasporic consciousness mainly as a way of understanding one's African Americanness, not as a way of understanding other places in the African diaspora. Avey merits a praisesong because the journey toward African American cultural nationalism is a struggle to engage with a history both joyful and tragic, both individual and shared. Her trip to Carriacou, though worth celebrating, depends on cultural tourism, particularly since she crosses class boundaries to achieve a sense of connection before, presumably, returning to her comfortable middle-class life in the United States.[26] Avey travels in the well-worn grooves of associating the Caribbean with a kind of license, with a set of freedoms in a vacation paradise intended explicitly as a break from one's daily reality. Her promise to pass on her cultural nationalism depends on her return to a more buttoned-down existence and to ownership of a house and land in Tatem. She can tell stories to her grandchildren from the space of her homeland only because she has time to vacation and a house on the island for them to visit. Marshall obscures this element of Avey's journey by ending the novel before Avey returns to the United States. Productively and problematically, Marshall focuses little on the class differences between Avey and the islanders that make the protagonist's travel and transformation possible. Because the specificity of Carriacou is less important to Avey than its relationship to her selfhood in the United States, Tatem is ultimately the more important home space. Marshall's elision of class politics allows her to define Tatem through its relationship to Carriacou.

It is no coincidence that Avey's separation from self, her discontent with life, surfaces and increases beginning when, a few years after her children are born, she stops visiting Tatem each summer. The dance on one island allows her to claim another. In deciding to return to Tatem and to invite her grandchildren to this homeland, Avey will consolidate her cultural nation. Her personal restoration to self and health urges African Americans to claim diasporic consciousness as a means of collective healing. Avey makes the kind of "return" Marshall envisioned a decade before *Praisesong* was published: "I am not really talking so much about an actual return. . . . The physical return described in the novels is a metaphor for the psychological and spiritual return back over history, which I am convinced Black people in this part of the world must undertake if we are to have a sense of our total experience and to mold for ourselves a more truthful identity" ("Shaping" 107). This "return" is indeed mostly a metaphor in Avey's case. It is not only a literal journey back through history; rather, Avey's trip is future-oriented: it sows the seeds of an African American cultural nation reliant on traditions forged in the United States. Avey visits Carriacou as a way of making sense of her individual and collective past, but Tatem, just off the American coast and a place of Avey's actual experience, is the promised site of physical return.

*Praisesong* defines diasporic consciousness as difference understood in moments of unity. This diasporic consciousness is both uniquely redemptive for one African American and potentially useful for many others, perhaps especially those who never leave the continental United States. Carriacou is the place where a traveler arrives at an awareness of "the larger world of darker people." This awareness is a stepping stone to a cultural nationalism rooted in the United States but loosely tied to other routes of identification. Tatem is neither birthplace of Garvey's working-class nationalism nor a site of the urban, northern, and masculine cultural nationalism of the black arts movement. Instead it is a space of a black women's cultural nationalism that imagines itself in relation to the "larger world of darker people."

In the last pages of *Praisesong*, Avey plans to take up the work of spreading the gospel of collectivity everywhere she goes, expanding her map of nation to cover a growing "territory" that includes "their small section of North White Plains. And the shopping mall and train station. As well as the canyon streets and office buildings of Manhattan. She would haunt the entranceways of the skyscrapers" (255). In Naylor's *Mama Day* and Marshall's later novel *Daughters*, the difficulty of transporting a diasporic consciousness like Avey's to these urban spaces is more clear than in *Praisesong*, which ends before Avey's return to her actual native land. Avey's efforts to act on her awareness of the "larger world of darker people" do not actually appear in *Praisesong*.[27] She promises to return to Tatem, to bring her descendants there and tell them the story of Ibo Landing. She plans to retell this particular story because it is an archive that has prompted her connection to a broader literal and spiritual homeland. This use of a foundational myth is Avey's work to make her diaspora usable for others, beginning with her grandsons. This woman's work as a griot remains potential in *Praisesong*; as Velma Henry's labor as a healer lives beyond the text in *The Salt Eaters*, *Praisesong* promises, but does not narrate, Avey's storytelling.

Christian writes, "Paule Marshall, like Avey Johnson, must continue the process by passing on the rituals. And this function is finally the essence of *her* praisesong" ("Ritualistic Process" 83). Writing, like dancing, is a ritual for articulating individuality and community in the New World. Avey Johnson and Paule Marshall dance and write a nation in the island spaces and water crossings of *Praisesong for the Widow*. This cultural and geographical space born of women's work makes room for Avey and offers a homeland for Marshall and her readers as well. As Wall puts it, "Reading becomes a ritual of cultural preservation," a ritual each reader of *Praisesong* repeats (*Worrying* 184). Marshall writes of Avey, "She had finally after all these decades made it across" (248). This is not a crossing to Africa or a movement in geographical space, but a journey "across" Avey's lifetime to reach home. Following Avey's travels, the reader too has "made it across," has followed the novel's theory of an African American nation as a community dependent on individual and collective memory, performed in repeated rituals, defined in relationship to "the larger world of darker people," and rooted in spaces that are both part of the United States and apart from it. In Avey's journey toward understanding herself as part of this alternative nation, Marshall moves from individual to community, defining a cultural nationalism informed by the African diaspora.

Marshall's threads of connection migrate in Gloria Naylor's *Mama Day*. Naylor, using Marshall's Sea Islands but not her transnational encounter, builds on diasporic consciousness to articulate a portable African American cultural nationalism. The difficult work of practicing a cultural nation in disparate spaces becomes increasingly visible in Naylor's novel.

# 4 / Mapping and Moving Nation: Gloria Naylor's *Mama Day*

For Gloria Naylor, cultural nationalism is not Avey Johnson's diasporic travel in *Praisesong for the Widow,* nor is it a political movement among black male poets and playwrights in the urban North of the 1960s and 1970s or the Afrocentrism of the 1980s. Naylor's nationalism is, rather, an ongoing effort to build a distinct African American community in disparate geographical spaces. Defining cultural nationalism as daily practice, she says, "I have often said that I am a cultural nationalist. That means that I am very militant about who and what I am as an African American. I believe that you should celebrate voraciously that which is yours. That begins with something as basic as our skin color or our peculiar past. And we do have in this country as black Americans a peculiar past that springs from that peculiar institution of slavery. . . . So that's what cultural nationalism means to me. To be militant about your being" (Bellinelli 107). This vision of nationalism depends on vocal and visible allegiance to African American history and culture. Naylor imagines collectivity based on skin color and history. Her statement demands that members of a distinctly African American nation "celebrate voraciously" the "I" and the "we."

Naylor's 1988 novel *Mama Day* defines mapping as a practice of this mode of cultural nationalism. *Mama Day* deploys the South as a practiced space that invites the participation of those who have not actually lived on southern soil. For Naylor, one advantage of a cultural South is portability. Because it is neither nostalgic for segregation nor primarily invested in a static culture, the fictional island Willow Springs becomes a mutable and mobile alternative homeland. The portable homeland pushes beyond the United States, freeing the African American nation from land-based borders. Rather than follow readers who interpret Willow Springs as a nostalgic portrait of segregated space or as primarily an argument for African American autonomy, I investigate the way this island redefines spaces beyond its geographical boundaries, constructing home as a portable concept that replaces the nation-state as a route of identification.

## Maps of Home: Sea Islands, the South, and the Nation

*Mama Day* marks geography in terms of both topographic and cultural territory. Naylor, like Marshall, uses the Sea Islands off the coasts of Georgia and South Carolina to write a space of power that is not on conventional maps and thus lies partly outside the power structures of the United States. Stretching against the borders of the United States toward the shores of Africa, Willow Springs "ain't in no state" (*Mama Day* 5) and cannot be claimed fully by either continent. Naylor refuses a problematic portrayal of Africa as a monolithic, romanticized site of alternative identity. Instead she chooses the Sea Islands, which are rich with African inheritances, suggestive of the Caribbean, and the part of the United States geographically closest to Africa. Willow Springs serves as a near, unmapped, portable southern homeland for people of African descent. The Sea Islands, both connected to and apart from the mainland, engage the logic of nation without being fully incorporated into the nation-state. Following Naylor's practiced cultural nationalism, Willow Springs relies on the logic of nationhood; Naylor calls it "a microcosm for building a nation" (E. M. Smith 1435). The site of Naylor's nation is aligned with and resistant to the United States; Willow Springs is geographically located in the rural South but migrates culturally to the urban North. Naylor writes the island as "the ideal black community" defined by the fact that it is "separated from the mainland" but with a bridge that allows residents to "go back and forth" (Ashford 77). "A redemptive place" (77) both apart and connected to the United States, Willow Springs is the starting point for the African American nation in *Mama Day*.

Unmapped and bound to no nation-state, Naylor's southern homeland is liberated from the drive to gain legal rights to land.[1] African Americans have been struggling for ownership of southern soil at least since David Walker's *Appeal* claimed in 1829 that the blood and sweat of those who labored there were as good as a deed to the land of the U.S.

South. Instead of engaging in this battle for literal parcels of land, Naylor lays claim to a cultural geography, taking control of the narratives that construct nation and community. Narrative control in contemporary African American women's novels often manifests as a return to southern soil.[2] Naylor's South is less literal; she says, "I grew up in New York in a hothouse of transplanted southerners" (Naylor et al., "Finding Our Voice" 193), asserting that she experienced a southern upbringing in a northern setting.[3] Cultural migrations in *Mama Day*, like Naylor's own experiences, rope New York City and Willow Springs into the same African American nation.

The love story of *Mama Day* takes place on these two islands. George grows up in New York, and Willow Springs is Cocoa's literal and spiritual birthplace.[4] In a retrospective tale, their voices entwine with the first-person plural voice of Willow Springs to narrate the story of their lives, meeting, and marriage. The island is home to Cocoa's grandmother Abigail and great-aunt Miranda "Mama" Day, a midwife, rootworker, and healer. "The Other Place," childhood home to Abigail and Mama Day, once housed the conjure woman Sapphira and her owner, Bascombe Wade, as well as their seven sons and subsequent descendants. The Other Place is the site of Mama Day's most powerful labors: impregnating an infertile woman and saving Cocoa from a conjured illness. The Day ancestral home is both part of Willow Springs and a separate space, a site Mama Day reclaims to unveil and confront family history, cultivate a garden, perform rituals, and gather power. The Other Place models the portability of Willow Springs, enacting the role of cultural wellspring that the whole island ultimately performs in the novel. The Other Place has far-reaching influence, evoked directly or obliquely by every character in *Mama Day*.

The reach of a cultural nation germinated in the Other Place and Willow Springs implicitly critiques the United States by rejecting it as an adequate route of identity. Naylor's portable South remaps space, speaking to a persistent effort in African American writing to create alternative homelands. In *Ride Out the Wilderness*, Melvin Dixon claims "alternative spaces" as a tradition reaching back to the beginnings of African American literature. Dixon describes what is at stake in these geographies:

> More than merely describing place, Afro-American writers
> have vigorously analyzed what kind of behavior or performance
> occurs in alternative spaces and leads to control over self and

environment. Writers and protagonists stake their claim to a culture that sustains individual and group identity. Passage into the alternative space is but one step toward the recovery of wholeness. Writers depict place and performance to set the narrative in motion and encourage reader participation. The open-ended structure and ironic closure . . . invite readers to complete performances in and of the narrative. (5)

The island fits squarely into this tradition of claiming "a culture that sustains individual and group identity." In the mode Dixon identifies, Naylor does "invite readers to complete performances in and of the narrative." *Mama Day* concludes with the title character "ready to go in search of answers" (312). Like Bambara, Shange, Marshall, and Morrison, Naylor leaves the reader with the kind of open-ended moment Dixon describes. Naylor's ending suggests that the reader might work to continue the story by allowing the culture of Willow Springs to shape her own space. At stake in the portable homeland Naylor constructs is the possibility that it might provide a "recovery of wholeness" for people outside the text.

Dixon reads these practices as common to male and female African American authors. For Naylor, on the other hand, only women can forge the "alternative spaces" that will sustain identity. Rather than focusing on control, Naylor emphasizes discovery and celebration. She claims "place and performance," the social map of Willow Springs and the rituals that occur there, as women's work. The place and performance that foster "recovery of wholeness" falls exclusively to women in *Mama Day*, whether it be Mama Day conjuring fertility and unearthing a matrilineal history or Naylor mapping a nation in the pages of her novel. Naylor and her contemporaries revise the tradition that Dixon identifies, positing "recovery of wholeness" as women's work. America fails to speak to and for many who live within its geographical borders; Naylor and her literary kin offer wholeness, history, and community in a novelistic nation apart, a collective dependent on a portable homeland where recovery can occur.

This kind of identity formation through spatial imagining has long been the work of novels. Naylor's innovation is to use the novel to reject the nation-state in favor of a portable cultural nation. *Mama Day* depicts a nation unmoored from governmental institutions and political structures, rooted instead in social relations and local, daily practices. In Naylor's novel, Willow Springs is Steven Hahn's "stunningly distinct"

(9) African American nation apart that reaches beyond its own borders to engage with the U.S. nation-state. Willow Springs borrows from and revises customs and ideologies of the United States. The island reaches out to create change in the nation-state, exhibiting familiarity with national customs, but offers "stunningly distinct" practices of community in the face of America's failure as a home for African Americans. Naylor creates an imagined homeland in *Mama Day* that supplements, complements, and subverts the nation-state to forge a portable cultural homeland for African Americans. Like the grassroots, largely southern, local organizing practices Hahn describes in his work on "nation-peoples," site-specific rituals, including Mama Day's conjure works at the Other Place, constantly produce Naylor's fictional homeland. The nation in *Mama Day* follows a tradition of African American activists who imagine collectivity as "not so much about nationhood as about peoplehood, not so much about structures as about solidarities" (Hahn 473). Willow Springs engages with the United States in the type of diasporic practice Robin Cohen describes: "The nation-state is being used instrumentally, rather than revered affectively" (195). Naylor's novelistic space illuminates this shifting use of the nation-state as the story of Willow Springs unfolds in *Mama Day*. She pushes against and draws from the nation-state "instrumentally" to develop her own map of nation.

With an emphasis on "peoplehood" and "solidarities" over state institutions, *Mama Day* demands a mental map of nation where topography is marked by relationships rather than imposed borders.[5] This narrative depends on the assumption, sincere or strategic, that the reader knows the place evoked. Naylor constructs Willow Springs with its past very much in the present but leaves the reader in suspense as to many details of both time frames. *Mama Day* demands that the reader assemble a feeling for this past through events and relationships. The reader's sense of place relies on fragments that coalesce in the novel as a social map. Naylor introduces her island with a map, a chart of Cocoa's genealogy, and a bill of sale for Cocoa's ancestor Sapphira, all textually set apart before the action of the novel begins.

The genealogy, the geographical map, and the bill of sale chart relationships, space, and history, respectively. The family tree records lineage, the map defines space through local landmarks like "the graveyard" and "Mama Day's trailer," and the bill of sale documents the slave history of the community. Though Naylor joins a tradition of novelists who have mapped space at least since the early nineteenth century, she strains against novelistic conventions by including these nonnarrative documents. The first pages of *Mama Day* mark a departure from conventional narrative strategy, alerting the reader to both formal innovation and the work the text will require. These documents suggest a discourse of nation. Daphne Lamothe notes that the map and the family tree are "tropes conventionally used to signify a cultural nation" (159). The bill of sale puts some pressure on the "cultural nation" visible in the map and record of kinship. From the start, the sense of connection implied by the map and the family tree is threatened by the violence and forced separation that the bill of sale reveals.

Willow Springs, as mapped in these fragments, appears isolated, difficult for outsiders and even its own people to understand. The novel's opening tale, an additional framing device, illustrates this illegibility. A well-intentioned ethnographer from the island attempts to record the culture of Willow Springs for an academic audience. The island's communal voice reports that he "was running around" with a tape recorder, "sticking that machine in everybody's face" (8) but gaining no real understanding of his birthplace.[6] *Mama Day* goes on to do similar work in a less obtrusive way, allowing the history of the island to unfold in its own voice. The map, bill of sale, and genealogy at the beginning of the novel call for an engaged reader; the framing narrative insists that the reader's engagement be participation rather than observation. If the reader is to avoid the trap of "gaining no real understanding," she must not be like the anthropologist, looking in from the outside, but instead must look around from inside the map of Willow Springs.[7] The island becomes increasingly legible to the invested reader. The text implicates the reader, forcing her to become literate in its spaces and language. She must surpass the naïve ethnographer to listen to and understand the voices of the novel.[8] *Mama Day* refuses to simply deliver ethnographic knowledge and instead teaches a spatial practice of reading dependent on understanding and participating in a mutable social network. The novel does not trade on the diasporic consciousness Avey Johnson achieves in *Praisesong* but reads the African American nation through the lens of a single island. Cheryl Wall writes, "Drawn to a scale that makes the island dwarf the states of South Carolina and Georgia, the map reflects the islanders' sense of their world and the relative lack of importance of the world beyond the bridge" (*Worrying* 166). Willow Springs works like Velma's healing in *The Salt Eaters*, Shange's replicable recipes, and Marshall's "manageable landscapes": the island is a small locale that radiates outward to establish community and nation.

Acknowledging the island's initial isolation, Wall calls Willow Springs "a world elsewhere" that "can be located only on the map that the front matter of the book helpfully provides" (*Worrying* 162). This characterization reveals that this site of origin for the African American nation is a place apart (it exists "elsewhere") that *Mama Day* puts on the map, literally in the front matter and figuratively by making its culture central to the novel. In addition to being both central and "elsewhere," Willow Springs has a distinct relationship to the past. The past in the present is signified by local use of the term "18&23" to refer to various events, situations, and actions but always, sometimes unconsciously, keeping present the year 1823, when Sapphira "persuaded Bascombe Wade in a thousand days to deed all his slaves every inch of land in Willow Springs" and "poisoned him for his trouble" (3).[9] Every repetition of "18&23" in *Mama Day*, always run together as a single term, keeps this moment of female slave rebellion palpable in the present. The colloquialism saturates the novel's framing narrative, building suspense regarding its meaning while simultaneously making the term and its origins intensely present for the reader.

The reader is immersed in "18&23" without quite grasping its meaning at first. Sapphira's story is similarly foundational for the island but both known and unknown; Willow Springs locals say, "Sapphira Wade don't live in the part of our memory we can use to form words" (4) and "Nobody here breathes her name" (10). Karla Holloway writes, "Sapphira's (absent) presence is the single most powerful image in the book. . . . Sapphira Wade's grandchildren have no choice but to re-collect the significance of their ancestor's living into their own" (86). The island's past has materiality in the present; its residents interact repeatedly with this past both consciously and unconsciously. Enmeshed in history, the island is the site where the contemporary Day women can begin the work of nation building by "re-collect[ing] the significance of their ancestor's living." The Day women unearth and privilege Sapphira's legacy of female power, bringing to consciousness her "(absent) presence" that has all along been at hand for residents of Willow Springs in their constant use of the catch-all term "18&23."

In *Who Set You Flowin'?*, her study of migration narratives in African American arts and letters, Farah Griffin describes the ways alternative temporalities shape space in Naylor's work. Griffin counts Naylor among a group of African American authors whose work "asserts the vital necessity of women-centered ritual and community for black women." "Naylor's safe spaces," she writes, "challenge realism as an adequate form for portraying the lived experience of black women" (119). Space in Naylor's fiction depends on extrareal or magical practices, such as the variety of rituals that are part of everyday life in Willow Springs, especially as practiced by Miranda "Mama" Day. Ritual subverts linear narrative time and realist interpretations of space. In other words, acts like placing moss in one's shoes before stepping into the Day family graveyard have been performed in the past, exist in the present, and will be practiced in the future, making three time frames simultaneous with each instance of the ritual. This is an especially rich practice because it occurs in the graveyard, a sacred and separate space one must cross to reach the Other Place, the site of death, enslavement, and insurgency in Cocoa's maternal line.

Wall reads the Other Place as "a site of transition, both for the ancestors of the Days who are buried there and for all the descendants who are attuned to its soundings. The map [in the beginning of the novel] establishes the relation of the residents of Willow Springs to each other and to the past" (*Worrying* 166). As Wall suggests, space in Naylor's novel is relational. The map charts not standard geography but "the relation of residents of Willow Springs to each other and to the past." This map includes the Other Place, landmarks like "Dr. Buzzard's Still" and "Abigail's House," which are meaningful only within the social network of Willow Springs. This is a map of community, of spaces determined by people rather than geography.

Naylor's social map uses what Michel de Certeau terms "tactics" and "strategies." For de Certeau, these acts are radically opposed; Naylor uses aspects of both in her mapping. De Certeau writes, "A *tactic* is a calculated action determined by the absence of a proper locus. . . . The space of the tactic is the space of the other." The tactic has "a mobility that must accept the chance offerings of the moment" (37). Mama Day baking in her trailer and Dr. Buzzard brewing at his still shape the space of the novel through tactics. Their practices are "of the moment" and mobile (both the trailer and the still can relocate at a moment's notice) but invested in history as well. While for de Certeau the map is an instrument of looking from without, *Mama Day* constructs the map as legible only from within. The novel employs the subversive mode of the tactic but gives it the traction of a strategy, the latter usually reserved for preserving hegemony in de Certeau's definition. Naylor does locate and reproduce identity in the mode of a strategy, but she does so to revise and resist the strategies of the nation-state. For de Certeau, "space is a practiced place" (117). Naylor's intervention is imagining nation, always a site of hegemonic strategies for de Certeau, as a "practiced place." Whereas the map in de Certeau's analysis is "a projection that is a way of keeping aloof" (92), the map for Naylor is a site of engagement. Mapping in Naylor's fiction uses some traits of the strategy to function as a tactic.[10] One cannot use the visual and textual maps in *Mama Day* unless one is in their culture. Unlike a traditional map, which functions as a tool for outsiders hoping to navigate, even colonize a space, Naylor's map requires immersion in a social network. The map of *Mama Day* cannot be appropriated into an existing system. Rather, it absorbs the characters and reader as each becomes versed in the ways of Willow Springs. George and the reader travel together, each attempting to attain the cultural literacy needed to make use of the portable homeland, to read an island determined less by imposed boundaries than by social landmarks like "Dr. Buzzard's Still" and "Abigail's House."

Tensions among social, topographical, and municipal mapping appear in African American novels both before and after *Mama Day*, especially in explorations of alternative homelands. In Martin Delany's *Blake* (1859), the protagonist works to establish a black nation in Cuba; a secret society plans to annex Texas as an African American nation in Sutton Griggs's *Imperium in Imperio* (1899); in Bambara's the *Salt Eaters*, Obie imagines "real estate near the woods," where a kind of progressive "brain-trust farm" could thrive (91); Shange's Sassafrass becomes a priestess on a separatist commune in Louisiana. Social maps, less concerned with geographical terms like *Cuba*, *Texas*, or *Louisiana*, appear with increasing frequency in novels by African American women in the latter half of the twentieth century. Naylor's system of geographical naming is especially close kin to the social and historical delineations of place in Toni Morrison's work. In *Song of Solomon* (1977), "Not Doctor Street" holds a deep history: "Town maps registered the street as Mains Avenue, but the only colored doctor in the city had lived and died on that street." So people take to calling it "Doctor Street." The post office refuses, for years, to deliver mail so addressed, until African American soldiers drafted into World War I give their addresses as "house numbers on Doctor Street." When city officials continue to insist that this road would always be known as Mains Avenue and not Doctor Street, the African American community starts to call it "Not Doctor Street" (4). Like Naylor's "18&23," "Not Doctor Street" tells a long history in shorthand with every repetition of the phrase. A social map, marked by the relational story held in "Not Doctor Street" or Naylor's "Other Place," resists the disenfranchisement, alienation, and losses often imposed by official maps marked by lines and numbers. In Ernest Gaines's *The*

*Autobiography of Miss Jane Pittman* (1971), for example, young Jane is flabbergasted when she finds that a map of Ohio is a tangle of lines and numbers rather than an image of freedom. Jane is looking for a map more like Naylor's, a map that will tell her where she can be safe, free, and at home (51–52).[11]

The feminist cultural geographer Doreen Massey writes that places "are not so much bounded areas as open networks of social relations" that change over time (121–22). According to Massey, "the geography of social relations forces us to recognize our interconnectedness" as definitional for individual and group identities (153–55). In "open networks of social relations," exchanges occur among New York, Willow Springs, and the Other Place. The Other Place shapes Willow Springs, and Willow Springs in turn shapes the island nation of *Mama Day*. "Interconnected" ancestors and descendants, men and women, slaveholders and slaves practice a geography constantly produced in relationships like those charted in the front matter of *Mama Day*.

Willow Springs relies on this idea of space as unstable, always produced in relationships. Naylor points to other traits of the island in an interview she gave the year *Mama Day* was published:

> My folks were from the South, like I said, and I was conceived there. I am the oldest of three girls. So I was born in New York, but I grew up in a very southern home. . . . Our foods were from the South and our codes of behavior as well. The speech I heard in my formative years was southern speech. It would take them many years to lose their accents, if you will. They've never quite lost their socialization and their worldview. That's totally southern. Our sense of family—how you're brought up to think about family and the importance of it—well, it's from the South. (Bonetti, "Naylor" 42)

Describing a southern childhood in New York, Naylor posits the South as a space origin for herself, her family, and a certain way of being, a "worldview" that emphasizes family. For Naylor, the South is defined more by culture (foods, "codes of behavior," speech, and upbringing) than by geography. The South is not a site of nostalgia or literal return. Rather, it is a portable homeland.[12] The portability of this complexly southern homeland becomes apparent as Naylor seeks, in the same interview, to arrive at a further explanation of the South:

> Not to have a center somewhere—I mean a geographical center somewhere in this country where there is a history for you, I think

definitely wrecks memory. We have no surviving relatives in the
South. . . . What stresses me is not so much our move as a nation
from the land to the urban area, from a land-based setting to a service economy. What I am more worried about is the fact that we
seem to have lost an emphasis upon ties—communal ties and spiritual ties. Those things can still be there. Those types of ties can be
there regardless of where your spiritual land base might be. (45)

Naylor restores "wreck[ed] memory" by making Willow Springs a source
of "communal ties and spiritual ties." The "there" where these connections "can still be" is in the pages of her novel, with Willow Springs as
its "spiritual landbase." These ties in *Mama Day* stretch from an imagined southern space to New York City, pushing through the borders of
conventional maps. Naylor's home base can be fictive, appearing on no
map but her own, because its portable culture of ties and memory is its
most important legacy.[13] Naylor thinks in terms of nation, using the first-
person plural to refer to African Americans as a nation, one that made
a great migration from the rural South to the urban North. The ties she
describes bind together a social entity forged by participation and cultural allegiance. This is a map not of a new territory to be conquered but
of a cultural community that gains solidarity with each use of "communal ties and spiritual ties."

A metaphorical or cultural South consistently informs Naylor's construction of national space. In order to portray this cultural South, she
chooses the real Sea Islands but creates a fictive singular island therein.
She describes the geography of Willow Springs and the Sea Islands as
an important imaginative space: "I needed, once again, a landscape to
demonstrate a state of mind, if you will, or a metaphysical situation. So, I
need a place that was part of the United States but not quite part of it so
there could be a bridge. And the bridge becomes very symbolic in *Mama
Day* because it bridges from reality to the world of magic" (Bonetti,
"Naylor" 58–59). The landscape as a "state of mind" allows Naylor to
use the southern cultural traits she values while neither replicating the
history of racial oppression rooted there nor exhibiting nostalgia for a
fictive southern past. Rather than functioning only as a site of mythmaking, finding one's roots, or directly critiquing the United States, Willow
Springs engages with the mainland nation-state in a dynamic relationship. The island resists the United States in favor of an African American
portable nation but needs the nation-state as its antithesis. The island is
"part of the United States but not quite part of it," demanding that the

reader and characters work to traverse the bridge between America and an alternative homeland.

## Crossing Over: The Portable Homeland

The first section of *Mama Day* concludes, "Any summer we crossed over that bridge would be the summer we crossed over" (165). As in novels by Bambara and Marshall, *crossing over* is a multivalent phrase; Naylor conveys this with repetition. George's impending death is one crossing over; George and Cocoa coming into an African American nation from the mainland is another. This journey off the North American continent reverses the direction of the Middle Passage but does not head to Africa or the Caribbean. The characters and the reader must make a new journey, must labor to cross over to Willow Springs.

The bridge, both the word on the page and the space between the two sections of *Mama Day*, represents the continued exchange between Willow Springs and the United States. The mainland creates the conditions that demand the island; the bridge allows the island to reach out and foment change in the continental United States, making a literal return to the South unnecessary. "The world of magic" can come to its people wherever they are. Just as the nation-state and the portable homeland are defined by their relationship, it is definitional for both reality and the world of magic that they are connected. The bridge goes two ways, carrying George and Cocoa to the island and carrying the magic and southernness of Willow Springs into George's New York. Naylor ultimately refuses nostalgia by making Willow Springs not a static site of southernness but a place of permeability and exchange.[14]

New York unfolds during George and Cocoa's first dates, a series of explorations of the city's five boroughs. George shows her his city and, in doing so, reveals that New York is not as far from Willow Springs as Cocoa might think. She narrates, "You had said you wanted me to see New York, and you did your damnedest. Every inch. Any schoolkid knows that Manhattan is an island, but you have to stand in the middle of the George Washington Bridge on a clear day to really understand" (98). Naylor insists on specific places, locating Cocoa's direct address to George firmly in New York, Manhattan, and "the middle of the George Washington Bridge." They walk the city, "every inch," practicing walking as disruptive cartography, as de Certeau describes it: "The operation of walking, wandering, or 'window shopping,' that is, the activity of passers-by, is transformed into points that draw a totalizing and reversible line on the map" (97). In their walks, George and Cocoa "draw" a map of New York that defines it, like Willow Springs, by sites of experience. The George Washington Bridge is one such marker, a particularly important one because it makes the topographic similarity between Manhattan and Willow Springs tangible, tied to the same awareness of isolation that was part of Cocoa's youth. The couple refutes de Certeau's notion that the city map is always a means of remaining "aloof." Rather, George and Cocoa walk a new map that charts the city in a social geography. They are, as de Certeau describes walkers, "articulating a second, poetic geography on top of the geography of the literal, forbidden or permitted meaning" (105). Both Willow Springs and Manhattan become sites of the portable homeland, of a "second, poetic geography." After George and Cocoa have remapped the city in their walks, New York can participate in exchanges with Willow Springs and partake of the portable homeland.

Naylor's New York proves receptive to Willow Springs. Mama Day sends the island to George via something as seemingly ordinary as postal mail. George and Cocoa meet in a job interview. He promptly forgets her until she sends a follow-up letter laced with magic by Mama Day. George recalls:

> The small envelope was stuck between a batch of project proposals and I split it open without a glance at the return address. Too bad, lady, the job is taken, but you'll survive—we all will. And it would have stayed in my trash basket if I hadn't noticed the film of yellow powder on my hands. It was the consistency of talc and very sparse—as if I'd touched a goldenrod.
>
> I frowned and retrieved the crumpled letter and envelope—it had been mailed from Willow Springs. Now, where had she said that place was again? South Carolina? Georgia? No, she had said it was in no state, and there were no state initials on the postmark, just Willow Springs and a zip code. Strange. Had she put a sachet on the letter? I brought it to my nose, but there was no scent. And the only trace of extra powder was on my fingers. It didn't rub off easily, and for some reason I felt uncomfortable about brushing it off on my pants. I left the phone ringing and went to wash my hands in the bathroom. As the water ran and the powder finally dissolved from my fingers, it all came back, a movie being played in reverse from frame to frame: the defiant set of your back and my overwhelming relief when you walked out of my office, your spunk, the story of your cousin's death, your grandmother, Willow

Springs, the suppressed accent, the hand rising to move stray hairs from your neck. Your neck. (54)

George's recollection charts his transition from a man striving for the American Dream to someone who, when touched by a bit of the flora from an alternative site of identification, slows down and lets in the power of memory.[15] George's voice shifts in tone from the hard stance exemplified by "too bad lady" to a romantic recollection of Cocoa's neck and "stray hairs." The intimacy of direct address enables a connection that reaches far beyond these two characters. George uses specific individual experiences of opening mail and washing his hands to arrive at collective memory. His recollection becomes a portrait of Willow Springs as he recalls Cocoa's "story of [her] cousin's death," evoking storytelling and family history; her grandmother, calling on family ties and spiritual power; Willow Springs as the space of this culture; and her "suppressed accent" as a mark of her southernness. The zip code with "no state initials on the postmark" reiterates the island's complex relationship with the United States. Willow Springs is simultaneously marked by and outside of the nation-state. It converses with the nation, literally corresponding through official routes of zip code and postmark, but resists complete identification by marking nation without state.

Mailed from the nation to the nation-state, the memory Mama Day sends to George in the yellow powder evokes a layered portrait of Willow Springs, where George will ultimately find a spiritual home. This conjure work follows Bambara's model in *The Salt Eaters*, making use of varied forms of knowledge to ignite a new mode of collectivity. George involuntarily experiences not just his own memories but memories of Cocoa and her birthplace as well. In this vision of a nation's people, memory is always intersubjective; recollection relies on entangled individual and collective experience. George begins to claim these memories as one means of accessing the portable homeland. Eager at first to wash away the conjure powder, he begins to access the culture of storytelling, narrating his own life, from childhood in an orphanage to his death in Willow Springs. George seeks a scent and a postmark but abandons traditional signals in favor of memory and desire. He shifts from one who would discard the homeland, literally putting its gifts in the trash, to one enmeshed in its culture. He shows the reader how to make use of Willow Springs for sustenance rather than just to survive. He takes on traits of the portable homeland, embodying migration without movement, experiencing the South in the North. This passage marks George's entry as a narrative voice, indicating the importance of men in fashioning the African American nation. Their job is not to found and defend a nation but to inhabit the nation practiced by women. George crosses over into narrative authority before he crosses over into Willow Springs.

Willow Springs again reaches into New York when Cocoa celebrates the island's winter holiday, Candle Walk, with George in the city. Candle Walk began as a night parade lit with candles to emulate stars that Sapphira Wade, "the greatest conjure woman on earth," asked God to leave on the island that she might "lead on with light" (110).[16] The holiday changes with each generation; communal narration asserts it "was different still" repeatedly throughout the novel. Even its first appearance and initial meaning are up for grabs. Asking, "What had daddy said *his* daddy said about Candle Walk?" (118), Mama Day thinks the light may have been Bascombe Wade's candle as he combed the woods of Willow Springs, searching fruitlessly for Sapphira. This "worshipping" (111) of Sapphira is not a static ritual, though each incarnation remains marked by the same greeting—"a lift of the candle and a parting whisper, 'Lead on with light'" (110)—even when the candle has been replaced by a battery-operated flashlight. The holiday is perhaps less a "cultural tradition" that threatens to "deteriorate," as Madhu Dubey asserts (*Signs* 161), than a mutable practice, simultaneously traditional and flexible. Willow Springs neither depends on nostalgia nor insists on preserving a fixed, autonomous culture, as the "different still" manifestations of the island's primary holiday suggest.

Candle Walk evolves into a gift exchange. Community members use the holiday to offer one another material support. The gift exchange is a ritualized tactic for sustenance and survival. As with de Certeau's tactics, Candle Walk is mutable, seizing on opportunities of the moment to fit changing needs. Unlike de Certeau's tactics, however, Candle Walk is a repeated ritual. Naylor manages to make a tactic into an institution while resisting the static aloofness of strategies. The communal voice of the island asserts, "Used to be when Willow Springs was mostly cotton and farming, by the end of the year it was common knowledge who done turned a profit and who didn't. . . . Candle Walk was a way of getting help without feeling obliged" (110). The community is a source of help rooted in an agrarian history. Gift exchange offers an opportunity for giving back without participation in a profit economy: "Only had to be a little bit of something, as long as it came from the earth and the work of your own hands. A bushel of potatoes and a cured side of meat could be exchanged for a plate of ginger cookies, or even a cup of ginger toddy"

(110). Each of these gifts is handmade; no mass commodities are a part of Candle Walk at first. Later, "young people" (111) exchange some purchased goods during the holiday. The centrality of food makes Candle Walk a source of sustenance. Even as it evolves, Candle Walk remains, perhaps unconsciously, a means of maintaining Sapphira's legacy and fostering collaboration in Willow Springs.

Willow Springs's formal and institutional independence, as Dubey notes, is a "mechanism of social order" in *Mama Day* that effectively erases "the realities of class stratification within segregated black communities" (*Signs* 160). In this regard, *Mama Day* elides economic factors, internal and external, that shape this community. The novel never quite acknowledges that gift exchange during Candle Walk is partly a response to poverty. Naylor narrates Cocoa's difficulty finding employment early in the novel, but she sets this dilemma aside to focus on Cocoa's relationship with George and Willow Springs. Like Morrison's mourning for African American neighborhoods, which I discuss in chapter 5, Naylor's vision of community places the responsibility of repairing damages wrought by institutionalized racism and class oppression largely on its victims. The restorative possibilities of Naylor's portable nation depend on an erasure of class boundaries and structural economic oppression.

Making productive use of this erasure, Candle Walk travels with Cocoa beyond Willow Springs. The novel does not explicitly address the economic differences between the relatively poor gift economy of Willow Springs and the middle-class, corporate context of Cocoa and George's New York. (George is a partner in an engineering firm, and Cocoa's job search ultimately lands her the position of wife.) This elision allows Candle Walk to take place in the city with no apparent obstacles. The exchange goes both ways when, bringing Cocoa back to New York after George's death, Mama Day buys "plastic ashtrays shaped like footprints, Mario Cuomo dolls, drinking cups from the hollowed-out head of the Statue of Liberty, [and] 'Hug Me—I'm Jewish' T-shirts" in order to give them as gifts during Candle Walk in Willow Springs (304). Here the island is permeable, its traditions flexible enough to encompass other spaces of the African diaspora, as indicated by the distinctly New York nature of these gifts. Naylor uses an unsubordinated list to suggest abundance; Candle Walk can expand to accommodate infinite variety. The objects are intensely ordinary, urban, and contemporary, refusing a nostalgic portrait of Mama Day. She is not hermetically sealed in romanticized southern folkways; her cultural nation can make use of the urban North. Just as her yellow powder draws George into the culture of

Willow Springs, her practice of Candle Walk takes in New York and its objects. The changing, absorptive portable homeland incorporates the most mundane of New York souvenirs.

The adaptability of Willow Springs enables it to include not just objects of the city but people as well. Willow Springs is home to George even before he gets there. He admires Cocoa's relationship to her history and family long before he visits the island: "New Orleans. Tampa. Miami. None of those cities seems like the real South. Nothing like the place you came from. I was always in awe of the stories you told so easily about Willow Springs. To be born in a grandmother's house, to be able to walk and see where a great-grandfather and even great-great-grandfather was born. You had more than a family, you had a history" (129). George names southern cities and then speaks of a different sort of space, one he imagines as "the real South," thick with stories, steeped in family history, and saturated with connections among people, past and present. George, a football fan who travels to games in New Orleans, Tampa, and Miami, thinks that these southern cities are not the real South. He yearns to inhabit the very traits of Willow Springs already conveyed in the novel's opening pages. Raised in an orphanage, George wants a lineage, wants a "grandmother's house" to return to; Mama Day's trailer becomes that home for him. His wish for a paternal line, a "great-grandfather and even great-great-grandfather," is less available. The lineage of the real South in Willow Springs is strictly female, although little biological mothering occurs in the novel. George embodies a spiritual or emotional need that the portable homeland can partially fill, particularly if he accepts the primacy of women. While his view of the South is clearly romantic, it also motivates him to make use of a portable culture. As Dubey notes, this South is "a literary construct" "not meant to be taken as a putatively real place that existed in the past, but as a fictive terrain charted by the literary imagination" (*Signs* 165). This break with realism, and with the geography of the nation-state, makes George's real South a usable construct for practicing community. Dubey explores the ways *Mama Day* and Morrison's *Song of Solomon* "admit, often self-reflexively but sometimes inadvertently, the difficulties plaguing their own use of the rural South as a device of literary resolution to postmodern urban problems" (*Signs* 145). Naylor creates Willow Springs as a space of connectedness, family, storytelling, and emphasis on the past, a wellspring for Cocoa and George. This does suggest that the island is a romanticized version of a literary rural South. However, the complex set of exchanges between New York and Willow Springs, the specificity and evolution of practices on the southern island, and the ways both spaces change for the characters and readers who become literate in Naylor's social map complicate Dubey's reading. While Naylor does make instrumental use of the rural South, *Mama Day* also works, and not necessarily "inadvertently," to reveal the possibilities and limits of a dynamic exchange between the rural South and the urban North to inform concrete, lived practices of cultural nationalism in both places.

When George finally travels to Willow Springs, it is a homecoming, a chance to physically access the portable homeland he has already practiced in celebrations of Candle Walk and walks across New York's bridges. As George and Cocoa cross over into Willow Springs, they travel on a literal and metaphorical bridge, represented textually by a section break. Eventually George, the loner and lifetime New Yorker, comes to value the alternative temporality and communal focus of Willow Springs. He notes, "A week in Willow Springs was enough to understand that words spoken here operated . . . through a whole morass of history and circumstances" (256). Just as *Mama Day* is initially opaque for the reader in the framing documents and story, the island's "morass of history and circumstances" demand that George struggle to attain a new cultural literacy. Attempting to navigate this morass and make sense of the homeland, George is a figure for the invested reader.

Born as a beacon of hope at the end of Naylor's novel *Bailey's Cafe* (1992), George is a fitting figure for the inclusion of men in the African American nation. This authorial return in a later novel creates a history for him. His is the first birth in Bailey's Café, a way station that is "real real mobile," appearing when people need it (28). The café provides a temporary home, a place where people come when they have reached the end of their rope. Bailey's Café helps them die or return to their lives, either of which can be achieved by walking out the back door of the restaurant into the fluctuating space that lies just beyond the threshold. The café can be found "in any town" (112), appearing when it is needed. George's mother, an Ethiopian Jew named Mariam, is rejected by her community for insisting her conception is immaculate. She walks a magically short distance from Addis Ababa to Bailey's Café. George, though he does not know it, has African origins and was born into a powerful portable space. This history makes him especially suited to access the African retentions in the culture of the Sea Islands. Born to a virgin, George is also a Christ figure, one who ushers in "a whole new era" (160) for the patrons of Bailey's Café. He may bring salvation to these diners, who come to the café running from lives stunted by economic, racial, and gender oppression. The shift promised by George's birth is as ambiguous as the stormy change that concludes Bambara's *The Salt Eaters*. The proprietor of Bailey's Café speculates, "Maybe when it [the baby] gets here, it'll be like an explosion of new hope or something, and we'll just fade away" (160). Mariam gives birth just beyond the back door of the café, in a world of many colored lights. The birth creates celebration and joy, a "ceremony" of "survival" (226) in a space of limbo. Carrying this legacy of change and magic, George is sent off to a boys' shelter in New York. Born in *Bailey's Café* in a portable homeland to an African mother, George begins the life that will lead him to Willow Springs in *Mama Day*.

Although George does not ultimately survive on Willow Springs, Naylor holds him out as a sign that men have a key role to play in practicing a cultural nation. Like Bambara's Dr. Julius Meadows, George becomes increasingly open to many ways of knowing. In his last days alive, he has a prophetic dream about Cocoa's coming illness and his own painful attempts to save her. Born in a space of diasporic crossing, George demonstrates the centrality of African connections to the nation imagined through Willow Springs. The island could not be portable without the presence of this African interloper. While conjure remains a difficult aspect of Willow Springs for George to fully accept, Naylor depicts an immersion in the portable homeland that leads him to a fuller sense of self. This shift manifests in George's changed experience of time and his somewhat fanciful desire to move permanently to Willow Springs. The failure of the island to completely save him only increases the novel's sense of longing for a successful homeland. By holding out the hope of a mutable cultural nation for African American men and women, Naylor builds urgency in her demand for such a space.

Though it cannot quite save or fully include George in life, Willow Springs becomes his final homeland.[17] The change in daily practice promised for Julius Meadows does not quite appear on the page in Bambara's *The Salt Eaters*; George's work in the cultural nation, on the other hand, takes place in *Mama Day*. In death, George resides permanently in Willow Springs, narrating his part of the story from the island, where both Cocoa and Mama Day converse regularly with his spirit. While Sapphira travels "back to Africa . . . some say in body, others in mind" (206) after death, George replaces an afterlife in Africa with one in Willow Springs. The stories of escape or return (salt eaters, flying Africans, and Ibo Landing) shift here to make the Sea Islands a mythic and real homeland for African Americans. Naylor implicitly asks the reader to partake of the broad reach of the island, to correct George's death by total immersion in the alternative nation, by choosing this marginally American space over Africa as a promised land.[18]

## Alternative Homelands, Alternative Archives

Broad connections prove the most far-reaching aspect of the island's culture. Late in the novel, a violent storm begins to rise. The communal voice of the island and Abigail's thoughts intertwine, narrating a coming storm that courses across time and the African diaspora:

> The old walnut clock ticks on behind the soft murmuring of Abigail's voice, while far off and low the real winds come. It starts on the shores of Africa, a simple breeze among the palms and cassavas, before it's carried off, tied up with thousands like it, on a strong wave heading due west. . . . It rips through the sugar canes in Jamaica, stripping juices from the heart, shedding red buds from royal poincianas. . . . A center grows within the fury of the spinning winds. A still eye. Warm. Calm. It dries a line of clothes in Alabama. It rocks a cradle in Georgia. . . . A buried calm with the awesome power of its face turned to Willow Springs. It hits the southeast corner of the bluff, raising a fist of water to smash into them high rocks. It screams through Chevy's Pass. . . . The tombstone of Bascombe Wade trembles but holds. The rest is destruction. (250)

*Mama Day* thus ties Willow Springs directly to the broader history of the African diaspora. Naylor evokes the Middle Passage with the imagery of a wind "on the shores of Africa" that is "carried off, tied up with thousands like it," like a body seized into slavery. Jamaica might be the next destination for these "thousands." The Jamaican sugarcane fields are a space of pain and forced labor, where the storm "rips through." Like people of African descent, the hurricane comes to the American South: Alabama, Georgia, and Willow Springs.[19] The island's past includes not just the history of Sapphira and Bascombe Wade but the history of slavery as well. The walnut clock is marking not hours but centuries. The history and sense of connection in Willow Springs are grounded in a geography much larger than a single island. Like *The Salt Eaters*, *Mama Day* warns of an apocalyptic "destruction" that is both threatening and a possible step toward renewal, toward the rebirth of an African American nation.

Wall describes the possibilities for renewal wrought by events in Willow Springs, emphasizing the promise of the portable nation: "It offers a heritage, both to those African Americans who, like the novel's male protagonist, George, are culturally orphaned, cut off from any traditions other than those of mainstream America, and to those who, like Cocoa, are linked genealogically to the wellspring of black American culture. Yet it emphasizes that anyone who can hear the sound of that culture can partake of its balm" (*Worrying* 165). That "anyone" includes not just the characters in the novel but the reader as well; *Mama Day* invites the reader to, like George and Cocoa, draw from the "wellspring" and adopt the "heritage" of Willow Springs. Naylor's map demands an imaginative journey, an immersion in social space. Willow Springs rewards the reader by showing her how to imbibe its "balm." The communal geography of Naylor's portable South yokes Willow Springs, Jamaica, Africa, Manhattan, and the space of the reader into a single map. Mapping thus becomes a practice of cultural nationalism.

Naylor's fiction, like each text considered in this study, also defines archiving as a practice of cultural nationalism. Like Ibo Landing in Marshall's *Praisesong*, Willow Springs is a repository of African American history that characters must uncover and use. The archive in Naylor's writing takes several forms, but appears most often as a written text that must be discovered. Readers can see the map, family tree, and bill of sale in the front matter of *Mama Day*, but characters must work to access the history archived therein. Hélène Christol writes that the "old ledger kept in an attic" in the Other Place "forms the core of the narration" in *Mama Day* and allows for simultaneous narration of the past and the present (159). For Christol, Mama Day's search for an ancestor's name leads to genealogy, to the family tree printed in the front of the novel: "What she discovers is a string of women's names: Savannah, Samarinda, Sage, who are Sapphira's sisters, thus creating the large family of women slaves who had escaped, if not in body, at least in mind, from slavery" (162). As its diasporic reach indicates, Willow Springs and the Other Place are sites of cultural memory. Women's work on Willow Springs both unearths past memories and constantly creates new ones. The archive in *Mama Day* values the list of women's names, but treats that list as a work in progress; Mama Day, Abigail, and Cocoa are implicitly added to the list. Just as Ibo Landing is a key archival site on Marshall's Tatem, the Other Place on Willow Springs is a spatial archive. This homestead records radical imagining and liberation that contemporary Day women must struggle to reclaim. They access this record through the textual archive of the ledger.

In *Linden Hills* (1985), Naylor's textual archive is intensely local and purports a less mobile culture than Shange's Carolina recipes for

"Manhattan Nights," Marshall's Ibo Landing, or her own Willow Springs. Recipes in a basement trunk record family history. Willa Prescott Nedeed, a daughter of Willow Springs and a descendent of Mama Day, uncovers the history of her predecessors. Locked in the basement for suspected adultery, she discovers a women's lineage of resistance: "She was on her knees, surrounded by piles of dusty, yellowing cookbooks. . . . She tore open the third cardboard box and found another stack of wire-bound recipes. . . . At the bottom, there were two slim volumes covered in black silk. They were also recipe books, but their thickness and width set them apart from the others" (139–41). Willa finds the recipes of Nedeed wives who cooked compulsively, often chopping onions as an excuse to cry, and the "two slim volumes" that record the many ways Evelyn Creton Nedeed tried to surreptitiously poison her husband.[20] As I discuss in chapter 2, recipes strain against the text, pushing beyond the boundaries of the page by demanding performance in the kitchen. The archive may seem a static text but actually calls for dynamic performance of domestic ritual, for reenactment of these resistive cooking practices and for archiving as women's work.

Naylor's male contemporaries also work to define an African American archive. David Bradley's *The Chaneysville Incident* (1981), for example, narrates historian John Washington's attempt to reconstruct his paternal inheritance. Like Mama Day, Washington finds a ledger, but his is a history almost exclusively about men. Rather than employ history to act in the present, as Naylor's women do, Washington obsessively documents the past on index cards and a loose-leaf notebook in a mostly frustrated attempt to pin down past events (144).[21] His efforts to piece together and fill gaps in history are a failed cooking experiment: "Like a poor cook trying to salvage a culinary disaster, [the historian] peppers his report with deceptive phrases . . . and salts it with obscure references and then he pretends (to no one in particular because no one in particular usually cares) that the seasoned mess is chateaubriand instead of turkey hash" (49). In the creation of history as Bradley depicts it, cooking serves as a metaphor for attempts at building an archive. For Naylor, cooking is the work of putting the archive into practice. While Bradley's metaphorical dish is addressed "to no one in particular," Naylor's recipes imply audience; food will be consumed, whether by unsuspecting husbands drinking love potions and poison in *Linden Hills* or by Cocoa, who comes happily home to her great-aunt's coconut cake in *Mama Day*. Turkey hash cannot pass for chateaubriand in Naylor's work because someone will eat the dish.

Bradley suggests that a mass of ledgers, newspaper articles, and county records are the territory of men. Protagonist John Washington's mother maintains a room full of family photos (126–32). Though Washington pores over them, this visual archive does not make it onto his index cards. Created by a woman, one whom he often disparages, the photographic archive remains confined in the domestic sphere, pushed out of his official history. The books in his father's attic hideaway are far more important to this archive. In another alternative to the textual archive, Washington's wanderings through his Pennsylvania hometown begin to suggest a spatial archive not unlike those in Marshall's and Naylor's novels; however, he tells the story of the town through official buildings and monuments. This is not the dynamic social map marked by "Abigail's Trailer" and "Doctor Buzzard's Still" but a place of churches, streets named for colonists, and the County Courthouse (167–69). In *The Chaneysville Incident*, official landmarks chart history. The familial story Washington seeks to tell lies beneath the official version; it winds like a double helix in and around a public, mostly white history. Naylor's notion of familial history, on the other hand, stands deliberately apart from the nation-state and its documents, especially its maps, suggesting that the usable archive of African American women lies outside official documentation. The bill of sale in the front of *Mama Day*, the single public printed document in the novel, points to slavery as the reason for this separation. Official documents record the violence that necessitates a separate African American archive and nation.

Naylor implicitly revises the version of African American women's archives that Deborah Gray White describes in her study of black women's organizations. White writes that "club women," members of the National Association of Colored Women and other groups, left behind collections "filled with public memorabilia rather than personal materials" as part of an attempt to "be one's own best argument" for black womanhood (88). Velma Henry's illness in *The Salt Eaters* arises from the ongoing sacrifice of her private self (her "inner nation") for public political work. The strain of maintaining a public persona determined by a very narrow femininity creates an archive that erases or hides any private self. Naylor restores the private dimension to the African American archive by focusing on the recipes of resistance clubwomen would certainly not include in their cookbooks. The photographs on the periphery of Bradley's archive would fit easily into Naylor's matrilineal repository. In turning to recipes, photo albums, and handwritten ledgers, Naylor insists that an archive of the African American nation must be unearthed and practiced by women. Recipes in particular, because they beg to be performed and revised, resist the fixed notion of an archive pursued throughout Bradley's novel.

Maxine Lavon Montgomery articulates the stakes of Naylor's recipes, claiming "women's culinary art" as "a subversive medium." "The kitchen," Montgomery continues, "becomes a battleground in the war between the sexes. . . . The documents that the Nedeed wives author attest to the home as a place of bondage and subjugation" (61–62). *Mama Day*, unlike *Linden Hills*, recovers women's work as celebratory ritual. According to Montgomery, women's work creates conditions in which "the home place exists without boundaries and offers the possibility for rebirth and renewal. Not necessarily mundane or burdensome, women's work takes on spiritual dimensions, allowing black women to transcend imposed notions of female place. *Mama Day* is a key text revealing women's expanding sphere of influence" (64). For Montgomery, the culture of Willow Springs is crafted entirely by women's work in their own homes.

Montgomery's formulation follows Houston Baker's and offers a similarly problematic romanticization of women's labor in the home. Cooking is part of what Baker calls "Afro-American women's expressive production" (9). Montgomery and Baker attempt to walk a fine line between celebrating women's work and eliding the oppressive, patriarchal conditions that often contextualize that work. Naylor gets out of this bind by presenting housework as both imprisonment (*Linden Hills*) and liberation (*Mama Day*). Women's work in *Mama Day*, from mapping to cooking and conjure, creates an "expanding sphere of influence." "In the fiction of Gloria Naylor," Montgomery declares, "home is not a neutral space but is relevant in the struggle for freedom from oppression. . . . Naylor's texts imply that such routine tasks as cooking, cleaning, and mothering can be means of furthering the cause of freedom" (67). Partly because "cooking, cleaning, and mothering" done by African American women has often been slave or poorly paid labor in white homes, doing such labors for one's own family can be a liberating redefinition of women's work. For Naylor, these tasks gain power in the home but extend well beyond the kitchen.

Recipes thus become archival practice to build a cultural nation. By resisting the static archive of Bradley's *The Chaneysville Incident*, Naylor turns recipes into something more than Baker's "Afro-American women's expressive production." As I explored earlier, Ntozake Shange seizes on this culinary field of possibility and revises Baker's configuration. These recipes are part of an attempt to define not just the self but the African American nation as well. Though they begin in the domestic sphere, the influence of these archives knows no bounds. These archives, the ledger of *Mama Day* and the cookbooks of *Linden Hills*, record struggles for liberation, both from the literal bondage of slavery and a locked basement and from many of the same limitations placed on African American women that motivated Bambara to declare their wild diversity and possibility in *The Black Woman*. These records, like Bambara's anthology, raise the possibility of women's collective action. Uncovered, the archive can form a coalition of women, beginning with the cross-generational ties that Naylor's documents create.

Barbara Christian sees hope for expansive allegiances in Willa Nedeed's uncovering the archive in *Linden Hills*: "The imprisoned Mrs. Nedeed remembers *her* real name because she discovers the record left by her predecessors, letters, recipes, and photographs—as the mothers cry out to be heard, to be reckoned with, to exist. As Willa Prescott Nedeed relives the herstory so carefully exhumed from the Nedeeds' official records, we realize how the experiences of the women are a serious threat to the men's kingdom" ("Naylor's Geography" 111). That herstory in the Nedeed basement is the archive that Naylor spatializes and makes portable in *Mama Day*. Toni Morrison, as I show in the last chapter of this study, seats a similar archive in spaces both hidden and visible. The "serious threat to the men's kingdom" that herstory and female coalescence pose is the central dynamic of Morrison's *Paradise*. This "threat" is the stakes of the struggle to unearth a women's archive. Nothing less than dismantling patriarchy is at stake in Naylor's map, family tree, and recipes. These are not only individual expressions, but also demands for collective resistance to oppression. Rather than simply positing women's work in the kitchen as vaguely meaningful, Naylor recasts recipes as part of an African American archive in practice. Women's work becomes not cooking as only self-articulation but also the discovery, preservation, and use of this archive. Willa Needed is as much a family archivist as she is a cook.

The far reach of the archive and the nation in Naylor's fiction are built on local daily practices. Cooking sits alongside mapping and archiving as women's work of cultural nationalism in *Mama Day*. By treating these labors as equally visible work in the female domain, Naylor simultaneously elevates domestic labors and normalizes the potentially abstract work of mapping and archiving. Women's daily acts gain subversive power in Naylor's writing precisely because they are a group of seemingly disparate practices that particularize the "expressive production"

Baker describes. Naylor's intervention is to make mapping, archiving, and cooking a few among many detailed and material forms of women's work, each a crucial practice of cultural nation.

In *Linden Hills* and *Mama Day* Naylor writes fiction that "celebrates voraciously" the cultural grounds of African American nationalism. As we will see in Morrison's *Paradise*, the disagreements, alienation, tensions, and failures that plague women in Naylor's *The Women of Brewster Place* and *Linden Hills*, if not *Mama Day*, remain major obstacles to creating collectivity. Larry R. Andrews suggests the limits of women's collaborative work in Naylor's fiction: "At its best, this bond among women confers identity, purpose, and strength for survival. But although it is dramatized in the novels as clearly desirable, the success of female friendship, of the black womanbond, remains limited and potential" (285). Ties forged from Andrews's "matriarchal mythmaking" are both desirable and troubling. There is no clearer example of the matriarch and the myth in one body than Sapphira Wade of *Mama Day*. She fosters a bond among the Day women that, in Andrews's terms, depends on "historical connection" and ties to mother nature, both handed down from Sapphira, through generations, to Cocoa (286). Just as Willa Nedeed unearths an archive in *Linden Hills* to remember she is of the Day family, Mama Day finds the ancestor's name, Sapphira, digging in the attic of the Other Place. Sapphira's story of resistance, like that of the culinary tactician Evelyn Creton Nedeed, is a buried story that must be uncovered, recalled, and named as a practice of community. Naylor's "matriarchal mythmaking" writes the founding documents of her African American nation. The "womanbond" indeed "remains limited and potential" in *Mama Day*, just as it does for the Seven Sisters of Bambara's *The Salt Eaters*. Female coalescence is the way to an alternative cultural nation in these novels, but that nation is never fully realized. The "limited and potential" power of female alliances and the open-ended conclusion of these novels culminate in an insistence that the work of nation making continue beyond the text.

The stakes of "matriarchal mythmaking" are the use of Willow Springs as a portable nation. As Andrews notes, the power of the matriarchal myth holds fast as the novel oscillates between islands: "In *Mama Day* the rural South, alternating with New York scenes between George and Ophelia [Cocoa], offers a setting for a healing community with roots in female folk tradition and nature" (287). While this might seem too easy a panacea for all societal ills, Naylor insists that the portable culture, the foundation of nationalism present in Willow Springs, is hard-won and demanding, as George's death demonstrates. Partly because George does not fully follow its ways, "female folk tradition" is not a magical thread that stitches African Americans automatically into one nation. Rather, "female folk tradition" is one tool for building an African American nation. Naylor's fiction exemplifies a tradition of African American women's coalescence fraught with tensions that White describes as definitional for formal organizations of black women throughout the nineteenth and twentieth centuries. White asserts, "Black women's association history is . . . not a story of harmonious sisterhood, nor one about women selflessly sacrificing themselves for the good of the group. It is about women with missions that varied and often clashed, about women who aimed for progress and unity, but who sometimes fell short, about women who sometimes found the job of representing and fighting for themselves burdensome" (16–17). Sisterhood often proves an uneasy and difficult alliance. Women's work in *Mama Day* builds a portable homeland, but there are no guarantees that this homeland will accommodate the varied goals of all black women. White's study *Too Heavy a Load* charts the course of women's coalitions as necessarily changing and shifting over time to cope with the great diversity of African American women's needs, particularly in the face of political and economic change. Like the nation articulated by the authors in this study, "Black women's association" is always becoming, never being, never static. White suggests that African American women's collectives have historically been uniquely self-conscious, embracing diversity of opinion and tensions among their members (262). Naylor offers social mapping as a practice for constructing such a self-conscious, dynamic nation apart. Bambara, Shange, Marshall, and Morrison write in the grain of Naylor's efforts, each suggesting other forms of women's difficult work of imagining, creating, and changing this nation.

As I explore in the following chapter, Toni Morrison adds inscribing, markings of text and image, to Bambara's, Shange's, Marshall's, and Naylor's nation-making activities. Bambara organizes an inner and outer nation; Shange cooks up a nation with her kitchen practices; Marshall dances up her nation against a diasporic background; Naylor follows by mapping and moving nation. As White's study suggests, the collectivities they produce are no easy remedy for racial and gendered oppression. Reliance on class privilege and cultural tourism in Marshall's *Praisesong* and difficulty accommodating men and elision of economic factors in *Mama Day* are just some of the barriers to collectivity. Across these authors' works, failures of female coalescence become increasingly clear in the struggle to form an African American nation. Each text grows more exclusionist in terms of gender, culminating in the radically isolated, largely dysfunctional women's community of Morrison's *Paradise*. As the twentieth century draws to a close, the stakes become higher, the tensions in women's coalitions increase, diversity and dissent threaten to dismantle collectivity, and the nation Naylor maps struggles for its existence.

# 5 / Inscribing Community: Toni Morrison's *Paradise*

A letter composed in smeared lipstick, cuts on a woman's skin, a name scratched into the dirt, a lengthy genealogy burned rather than published, paintings of women's bodies on a basement floor—women in Toni Morrison's 1997 novel *Paradise* inscribe texts and images that struggle to become public or even legible. Created but rarely read, inscriptions in the world of the novel do not depend on an audience to create multiple meanings. In order to account for the obscured, hidden, and erased female writings in *Paradise*, I read inscription, as opposed to interpretation, as a key form of women's work in the novel. Inscription locates ambiguity of meaning—what might the letter in smeared lipstick say if it were legible? what was documented in the destroyed genealogy?—with the work of creating these markings rather than with the work of reading them. This calls attention away from men arguing over how to read the monuments and documents of their history and turns instead to women inscribing words and images as a means of fashioning self and community. Alongside organizing in Bambara's *The Salt Eaters*, cooking in Shange's *Sassafrass, Cypress & Indigo*, dancing in Marshall's *Praisesong for the Widow*, and mapping in Naylor's *Mama Day*, inscribing in Morrison's *Paradise* reclaims and redefines cultural nationalism as women's work, both everyday and extraordinary. At the close of the twentieth century, *Paradise* concludes two decades of fiction that claims nationalism as a practice of women.

## Inscribing Women's Stories

Inscription is not synonymous with Gerard Genette's paratext or Ashraf Rushdy's palimpsest, though it shares traits with both of these useful terms. For Genette, paratext is a "threshold" that permits entry into a text (1–2). The paratext "is empirically made up of a heterogeneous group of practices and discourses," including title, author's name, type-setting, dedication, epigraph, preface, and notes (2). As we will see in the case of *Paradise*, Morrison describes or narrates inscriptions but does not reproduce them in her novel. Paratexts, on the other hand, appear in, around, or beyond the pages of the primary text. In this sense, Naylor's map of Willow Springs and family tree in *Mama Day* are paratexts because they appear in the front matter of the novel, while Morrison's genealogy of the first families of Ruby in *Paradise* is an inscription because she describes the document and narrates its production and destruction without reproducing even an excerpt of its contents.[1] Genette also counts interviews, generic context, the date or period in which a work was written, literary awards, and information about a book or author as forms of paratext (7). This gets a bit closer to inscription because the paratext may be transmitted verbally (as in a classroom lecture or a radio interview, or otherwise told rather than printed) such that it, like Morrison's inscriptions, exists somewhere in the world beyond the text but has an important influence on how a reader receives the work. Genette's notion of paratext as a threshold provides another reason to use inscription as a distinct term. Genette imagines the paratext as an "airlock that helps the reader pass without too much respiratory difficulty from one world to the other, a sometimes delicate operation, especially when the second world is a fictional one" (408). For example, the "Oprah's Book Club" sticker and "Book of the Month Club Selection" banner on the current edition of *Paradise* are paratexts that invite in the reader who has enjoyed other books with these designations. Morrison's inscriptions are barriers to entry rather than thresholds. Inscription is the creation and function of markings rather than their actual content; for example, readers of *Paradise* see the impact, but not the words, of a lipstick letter that Seneca discovers as a girl.

Ashraf Rushdy's study of African American "palimpsest narratives" is useful here as well, but *palimpsest* is not a synonym for *inscription*. For Rushdy, palimpsest narratives are novels that are, in various ways, about slavery, "the family secret of America" that "haunts the peripheries of the national imaginary" (2). Inscriptions also trade in secrets that, like slavery, are simultaneously known and unknowable. Inscriptions, like palimpsest narratives, often try to work out or document "the meaning of the past for the present" for both individuals and their communities (5). Inscription differs, however, from the palimpsest narrative in important ways. It is not necessarily engaged directly with the history or impact of slavery. One "family secret" in Pat Best's genealogy in *Paradise*, for example, is intermarriage with Native Americans, as opposed to the white ancestor in an African American family line that is the "family secret" of slavery that shapes both Gayl Jones's *Corregidora* and Octavia Butler's *Kindred* in Rushdy's astute reading. Rushdy's palimpsests reveal "the hidden socialized illness in particular aspects of family life that are symptomatic of a national disorder caused by slavery" (19). This reading applies directly to Morrison's *Beloved* (1987), but the community in *Paradise* is an African American nation apart rather than the United States, and the symptoms of "national disorder" are fracture caused by any number of "family secrets" and collective histories that are not wholly about slavery.[2]

In terms of form, inscription describes acts performed by characters within a text rather than the complete novel Rushdy reads as a palimpsest. Accordingly the palimpsest narrative is legible and visible to readers, while inscriptions may not be. That said, Rushdy's "palimpsest imperative" (1) can shape inscription. When the women of the Convent in *Paradise* call Pallas by her mother's name, they effectively write over her birth name and the story it holds. Rushdy asserts, "The palimpsest also provides us with a fruitful metaphor for the intricate ways that contemporary lives and life stories are inscribed on parchments through which the slave past always shows . . . [and] the present is always written against a background where the past is erased but still legible" (8). As Rushdy's use of "inscribed" and "erased" demonstrates, palimpsest and inscription are close kin, both forms of composition that grapple with the materiality and effects of the past in the present. They are not quite synonymous, though; the burned, erased, and hidden acts of inscription in *Paradise* construct individual and communal history in ways that merit their own term.

Inscriptions, then, are the kind of women's writing Carole Boyce Davies describes in terms of "migratory subjectivity." Davies asserts that "migrations of the subject . . . can be conceived not primarily in terms of domination, subordination or 'subalternization' but in terms of slipperiness, elsewhereness" (*Black Women* 37). This "slipperiness, elsewhereness" is constitutive of inscription. Burned, erased, hidden, but constantly created in various places, inscriptions are, like Davies's "migrations," a vehicle of "the Black female subject refusing to be subjugated" (37). In *Paradise* this "slipperiness" and "refusing to be subjugated" "elude the terms of the discussion" in order to reimagine individual and collective narratives of self (37). As my claim that these inscriptions construct history suggests, I assume that African American authors and characters have agency in just the ways Davies describes.

Morrison's inscriptions write into a tradition of African American literacy narratives, of writing as a way to assume authority, from a slave learning to read in order to literally write his own free pass in Frederick Douglass's 1845 *Narrative* to James Weldon Johnson assuming the voice of "publisher" to rewrite the history of white authenticating prefaces in his *Autobiography of an Ex-Colored Man* (1912). Robert Stepto's study *From Behind the Veil* (1979) takes up Douglass, Johnson, and others to demonstrate that the literacy narrative as fact and metaphor is a crucial force shaping African American texts, including slave narratives, autobiographies, and novels. Stepto's case studies are largely about how African American authors and characters gain a voice through a journey of "ascent and immersion," where the work toward "freedom and literacy" is necessarily a "dual quest" (196). Morrison engages this function of the literacy narrative so that inscriptions carry with them this thick history of African American narrative. Coming after the tradition that Stepto charts, however, *Paradise* renders writing and reading somewhat more metaphorical. The stakes of inscription are, as for Douglass's and Johnson's writing, both literal survival and the ability to tell one's own tale, but inscription refers to a variety of markings in addition to text. In the reading of *Paradise* that follows, I assume, in the vein of Stepto, that inscriptions have power. However, Morrison's novel is neither Stepto's "classic ascent narrative" in which a protagonist journeys to a literal or figurative North to become an "articulate survivor" nor the "immersion narrative" of a journey to a literal or figurative South where the protagonist gains "tribal literacy" through reentry into community (167).

*Paradise* begins after immersion; the characters have found their way to an all-black town or an all-female community. Unlike many narratives of ascent and immersion, *Paradise* is not about African American agency in direct relationship to racial oppression; rather, Morrison examines the interactions among narratives of self and community in one exclusively African American context and one exclusively female context. *Paradise* ends neither with Stepto's "least oppressive social structure" that resolves the ascent narrative nor with the "most oppressive social structure" that concludes the immersion narrative (267). Rather, *Paradise* begins after the moment of immersion, after community has become definitional for self such that "tribal literacy" threatens to erase individual history. *Paradise* questions "tribal literacy" with a series of women's inscriptions that interrogate the possibilities and limits of a racially closed of community.

## "Before you erase this, *wait*"

Morrison turns from the diasporic horizons of Marshall's Caribbean journey and Shange's radical recipes toward increasingly conscripted communities. *Paradise* portrays women inscribing texts and other markings in two isolated communities: Ruby, Oklahoma, an all-black town, and the Convent, an all-female household. Through inscription, Morrison turns her gaze to 1976, when the civil rights movement had ended, black power organizations were on the wane, and the United States was celebrating its bicentennial with stamps, coins, a flag, and television specials about the signing of the Declaration of Independence. Anxious reaffirmations of Americanness at a moment of deep disillusion among African Americans make 1976 a marker of disconnect between the nation-state and its African Americans residents.[3] Morrison specifies this disconnect as one that threatened to erase women's stories: "Suppose everything turns out just fine? And in five years or ten years, boom, integration, whatever this movement was about *happened* and we all lived happily ever after? I said nobody's gonna get away with that; they're not gonna tell me it was that easy. . . . It was like they wiped out something. . . . It seemed to me that there was something somebody had forgotten. . . . Like, it was not easy being a black girl in 1940. . . . Before you erase this, *wait*" (Hatch and Billops). Morrison argues that "happily ever after" depends on erasing "being a black girl in 1940" and on forgetting an elusive "something." Women's inscriptions in *Paradise* tell of this "something"; Morrison writes what was "forgotten" during "integration" into the pages of this novel. An illegible letter, names scrawled in dirt and lipstick, cuts on hidden skin, a genealogy, and a group of self-portraits appear in *Paradise* as if to say, "Before you erase this, *wait*." Through fictional acts of inscription, Morrison reveals the content of "this": women's work to fashion self and community. She argues that the civil rights and black power movements depended on the erasure of complex and multivalent life as "a black girl."[4] Toward the close of the twentieth century, *Paradise* uses fiction to reiterate that claim; the novel thematizes erasure through a series of women's hidden, obscured, or destroyed inscriptions.

In this chapter, I examine scenes of women inscribing text and image to argue that these acts of inscription offer a portrait of the "something somebody had forgotten." These inscriptions critique both the integrationist goals of the civil rights movement and the isolationist logic of the black power movement. Finally, I inquire whether *Paradise* offers alternative visions of community grounded in women's work; the answer to this query lies partly in Morrison's 2008 novel, *A Mercy*. Inscriptions in *Paradise* say, "Before you erase this, *wait*" by asking readers to attend to the form and content of what might be lost in the dual movement toward integration and black nationalism in the latter half of the twentieth century.

The work of imagining collectivity in *Paradise* takes place not among men writing militant poetry and plays for public consumption in the urban North but among women inscribing their names and stories on spaces in the American West. This practice of community is under siege in the novel. Women's work to constantly produce a mutable cultural nation becomes increasingly conflicted as the turn of the century approaches. In *Paradise* the horizon of possibility promised by Bambara's *The Black Woman* narrows. This shift manifests in women's work of inscription. Not all writing in *Paradise* is inscription. I am concerned here with a group of texts and images created in private spaces by female characters in the novel. Inscription in *Paradise* creates individuals and community through multivalent storytelling. Because it depends on many layers and constant revisions and restatements, multivalent storytelling disrupts any single master narrative, be it the story of American Independence told in bicentennial celebrations or the oft-told tale of Ruby's founders.

*Paradise* defines inscription with a central counterexample. The motto on the large Oven in Ruby is everything women's inscriptions are not. "Old Fathers" "put most of their strength into constructing the huge, flawlessly designed Oven that both nourished them and monumentalized what they had done" in founding Haven, an all-black town (6–7). The Oven is not the site of work in the kitchens so important to Marshall and Shange; instead, the men of Ruby draw "nourishment" from a public monument. Their work to build the Oven displaces culinary labor; women do the actual cooking in private homes, most visibly in the expansive kitchen at the Convent. When Haven failed to thrive, these founding fathers carried "the bricks, the hearthstone and its iron plate two hundred and forty miles west" and rebuilt the Oven in Ruby (6). The "iron plate" bears a motto nailed by Zechariah Morgan into this potent symbol of men's labor to form a sovereign African American community. The motto, like the story of Ruby, is not transparent. Morrison sets "nourished and monumentalized" in the past tense, indicating that this former site of succor is losing power. The actual text of the celebrated "worn letters" (6) on the Oven does not materialize for about ninety pages. As the characters' attempts at interpretation suggest, "the half-dozen or so words" (7) are marked more by mutability and declining influence than any actual text. Rather than print the words themselves, Morrison first describes their shifting work: "Words that seemed at first to bless them; later to confound them; finally to announce that they had lost" (7). When the words on the Oven appear, they are already up for debate; language is already a site of ambiguity in the novel, but exclusively in terms of interpretation, of how it gets read.

Unlike the inscriptions of women in the novel, this bit of text is intensely public. As the novel finally reveals, the motto proclaims, "Be the Furrow of His Brow" or "Beware the Furrow of His Brow" to every passerby. This motto cannot be erased, smeared, burned, or hidden like women's inscriptions in *Paradise*. Rather, it is nailed into metal, hard, visible, and made by an "Old Father" whose grandsons, Deacon (Deek) and Steward Morgan, control most of the land and money in Ruby.[5] Taking up the work of interpretation, townspeople heatedly argue over whether the text on the Oven reads "Beware the Furrow of His Brow," suggesting a vengeful messianic Old Testament God, or "Be the Furrow of His Brow," suggesting that, as in the final words of the novel, those in the here and now can connect directly to a loving New Testament God to do his work where they are (86). Shopkeeper Anna Flood inquires whether it might be "Beware the Furrow of *Her* Brow" (159), meaning that violence toward women is a source of deathly karma for Ruby.

Amid debates over whether the text of this motto commands residents of Ruby to "be" or "beware," Steward's wife, Dovey Morgan, speculates: "Her own opinion was that 'Furrow of His Brow' alone was enough for any age or generation. Specifying it, particularizing it, nailing its meaning down, was futile" (93). Scholars interpret Dovey's thoughts as instructions for reading *Paradise*, noting that her insistence on ambiguity refers locally to the motto on the Oven but also more broadly to the text of the novel.[6] Dovey's assertion that "nailing its meaning down was futile" presupposes that a given text can be read. Her thinking serves as a useful guide for reading the motto because that particular text makes constant and visible claims for its authority. Her readerly work skips over the moment of composition. Many of the women's inscriptions in

*Paradise* share a degree of ambiguity with the motto, but women's works are often illegible, rarely public, and not strictly textual and assert ambiguity of meaning even if they are never read. The motto polices a coherent, sovereign, and religious community. Interpretation usefully destabilizes its narrow conception of African American identity. Each instance of inscription in the novel is already unstable as a practice of composition rather than a static piece of text. The motto, even with two possible readings, is rigid, while such inscriptions as letters, names, and genealogies are fluid. Whereas interpretation assumes an audience, inscription makes room for those markings that may never be published or otherwise public. In contested moments of inscription, possibilities emerge for collectivity based on something more mutable than the masculine master narrative marked by Ruby's Oven. Each instance of inscription in the novel is already the "deployment of rebellious local knowledges and memories that," according to Stéphane Robolin, "assist in loosening the paternalistic grasp of the powerful" with "a vast peopling of the discursive terrain with multiple memories or stories" (312) in *Paradise*. This "rebellious" "vast peopling" shapes women's work of creating stories; "deployment" is in the making, not the consuming, of inscription. A text can be ambiguous from the moment of composition, even if it is never read. Women's work in *Paradise* makes neither the cultural nation of *The Salt Eaters*, the portable homeland of *Mama Day*, nor the transnational community of *Praisesong for the Widow*. Women's work in Ruby and the Convent instead makes a temporary family constituted by tension, dissension in the ranks, resistance to patriarchy, and constant, ongoing labor "down here in paradise" (318). To be seen, women's work in Ruby and the Convent demands a framework other than Dovey's focus on interpretation. We must attend to the work before reading: the work of composition.[7]

Ruby's Oven is a site of contested reading or interpretation; the Convent outside Ruby is thick with inscriptions. Once a Catholic school for Native American girls, it has become a refuge for women. Convent inhabitants include the racially ambiguous Connie, brought to the Convent school from Brazil by missionary nuns; the political activist Gigi (born Grace); the runaway and recent rape victim Dee Dee (short for Divine, birth name Pallas); Seneca, who mourns her lack of family with self-mutilation; and Mavis, who flees motherhood in her daughter's rain boots and her husband's Cadillac.[8] Despite the chaste implications of their home's name, these women all have sexual appetites apart from a drive to procreation. This causes anxiety among the men of Ruby, especially those who have been intimate with Convent women. The men attempt to fix "danger or natural evil" onto the Convent. Like the title character of Morrison's *Sula* (1973), the Convent is a repository for a vague and sexual danger. Both Medallion in *Sula* and Ruby in *Paradise* depend on their pariahs for their collective identity.

Dangerous outsiders are crucial to Morrison's novels. Ruby's rigid identity is so fragile that it needs a whole group of outcasts to define itself against. From the Peace women of *Sula* to the Convent women of *Paradise*, the function of the outsider changes. This shift marks an important set of losses charted in Morrison's novels. She says, "The community in *Sula* let [Sula] stay. They wouldn't wash or bury her. They protected themselves from her, but she was part of that community. . . . There were some really interesting people who were willing to be whatever they were. People permitted it. . . . They had an enormous span of emotions and activities" (LeClair 125). Between the pre-integration era of *Sula* and the mid-1970s moment of *Paradise*, the aperture of this "span of emotions and activities" narrows. While the people of Medallion, Ohio, would not "wash or bury" Sula after her death, they would never contemplate the violence that Ruby ultimately rains down on its pariahs in *Paradise*. *Sula* elegizes segregation, mourning the loss of an all-black community. The first sentence of the novel alerts us to something lost, "a neighborhood": "In that place, where they tore the nightshade and blackberry patches from their roots to make room for the Medallion City Golf Course, there was once a neighborhood" (3). *Paradise* shines a light on problematic outcomes of attempting to stave off this loss in two segregated communities, one determined by race and the other by gender.[9] *Paradise*, though written at the turn of the twentieth century, looks back at the last gasp of segregated communities thirty years before.[10] In the years following the civil rights movement and integration, racially isolated communities like Medallion and Ruby become increasingly impossible to preserve. Though outsider women in both novels are "part of that community," the horizon of possibility for people's "emotions and activities" fades in Morrison's novels as the twentieth century draws to a close. When, in the last lines of the first chapter of *Paradise*, "the men take aim. For Ruby" (18), they are, as the double entendre indicates, destroying their town in an attempt to protect it.[11] As Sula is blamed for everything from a twisted ankle to a "plague of robins" (89), the posse of men blame the Convent as the source of all that threatens their way of life. They stage a raid meant to destroy that elusive something, a complex range of women's creation of self and community that Morrison cautions us not to erase.

## Neighborhood and Nation

Morrison had long contemplated the nascent dangers in the ways neighborhoods define and interact with their outsiders. In a 1976 interview with Robert Stepto, she says:

> More with the second book [*Sula*]; and very much with the one I'm working on now [*Song of Solomon*]—I felt a strong sense of place, not in terms of the country or the state, but in terms of the details, the feeling, the mood of the community, of the town. . . . My tendency is to focus on neighborhoods and communities. And the community, the black community—I don't like to use that term because it came to mean something much different in the sixties and seventies, as though we had to forge one—but it had seemed to me that it was always there, only we called it the "neighborhood." . . . Responsibilities that agencies now have, were the responsibilities of the neighborhood. So that people were taken care of, locked up, or whatever. If they were sick, other people took care of them; if they needed something to eat, other people took care of them; if they were old, other people took care of them; if they were mad, other people provided a small space for them, or related to their madness or tried to find out the limits of their madness. ("Intimate Things" 10–11)

In the same year she would later use as the time frame of *Paradise*, Morrison abstracts "community" as "a mood" and a "felt . . . sense of place." She explicitly rejects "the country" and "the state." That "people were taken care of" in the sense of being "locked up" rings of the same threat to life and freedom that the men of Ruby pose to the women of the Convent. Morrison mourns the "responsibilities of the neighborhood" but also foreshadows the dangers that emerge in *Paradise*.[12] The neighborhood model implicitly forecloses the possibility of any positive governmental or state aid, placing the responsibility of coping with institutional racism on its victims rather than its perpetrators. Morrison's elegies for the neighborhood depict it as unsustainable and never entertain the possibility of outside assistance. Following the logic of the neighborhood as a self-sustaining community, adults in Ruby go without necessary medical attention, and children learn the history of Ruby's founding families to the exclusion of other subjects. Residents of Ruby once "related to" the "madness" of the Convent women; they bought produce, livestock, and baked goods from Connie and maintained friendships, or at least neighborly relations, with Convent women. By 1976, when a racially defined community is increasingly difficult to maintain, the men of Ruby absolutely refuse to "provide a small space" in their neighborhood for these outsider women.

There is never any question for Morrison that there is a first-person plural, "our group," that refers to African Americans. There was no need to "forge" a community in the 1960s and 1970s because one already existed well before the civil rights and black power movements. Morrison's "our group" was a self-sustaining community long before the advent of 1970s cultural nationalism. Like other black cultural nationalists, she makes a separatist gesture. Her "we" is a nation within a nation, residing outside any designation as "citizen" of the United States. She aligns not with the African diaspora or the U.S.-wide black nationalist effort but moves from the geography of nation to increasingly smaller collectives. The neighborhood, the family, and the household are "the community" that matter in her novels.[13] She repeatedly points to government intervention as an insidious force that divorced African American communities from the work of caretaking. Her fiction suggests that integration and enfranchisement drained a sense of pride in everyday work from an African American collective that "never needed definition."[14] While her novels do not demand a return to segregation or eschew civil rights, they ask readers to *wait*, to attend to what might be lost or erased in the move away from a practice of neighborhood that included both Ruby and the neighboring Convent.

If *Sula* mourns a "mood" of community lost by integration, *Paradise* charts the violence required to preserve that segregation beyond the midcentury moment of *Sula*. *Paradise* demonstrates that it is dangerous, "slippery," as Carola Hilfrich asserts, "to enlist the politics of everyday life and countermemory in efforts to criticize, oppose, subvert, or escape the racialized and gendered nation-orders we know" (323). One danger, as I suggested in earlier chapters, is that a focus on "the politics of everyday life" can result in a version of Houston Baker's "Afro-American women's expressive production" that elides the actual women's work at hand. Another concern is that "politics" can easily fall out of the "everyday." Most pressing in *Paradise*, however, is the concern that practices of community often re-create "the racialized and gendered nation-orders we know" or fracture under the pressure of those orders. Patriarchy is constantly rewritten in Ruby, where the dissolution of community, as much as its practice, determines the inscriptions marked in *Paradise*. Morrison is keenly attuned to these dangers. In a particularly candid moment, she says, "There was a lot of macho stuff in that [black power] movement. . . . There was a heavy weight of men with dicks. . . . The earnest *desperation* for proof of maleness, proof of manhood for black men, was at the heart of that movement" (Hatch and Billops). Although the Morgan twins and their peers suppress black power politics in Ruby (as they shun any identification with a collective beyond the borders of their town), they share the "*desperation* for proof of maleness" that Morrison describes. In this 1983 oral history interview, her voice is thick with tones of both disgust and sympathy as she describes this male desperation. This crisis of masculinity is both dangerous and a rational response to the marginalization and emasculation long forced on African American men by U.S. institutional and cultural forces. This desperation forges a cross-generational alliance and inspires the raid on the Convent. "Macho stuff" manifests in *Paradise* as Deacon and Steward Morgan's efforts to determine the lives of young people, control the town's purse strings, and tell and retell Ruby's founding narrative, editing as they choose.

Despite every effort of the Morgan twins, it proves impossible to keep the world at bay. Ruby residents and Convent women are certainly aware of a larger world. Boys of Ruby come home from Vietnam in body bags, and a calendar in the Convent bears large X's to mark the dates of death of Martin Luther King Jr. and two Black Panther leaders. Though this particular piece of writing has no specific author, the markings on the Convent calendar might be read as another instance of women's inscription, a counternarrative that replaces the U.S. national holidays often found on printed calendars with records of these deaths. All Morrison's novels are informed by a degree of isolation, sometimes as a result of violence, like those assassinations inscribed on the Convent calendar, but *Paradise* uses its neighborhood as the limit case of sovereignty. The novel's critique of a black nationalist project pushes against the racially closed circles of Haven and Ruby but also sympathetically portrays the decline of both towns as a result of engagement with the nation-state. In other words, both racial separatism and aspiring to national citizenship are dangerous choices in *Paradise*. The story of Haven and Ruby makes the problems of both integration with and divorce from the nation-state clear:

> From Haven, a dreamtown in Oklahoma Territory, to Haven, a ghosttown in Oklahoma State. Freedmen who stood tall in 1889 dropped to their knees in 1934 and were stomach-crawling by 1948. . . . All the others he knew about or heard tell of knuckled to

or merged with white towns; otherwise, like Haven, they had shriveled into tracery. . . . One thousand citizens in 1905 becoming five
hundred by 1934. Then two hundred, then eighty, as cotton col-
lapsed or railroad companies laid their tracks elsewhere. Subsistence farming, once the only bounty a large family needed, became
just scrap farming as each married son got his bit, which had to be
broken up into more pieces for his children, until finally the owners
of the bits and pieces who had not walked off in disgust welcomed
any offer from a white speculator, so eager were they to get away
and try someplace else. A big city this time, or a small town—anywhere that was already built.

But he and the others, veterans all, had a different idea. Loving
what Haven had been—the idea of it and its reach—they carried
that devotion, nursing it from Bataan to Guam, from Iwo Jima to
Stuttgart. (5–6)

Morrison tells the story of Haven and Ruby by focusing on an ambiguous "he" who could be any of the men raiding the Convent. The singular pronoun refers to Deacon, Steward, and all the men because what
matters is not their individual identities, but their united, masculine
desperation to save the town they have built. The shift from territory to
state, incorporation into the United States, was the death knell of Haven,
a black town founded by freedmen. Black towns that have "shriveled into
tracery" haunt Rubyites; there but for the grace of God (who has so far
protected them even from death) go they. The novel never contemplates
government intervention as a possible weapon in this fiercely independent fight against decline. Engagement with the nation-state always
breeds ill for Haven and Ruby. After emancipation and years of hard
labor, the Old Fathers went west, following the Homesteading Act of
1862.[15] They were turned away from communities of African Americans,
whites, and Native Americans; Ruby residents call this the "Disallowing." So the Old Fathers led their band of hungry migrants farther west.
They settled Haven, built the enormous Oven at the center of town, and
spawned the "new fathers," who, as Haven declined, moved even farther
into uncharted territory to establish Ruby (13–16). From taking advantage of homesteading to participating in U.S. wars on foreign soil, every
specter of national belonging in this novel is a threat rather than a source
of assistance. Haven and Ruby struggle throughout *Paradise* to untan-
gle themselves from the nation-state. Morrison distinguishes between
the "dreamtown" of territory and the "ghosttown" of state; mapping,

demarcation by government, is a mode of colonization that makes the space unfree, forces it into a relationship with oppressors.

References to World War II emphasize the impossibility of total divorce from the nation-state. This settler story appears again just pages later as the "powerful memories" of Deek and Steward. They are invested in this narrative, "the controlling one told to them by their grandfather" (13). The tale replaces mother's milk as the sustenance of their youth: "They listened to, imagined, and remembered every single thing because each detail was a jolt of pleasure erotic as a dream, out-thrilling and more purposeful than even the war they had fought in" (16). Each telling shores up this "controlling" narrative, which is "erotic" and intoxicating because it bequeaths a legacy of power and self-reliance to the Morgan men. They attempt to maintain and perpetuate this masculine history, referencing the story of fathers at every turn by using their substantial influence in the town. The "controlling" narrative absorbs many disruptions: residents of Haven think of the racism faced by African American soldiers returning from World War II as "the Disallowing, Part Two" (194), framing contemporary racial discrimination as an incarnation of family history. Even the annual children's nativity play is restructured as the story of Haven's founding, with the number of families changed each year to depict only those in the Morgans' favor (208–13). Because it is a highly visible, public performance consolidated by yearly repetition, the nativity play is a series of interpretations, not inscriptions.

The oft-repeated story of Haven and Ruby writes not only into and against the nation-state but also inquires into the limits and possibilities for other collective identities.[16] Exceptionalism, manifest destiny, and patriarchy are all aspects of the mythic history of the United States that contribute to Ruby's demise. Hewing closely to national myths proves a poor foundation for a cultural nation apart.[17] The men of Haven are "nursing" not children but the dream of an independent black town. They carry their vision and "devotion" "from Bataan to Guam, from Iwo Jima to Stuttgart."[18] The founding fathers of Haven and Ruby are veterans of American brutality, both as propagators of it abroad and recipients of it at home. They experience a slippage between defending their own homes and invading others'. This blurring of defense and offense travels back to Haven and Ruby with them, culminating in the false belief that an attack on the Convent is a justified defense of Ruby. All these men have fought in war to defend a nation-state that doesn't include them.[19] The rejection and disgrace that greeted soldiers returning from Vietnam augments this alienation. The desire to try again, to build a new "all-black town worth the pain" (5) is forged in war, and these soldiers bring a violent notion of what constitutes defense home with them.[20]

Men wage this defense in *Paradise* against women and their inscriptions. The raid on the Convent attempts to shut down inscription, to hold on to the realm of interpretation marked by the motto on the Oven and the annual nativity play. Private acts of inscription, even without readers, prove powerful enough in their palimpsestic nature to threaten Ruby's master narrative as performed on the Oven and in the play. Women's work of inscription appears in *Paradise* as a letter in smeared lipstick, self-inflicted cuts on a woman's skin, a name scratched in the dirt, a secret genealogy, and a group of self-portraits painted on a basement floor.

## Smeared, Scratched, Cut, Written, Painted: Women's Inscriptions in *Paradise*

Seneca carries a letter written in lipstick from her sister, Jean, her only proof of a lost familial connection. After days of waiting for Jean to return, Seneca breaks into a forbidden box of cookies and discovers a missive:

> Leaning against the box of Lorna Doones was an envelope with a word she recognized instantly: her own name printed in lipstick. She opened it, even before she tore into the cookie box, and pulled out a single paper with more lipstick words. She could not understand any except her own name again at the top, "Jean" at the bottom, loud red marks in between.
>
> Soaking in happiness, she folded the letter back in the envelope, put it in her shoe, and carried it for the rest of her life. Hiding it, fighting for the right to keep it, rescuing it from wastebaskets. She was six years old, an ardent first-grade student, before she could read the whole page. Over time, it became simply a sheet of paper smeared fire-cracker red, not one decipherable word left. (128)

*Seneca*, printed in lipstick both in this letter and later on her bedroom door at the Convent, is a textual repository of the past, a one-word inscription of childhood abandonment. The name of a tribe of the Iroquois Confederacy, Seneca serves as a reminder of Native American girls who once attended the Convent school. The Seneca resisted colonization, imparting a legacy of defiance to Morrison's character. Like the migrating fathers of Haven and Ruby, they were the westernmost part of their tribe. The character Seneca lives "fighting for the right to keep" her inscription of self, to preserve the text that records her connection to someone. Unable to read in early childhood, she carries the letter with her, its text smudged beyond legibility perhaps even before she can fully decipher it.[21] Whether or not there was "one decipherable word left" by the time Seneca could read the letter, its actual text never appears in *Paradise*. Dovey's lesson in reading teaches that, when it comes to any text, "nailing its meaning down was futile." In the case of Jean's lipstick letter to Seneca, and most women's writing in *Paradise*, this is not a choice but a statement of fact. There is nothing to "nail down," no details to "particularize" this important text.[22] Seneca's name is the only known detail of a letter that exists exclusively as composition. Jean's lipstick markings and Morrison's novel inscribe the letter as illegible, unread, a story of the impossibility of language to fully narrate abandoning a child. Even without its actual text, this "smeared" letter defines for readers the "something" erased: that "being a black girl" for Seneca mean a futile search for familial connection in a box of Lorna Doones.

Inscription is not necessarily freeing or positive, but it is always multivalent. From the moment of its composition, Jean's letter, for example, documents both Seneca's family connections and her abandonment. Seneca finds another form of inscription that is similarly complex: beginning in her youth in foster care, she cuts many "streets" into her body (260). In the face of abuse, she turns to this hidden habit. She maps experiences that are constantly denied or erased by others onto her body: "She entered the vice like a censored poet whose suspect lexicon was too supple, too shocking to publish" (261). These inscriptions are self-injury, a secret and "censored" language nearly erotic in its demands. Seneca's use of this "lexicon" demonstrates the pathology possible when women's stories are denied, erased, and hidden. Even in the sanctuary of the Convent, Seneca still needs to inscribe these escape routes: "Seneca did another street. An intersection, in fact, for it crossed the one she'd done a moment ago" (262). The "intersection" that "crossed" another on Seneca's thighs evokes Reverend Misner's and Steward Morgan's meditations on the various meanings of the cross (145–46, 154), but Seneca's secret cross, her "under garment life" (261), her geography of self, will never be read. As the cuts heal, they, like other women's inscriptions in the novel, are effectively erased. As inscription, they exist exclusively as composition. These cuts both document an alternative narrative of self and allow Seneca to mark her body as her own territory, a particularly crucial move for a victim of sexual abuse.[23] Seneca documents her history with inscription rather than narrating her experiences. Morrison questions the adequacy of language to describe a life like Seneca's by using inscription to tell that life. This is clear in part because Morrison ironically uses *lexicon* and *poet* to depict an instance of inscription in *Paradise* that is not writing, not words or letters.

Like Seneca and her streets, *Pallas* is an inscription of identity and territory in *Paradise*. Seeking escape from her life as well as her attackers, Pallas Truelove makes her way to Ruby sad, sick, and with a hair full of algae (174).[24] She has been on the run for months, having left her father's home to find her mother, Dee Dee, who subsequently has an affair with Pallas's boyfriend. Pallas keeps running until she is attacked by a group of men who rape and attempt to drown her. She arrives on the outskirts of Ruby traumatized and mute. Her first act is to write her name, only to immediately erase it: "Like a child alone in a deserted playground, she drew her name in the dirt with her toe. . . . [Then] she kicked her name away, covering it completely with red dirt" (175). Pallas's inscription, the name she writes and erases in the dirt, alludes to her resemblance to a wild animal. According to the OED, *Pallas* designates Pallas's warbler, a small Asian bird, and Pallas's cat, a wild feline native to a desert climate. In *Paradise* Pallas has migrated across such a desert, leaving both her father's home in Los Angeles and her mother's artists' retreat in the American Southwest. The bird, the cat, and one of the largest asteroids ever discovered are named for the goddess Pallas Athena. In Greek mythology, Athena is the goddess of wisdom and guardian of Athens. Gray-eyed like her namesake cat, she usually appears in military garb, with a helmet and shield bearing the image of the snake-headed Medusa. In the novel, Pallas's tangled hair on first appearance resembles Medusa's head of snakes; like Medusa, she becomes something of a warrior when men enter her home during the raid on the Convent. After months of wandering, she marks Ruby as her territory by inscribing her name in its soil.

Pallas's name, like Seneca's cuts, demonstrates that inscription is complex and contested. Keeping with the way inscription hides its literal content, Morrison does not reveal whether the "name in the dirt" is the birth name Pallas or the adopted name Dee Dee; both names hail this character in the novel. The women of the Convent write over a thicket of meaning when they decide to call Pallas "Divine" or "Dee Dee," forcing her mother's name on her (181). "Divine" titles Pallas's chapter and labels the card on her bedroom at the Convent. Rather than inscribe her true name, as Morrison's chapter title and the bedroom door do for Seneca, "Dee Dee" replaces "Pallas" both in the pages of *Paradise* and in a lover's arms. The nickname "Dee Dee" serves as a constant reminder of Pallas's hurt at her mother's hand; each iteration of her name tells this story in shorthand. When, after the raid, she returns briefly to her mother's home to retrieve a favorite pair of shoes, to metaphorically get what is hers, *Paradise* restores Pallas to her name, leaving "Dee Dee," and the history of pain and conflict therein, for her neglectful mother (311–12).

Pat Best's dense documentation of Ruby's genealogy is a more prolific site of inscription than Seneca's smeared lipstick letter or Pallas's name scratched in dirt. Pat, a schoolteacher, inscribes collective records of Haven and Ruby, creating a counternarrative to the story told and retold by generations of Ruby's founding fathers:

> It began as a gift to the citizens of Ruby—a collection of family trees; the genealogies of each of the fifteen families. . . . She had begun to supplement the branches of who begat whom with notes: what work they did, for example, where they lived, to what church they belonged. Some of the nicer touches ("Was Missy Rivers, wife of Thomas Blackhorse, born near the Mississippi River? Her name seems to suggest . . . ") she had gleaned from her students' autobiographical compositions. Not anymore. Parents complained about their children being asked to gossip, to divulge what could be private information, secrets, even. After that, most of her notes came from talking to people, asking to see Bibles and examining church records. Things got out of hand when she asked to see letters and marriage certificates. The women narrowed their eyes before smiling and offering to freshen her coffee. Invisible doors closed, and the conversation turned to weather. . . . She gave up all pretense to objective comment. The project became unfit for any eyes except her own. . . . Who were these women who, like her mother, had only one name? Celeste, Olive, Sorrow, Ivlin, Pansy. Who were these women with generalized last names? Brown, Smith, Rivers, Stone, Jones. Women whose identity rested on the men they married—if marriage applied: a Morgan, a Flood, a Blackhorse, a Poole, a Fleetwood. . . . The town's official story, elaborated from pulpits, in Sunday school classes and ceremonial speeches, had a sturdy public life. Any footnotes, crevices, or questions to be put took keen imagination and the persistence of a mind uncomfortable with oral histories. Pat had wanted proof in documents where possible to match the stories, and where proof was not available she interpreted. (187–88)

*Paradise* revisits the African American archive considered in all of the works in this study.[25] Pat's genealogy is a textual repository of "private information, secrets, even." Unlike most family trees, this is intensely private work "unfit for any eyes except" those of its author. Women's work in the home here is not the domestic labor of child rearing, cooking, or cleaning. The labor concealed from the public eye is a revision of the African American archive, albeit full of gaps and contested information. Pat domesticates the "public life" of the "town's official story," restoring private, secret, and female dimensions to the African American archive, including marriage and procreation with Native Americans and light-skinned African Americans. Women of Ruby, those who "narrowed their eyes" and shut "invisible doors," are, conversely, bulwarks supporting the "sturdy public life" of Ruby's master narrative. These women refuse to help Pat in her work, thus preserving a version of Ruby's history that largely excludes matrilineage.

The women with "only one name" are not ancestors in a single women's line, as in the attic ledger of *Mama Day*, but the foremothers of an entire town. "Generalized last names" appear separate from the first names that hailed these women, suggesting their distance from the founding fathers, even when the women were born or married into the rigidly defined myths of Haven and Ruby. This archive of women's names tells an incomplete story. What was the "Sorrow" that earned a woman such a name?[26] Which last name goes with which first name? What information fills the "footnotes, crevices, or questions"? Incompleteness and absence constitute this archive, but Pat does manage to fill some gaps. Hers is a "mind uncomfortable with oral histories"; she needs this written record even if no one else will ever read it.

As scholars point out, Pat is partly a figure for Morrison or the novelist more generally.[27] Resonance between Pat and Morrison gives Pat's genealogy a great deal of weight. Marni Gauthier acknowledges the ambiguity of narratives in *Paradise*, but interprets Pat's archive as an authoritative account, the one history that the novel "endorses . . . as a truthful account of Ruby" (399). Gauthier notes, "An astute genealogist, Patricia sees absence and silence as sources" (410). However, Pat's desire to fill those gaps rather than recognize them as constitutive of the archive makes her an unreliable authority, in part because of her drive to interpret, which is apparent in her participation in debates about the meaning of the motto on the Oven. Pat offers a close reading: "'Beware the Furrow of His Brow.' In which the 'You' (understood), vocative case, was not a command to the believers, but a threat to those who had disallowed

them. It must have taken him months to think up those words—just so—
to have multiple meanings: to appear stern, urging obedience to God,
but slyly not identifying the understood proper noun or specifying what
the Furrow might cause to happen or to whom" (194). Using the terms of
textual scholarship, Morrison's narration forecloses, or at least pokes fun
at, literary criticism. The text takes grammatical concerns as part of its
scope rather than leaving this sort of analysis to readers.[28] Lest Dovey's
lesson that "specifying" a single meaning of text is "futile" fail to reach
the reader, reviewer, or scholar, Pat reiterates the lesson by demonstrating the inadequacy of any attempt to fix the meaning of the motto. Her
attention to the understood "you" extends to identification of the vocative
case (the addressee of this "rule," "conundrum," "command," or "threat"
remains unstated). Pat reads the understood "you" as directly addressing
"those who had disallowed" Ruby's founders. The "him" in Pat's mind
is Old Father Zechariah Morgan, "slyly" concealing the "proper noun"
that would identify the object of rage. "His Brow" is God's, as the capitalization indicates, but the brow of vengeful Morgan men as well. Even
with her will to interpret, Pat's reading is mostly about words that do not
appear: the identity of the implied "you" and the owner of the furrowed
brow. Echoing her close reading of "Beware the Furrow of His Brow,"
Pat's editorial eye fills in gaps with extrapolation: "Where proof was not
available she interpreted." A lifelong Rubyite, Pat is not immune from
the will to interpret, to pin down a rigid meaning, even as she inscribes.

Giving Pat's documents greater authority than Jean's letter to Seneca,
Pallas's and Seneca's names, Seneca's cuts, or women's self-portraits at
the Convent elides some of the most important claims about history that
*Paradise* makes. Situated among many forms of inscription, Pat's archive
is just one account among many, one fruit of women's work in conversation with other accounts. Morrison says, "I know I can't change the
future, but I can change the past. It is the past, not the future, which is
infinite. Our past was appropriated. I am one of the people who has to
reappropriate it" (Taylor-Guthrie xiii–xiv). In her efforts to "reappropriate the past," Pat refuses to acknowledge that past as "infinite." She is
certain there is one true version of Ruby's history and one true meaning
of the motto on the Oven. *Paradise* takes this as a cautionary tale rather
than a model. Morrison's textual project necessarily exceeds Pat's genealogy by positioning that genealogy as one of many versions of history in
the novel. In thematizing acts of inscription, Morrison attempts to write
herself out of this authorial bind of preserving the infinite and polyvocal past in the work of a single author. She calls herself just "one of the

people" working to rewrite the past, but her published novel stands as the only form of public, legible women's writing by the end of the story. Morrison thematically destabilizes the authority of each inscription in the novel, while her own text necessarily dominates any other in *Paradise*.

Pat's inscription, on the other hand, meets a dramatic end: she burns it all. Only in the moment of its destruction is the full extent of her labors in the archive apparent: "One by one she dropped cardboard files, sheets of paper—both stapled and loose—into the flames. She had to tear the covers off the composition notebooks and hold them slant with a stick so they would not smother the fire. . . . At the kitchen sink she washed her hands and dashed water on her face. She felt clean" (217). She sheds the burden of history, feeling "clean" after burning this record of "the numbers, the bloodlines, who fucked who," all documented in piles of "files, sheets of paper," and "composition notebooks" (217). Pat's act of destruction is part of the work of composition. Women in *Paradise* have this mode of narrative control: they not only inscribe stories; they also destroy them, deciding what will be read.[29] This moment does not negate the value of Pat's work. Rather, her archive is meaningful because composed, whether or not others read it. Her story, as part of Morrison's published novel, changes the account of self, community, and history in *Paradise*. The documents that witness Pallas's rape, Seneca's abandonment, and "who fucked who" in the creation of Ruby's first families will never be read by Morrison's characters. This positions Morrison's readers as witnesses to inscription, even if they get only scraps of these texts. The reader can never quite know it all (Seneca's letter is illegible, Pat's archive burned), but she does see the acts of inscription, however partial or obscured, all over the text. Morrison's reader cannot fully interpret Seneca's letter or Pat's genealogy because their actual words do not appear in *Paradise*. Acts of inscription, rather than their products, are there to be read.

Beyond Ruby and its inability to accommodate the stories in Pat's archive, the Convent is a site for teasing out possibilities of coalescence and dissolution that inform women's inscriptions throughout the novel. Although the Convent is not quite the site of the murder and mayhem that men of Ruby suspect, it is a charged space, both threatening and liberating for the women who end up there in an uneasy female community. This collective has all the discomfort but little of the humor of the Azure Bosom dance troupe in Shange's *Sassafrass, Cypress & Indigo*. Scholars tend to read female households in Morrison's novels as utopian models of collectivity. The three prostitutes in *The Bluest Eye* (1970), for example, form the most successful household of that novel. Their home is the only place where young Pecola Breedlove is not harmed or ostracized. As Dubey notes, "The prostitutes constitute a kind of feminine folk community that is marginal even to the marginal community of blacks" (*Black Women Novelists* 45). Their home prefigures all-female households in *Song of Solomon, Beloved, Paradise*, and *A Mercy* as collectives of outsider women, but the gender exclusion in the later novels proves oppressive. The increasing polyvocality of these novels reflects this shift. Madhu Dubey notes the oscillation between free indirect discourse and Claudia's first-person voice in *The Bluest Eye* as a destabilization of authority (46); this strategy proliferates in Morrison's later work, shuttling among voices and points of view to formally depict the destabilization of community. Describing Pilate's home in *Song of Solomon*, the Peace home in *Sula*, and the prostitutes in *The Bluest Eye*, Susan Willis writes, "It is not gratuitous that in all these cases the definition of social utopia is based on a three-woman household. . . . These are societies which do not permit heterosexuality as it articulates male domination to be the determining principle for the living and working relationships of the group" ("Eruptions" 41). More in line with the households of *Beloved* and *A Mercy*, the women of the Convent in *Paradise* do not establish a "social utopia." Convent residents Gigi and Mavis fight constantly, often scratching and slapping one another; Connie descends into alcoholism and despair; and Seneca's self-mutilation continues well after she moves to the Convent. Women's collectivity in *Paradise* is a means of surviving, of maintaining a space outside of "male domination," and is thus defined partly by patriarchy. These efforts to create a home space are only partly successful; maintaining the Convent community demands constant struggle. Like Ruby's, the Convent's struggle for a sovereign existence is simultaneously divorced from and engaged with outside forces. An alternative community is necessary because male domination and racial segregation define Ruby; the Convent's female residents seek to create their own community apart from these forces. Their struggle proves productive, if not entirely successful.

The Convent explores the possibilities for utopia and dissolution in the all-female households of Morrison's earlier novels. Currently home to a community of outsider women, the Convent predates Ruby (223). Though it once served as a Catholic school for Native American girls under the direction of Mother Superior Mary Magna, it has a decadent past that informs the present residents' sensual rituals.[30] The remnants of the Convent's first incarnation as an embezzler's mansion lie strewn about the building. The women spot plumbing fixtures shaped like genitalia and sculptures of "nude women in polished marble; men in rough stone" (172). The classroom turned living room, ample wine cellar, and nude figures suggest a life of both girlish chastity and bold sexuality. The pieces of the Convent's layered past remain in this space, shaping the daily lives of the Convent women; they inscribe their identities on top of this history, writing over, but not erasing, these layers.

Connie, the Convent's oldest resident, observes, even judges, the ways outsider women occupy her home. She mourns the death of her adoptive mother, the nun Mary Magna, and silently resents the young women who come under her care. Connie experiences her gift for healing as devilment, fearing her abilities even when they prolong or save lives. In the eyes of the Convent women, she is an "ideal parent" (262), a loving embodiment of maternal care, but when she gets her own chapter, her grief over a long-past love affair with Deek Morgan and her anger at caring for lost girls emerge. The women become not so much individuals with their own stories as a collective framed by Connie. The chapter "Consolata," describes them:

> Over the past eight years, they had come. The first one, Mavis, during Mother's long illness; the second right after she died. Then two more. Each one asking permission to linger a few days but never actually leaving. . . . Consolata looked at them through the bronze or gray or blue of her various sunglasses and saw broken girls, frightened girls, weak and lying. . . . More and more she wanted to snap their necks. . . . Not only did they do nothing except the absolutely necessary, they had no plans to do anything. Instead of plans they had wishes—foolish babygirl wishes. (222)

Connie's drunken reverie initially identifies Mavis by name, but as the women accumulate, they become a collection of girls viewed through the colored lenses of the "various sunglasses" she wears. All the readerly sympathy accrued for Connie as a victim of the raid in the opening pages of *Paradise* drains away with the revelation that when she looks at the women she "want[s] to snap their necks." What might be read as independence and resistance becomes, in narration focalized through Connie, a bunch of "babygirl wishes" of infantile women. Seen through Connie's eyes, Seneca, Gigi, Mavis, and Pallas come to look more lost and desperate than rebellious. Perhaps most devastating, however, is the shift in the characterization of Connie. The woman who has seemed a strong, magical, loving force is also a bitter, angry drunk who has taken up residence in the basement, her eyes now too sensitive to bear any light.

*Paradise* refuses to let the reader rest comfortably in this characterization. Connie recovers credibility and power, particularly through stories of her bonds with women outside the Convent, Soane Morgan and Lone DuPres chief among them. Lone and Connie "practice" (244), an ambiguous term always without an object of the verb. *Practice* refers loosely to using gifts of second sight and healing. Connie, initially ashamed of her gift, learns through Lone's visits how to do powerful spirit work. Connie can "step in" to another person and bring her back from the brink of death, an act she performs for both Mary Magna and Scout Morgan (245). Only through Lone's visits does Connie stop thinking of her abilities as a curse to be suppressed at all costs and come to "accept Lone's remedies" (247). The link between Lone's second sight and Connie's healing powers reveals that the connection between Ruby and the Convent is not just men's use of a women's community as a psychic dumping ground but also a connection among women with magical gifts. Practice as supernatural work has crucial resonance for the broader practice of a cultural nation determined by connections among women. Connie's external eyesight fades as her "in sight" grows (247).[31] Following her internal rant, these stories of practice layer readerly sympathy and wonder on top of disdain. Her blindness becomes not a sad result of alcoholism and retreat from the world but evidence of supernatural gifts. She evokes a mix of emotions: affection, fear, disgust, admiration, and sympathy.

Third-person omniscient narration in many of Morrison's novels invites this type of layered response by putting the reader inside the thoughts of characters who might not otherwise invite much sympathy (Cholly Breedlove of *The Bluest Eye* comes to mind). *Paradise* continues and extends this narrative practice. Morrison says of *The Bluest Eye*, "I told it in third person in parts, in pieces like a broken mirror. . . . I introduced the two little girls and chose an 'I' for one of them, so there would be somebody to empathize with her at her age level" (Raus 97). While a first-person voice cracks through the third-person narration in *The Bluest Eye*, the "pieces like a broken mirror" of third-person narration make up all of *Paradise*, allowing for some sympathy but refusing identification with any one character. *Paradise* capitalizes on the possibilities of narrative fragmentation not to organize the choral coherence of Bambara's fiction but to refuse the reader and characters any safe home. The connection to first-person narrator Claudia that allows readerly empathy for Pecola Breedlove in *The Bluest Eye* appears nowhere in *Paradise*. Just as there is no single fixed meaning in any of the novel's inscriptions, there is no safe haven in identification with a single character or single interpretation. Accordingly Connie is neither completely a comforting mother nor fully an alcoholic madwoman.

## Inscribing a Binding Community

Thick with complexity created by the multifocal narration of *Paradise*, Connie emerges from the wine cellar and cooks an elaborate meal. Descriptions of her preparations appear interspersed with the women's self-examination and unraveling (Seneca cutting herself, Mavis negotiating a relationship with the ghosts of her children, Gigi hating herself in the bathtub). Just when the household seems most likely to disintegrate, Connie gathers the women to perform shared rites in the final weeks before the raid. Under her direction the women become, finally, the single entity promised in the opening pages of the novel. Connie calls them away from their private hurts and gathers them under her stern direction, saying, "I call myself Consolata Sosa. If you want to be here you do what I say. Eat how I say. Sleep when I say. And I will teach you what you are hungry for" (262). Reclaiming the name she last bore in her Brazilian girlhood, she enforces a new mode of institution and ritual to rescue herself and her charges from despair. Her authority inscribes a closed circle. After hearing these words and deciding to stay, the women "all came to see they could not leave the one place they were free to leave" (262). Like the self-segregated town of Ruby, this refuge is also a place of confinement as these women unify into a single being. The force of community is both sheltering and terrifying, as restrictive in its isolation as Ruby.

Having forged this binding community, Connie consolidates it through another kind of inscription: painting. She has the women "scrub the cellar floor" and lie "naked in candlelight" there, as she paints around each body to form a silhouette (263). She invites them into a ritual of collective consciousness called "loud dreaming":

> That is how the loud dreaming began. How the stories rose in the place. Half-tales and the never-dreamed escape from their lips to soar high above guttering candles, shifting dust from crates and bottles. And it was never important to know who said the dream or whether it had meaning. In spite of or because their bodies ache, they step easily into the dreamer's tale. They enter the heat in the

Cadillac, feel the smack of cold air in the Higgledy Piggledy. They
know their tennis shoes are unlaced and that a bra strap annoys
each time it slips from the shoulder. The Armour package is sticky.
They inhale the perfume of sleeping infants and feel parent-cozy
although they notice one's head is turned awkwardly. They adjust
the sleeping baby head then refuse, outright refuse, what they know
and drive away home. . . . They kick their legs underwater, but not
too hard for fear of waking fins or scales also down below. The
male voices saying saying forever saying push their own down their
throats. Saying, saying until there is no breath to scream or contradict. Each one blinks and gags from tear gas, moves her hand
slowly to the scraped shin, the torn ligament. (264)

Seneca, Pallas, Gigi, and Mavis "step easily" into one another's stories.
Mavis's memory of "the heat in the Cadillac" where she left her twins
as she entered the "cold air in the Higgledy Piggledy" becomes a collective experience. The women feel heat and cold, a slipping bra strap,
and a "sticky" package of hot dogs, just as Mavis did. The burden of her
twins' deaths disperses among them; it is no longer Mavis's alone to bear.
Without any signal of shift in consciousness—no break in paragraph or
change in voice—the women enter the pasts of their companions on the
cellar floor. "They kick their legs underwater," with Pallas losing "breath
to scream or contradict" her assailants. They feel the sting of the tear
gas that burned Gigi's eyes during urban uprisings. All of these pasts
become part of a communal sensory perception; the women are experiencing, rather than telling or hearing, one another's lives.[32]
    On the other side of this "loud dreaming," the women have access to a
new and nontextual mode of inscription: they inscribe their identities on
the silhouettes. With "tubes of paint" and "sticks of colored chalk," they
begin with "natural features: breasts and pudenda, toes, ears and head
hair" (264–65). Starting with the physical attributes that mark their sex,
the women move on to markings that reinscribe their collective story.
"Seneca duplicated in robin's egg blue one of her more elegant scars, one
drop of red at its tip. Later on, when she had the hunger to slice her inner
thigh, she chose instead to mark the open body lying on the cellar floor"
(265). As sharing her story with these women has lightened Mavis's load,
so distributing experience, putting it outside herself, allows Seneca to
share her story and stop damaging her body.
    The women paint revelations withheld in *Paradise* up to this point.
Seneca's self-representation causes her companions to ask whether Jean,

author of the lipstick letter, might not be her mother rather than her sister. The "locket around her body's throat" in Gigi's painting reveals pictures of the people she lost during urban rebellions. Pallas paints "a baby in her template's stomach," revealing that her rape resulted in pregnancy (265). Untold days pass as the women paint on and around their silhouettes, adding layers to the stories told in *Paradise*. Against the repeated nativity play or the tale of Ruby's founding, these strategies become a set of fluctuating, intertwining narratives. Echoing the layered and shifting African American archive posited in *Paradise*, "the body templates serve as a concrete reminder of the ways in which the body is a palimpsest, a historical record of overlapping traces," "a page that can be reinscribed" (Sweeney 58, 61). At the end of the chapter named for the woman who brings them together, "the Convent women were no longer haunted" (266). While doubt and danger simmer suppressed in Ruby, the women of the Convent have exorcised their demons through collective inscription.

When Morrison revisits the story of the raid on the Convent in the novel's penultimate chapter, the women have already figuratively escaped through this collective exorcism. The sanctuary of the Convent is under threat from the moment *Paradise* begins, but women's inscriptions remake this story before Morrison reveals its ending. Desperate to repair fissures in patriarchy and segregation, Deek and Steward lead the attack on the Convent, attempting to protect the community their fathers built. *Paradise* opens with the sentence "They shoot the white girl first. With the rest they can take their time" (3). The violence of this stunning first event, an armed raid on the Convent, frames the novel. Women's inscriptions populate the 250 pages between two tellings of the assault. "White girl" is ambiguous, never assigned to any specific resident of the Convent.[33] During the first telling of the raid, "white girl" seems to refer to Connie, but by the end of the novel the reader knows that, brought by nuns from Brazil in girlhood and aged into a kind of mystic mother superior in the years since her adoption and migration, Connie is neither white nor a girl. She is feeble with age and nearly blind and her ethnicity is ambiguous. Connie is Brazilian by birth, grows up amid Native American girls at the Convent school, and makes a multiethnic family of women who come there long after the school has closed; the narration refers to her as "not white" (223).[34] She goes unnamed in both descriptions of the raid; through "loud dreaming," she and her diasporic heritage become part of "the women" (285–87) rather than an individual entity. In the first pages of the novel, the omniscient third-person narration focalized through men collects the women under the single term *the target*, a collection of "detritus: throwaway people" (4).[35] These pejorative designations are a means of unification; the women are a community, an entity, a force to be reckoned with, even in the eyes of their would-be murderers.

A number of literary scholars read the unification of the women through "loud dreaming" as a hopeful model for individual and collective healing.[36] Working toward communal recovery and liberation shapes the other novels I have examined here, but *Paradise* seems less optimistic. While the Convent women drive out their own demons through "loud dreaming," the sphere of influence of this women's work remains unknown. This is not Bambara's *The Salt Eaters*, in which one woman's physical and mental recovery promises a hopeful future of communal work for change. The raid on the Convent frames *Paradise*; almost all of the action in the novel takes place between the moment Steward fires his gun at Connie and the moment the bullet hits her. Repeated tales of violence against women populate this suspended instant. The need for the Convent as refuge speaks again and again of misogyny, violence, and failures of community. The women work to create a new collective, but they do it in the belly of the beast.

Women's work of inscription in the Convent, while liberatory, seems not to change even their closest neighbors. Narration focalized through the men of Ruby takes on additional layers but does not suggest that these men could help dismantle racism or patriarchy. Attempting to justify violence, the men convince themselves that a white family found in fields near the road died at the hands of the Convent women rather than as a result of Ruby's refusal to offer aid. Their true grievance with these women emerges as well, freed into the space of consciousness in the final retelling of the raid. The men, having assumed a collective voice, think, "They don't need men and they don't need God" (276). This, of course, is the women's real offense. They are a single-gender community led by a woman with rituals divorced from the God whose furrow marks the Oven in Ruby. The men are furious not to be needed, not to be in control. Their collective stream-of-consciousness justification prior to the final narrative of the raid reveals their fear of being unnecessary and outdated. In deciding to stay under Connie's leadership, the Convent women have truly become something apart, no longer forced by their painful pasts to seek refuge but in the Convent by choice. As Lone thinks, "Not women locked safely away from men; but worse, women who chose themselves for company, which is to say not a convent but a coven" (276). The power in this choice of gender segregation, both dangerous and liberating, is that the women are "locked" only into the community of their choosing.

Perhaps most disheartening is that the women are no longer a community at the end of the novel. They radiate fracture rather than coalescence, division rather than kinship. As Hilfrich notes, "Morrison's closing chapter is skeptical about these specters' ability to generate a change that would exceed the limits of their own need for a repair or closure of their personal histories" (333). The community beyond the Convent includes no Dr. Julius Meadows drawing his "country mind" and "city mind" together, nor a Nadeen feeling "womanish" about to bring a life into the world. Rather than learning to see simultaneously with Bambara's "eye of the heart," "eye of the head," and "eye of the mind" as a route to coalescence, the denizens of *Paradise* come rapidly undone, disconnected from one another. The women of the Convent, "unlocked," have scattered by the end of the novel. If they are "specters," they occupy different planes from each other as well as from their former neighbors. They have practiced collective resistance to gendered and racial oppression as a community, but as individuals they are the disparate and fragmented, the very "psychically disengaged revolutionaries" *The Salt Eaters* attempted to heal seventeen years earlier.

Community in Morrison's novels is always in process and always fleeting. This theme recurs in *A Mercy*, which returns to a multiethnic group of outsider women. Though Florens, Lina, Sorrow, and Rebekka find some solace in fashioning a kind of family in the absence of landowner Jacob Vaark in the 1680s, their community too comes undone. The novel never fulfills the promise of collectivity among this motley crew. Toward the end of *A Mercy*, the view from the women's perspective breaks, focalized now through Vaark and two male indentured servants. The shift away from the point of view of women in their own community happens in *Paradise* as well. As the point of view diffuses, so do the women's communities. In *Paradise* the last two chapters take the reader out of the Convent women's consciousness after the "loud dreaming." In *A Mercy* a shift in focalization sets the stage for the damning conclusion that "the family [the four women] imagined they had become was false. Whatever each one loved, sought or escaped, their futures were separate and anyone's guess" (156). Although these words appear in a later novel, they aptly describe the dissolution of community at the end of *Paradise*. Even without the constraints of a separatist community, indeed before the United States became a nation or race a rigid social construct buttressing that nation, women in *A Mercy* cannot preserve their female household as a safe space.

Bambara uses a chorus in *The Black Woman* and polyvocality in *The Salt Eaters* to promise coherence; Morrison uses layering in *Paradise* to foretell dissolution. For Morrison, this is a matter of novelistic form, though she speaks to the layering possibilities in visual art as well.[37] The layers in the novel, the Faulknerian tellings and retellings, are specific to the novel form. Morrison speaks to the importance of the novel in her essay "Rootedness":

> It seems to me that the novel is needed by African-Americans in a way it was not needed before—and it is following along the lines of the function of novels everywhere. We don't live in places where we can hear those stories anymore; parents don't sit around and tell their children those classical mythological archetypal stories that we heard years ago. But new information has got to get out, and there are several ways to do it. One is the novel. . . . It should be beautiful and powerful, but it should also *work*. . . . Something in it suggests what the conflicts are, what the problems are. But it [the novel] need not solve those problems because it is a case study, it is not a recipe. (340–41)

The authors considered in earlier chapters of this study offer literal and figurative recipes for diasporic consciousness, African American cultural nationalism, and community formation. Morrison, on the other hand, presents a "case study" in *Paradise*. She asserts that her novels offer "new information" and new ways of accessing that information, replacing storytelling elders as archives of "mythological archetypal stories." The novel for Morrison is an active force. It has work to do, from enforcing an ambiguous perspective to building an archive always in production and outlining important problems. The violence needed to maintain communities defined by gender and racial separation is among the problems she holds up to the light in *Paradise*. Like the women of the novel, the text labors not to resolve anything but rather to offer a case study that illuminates important conflicts from multiple points of view. The reader too must work. Phillip Page writes, "The general effect [of ambiguity and difficulty in *Paradise*] is to require readers to work hard, so that they, like the characters and the author, become truly part of the fictional enterprise" ("Furrowing" 638). The novel teaches not just "new information" but how to enter "the fictional enterprise," leaving it to the reader to find solutions, to continue the work "down here in paradise" (318), beyond the final pages of the novel. As always in Morrison's writing (and in the work of her black arts movement predecessors), the reader's role is an active one. Almost twenty years earlier, difficulty was a hallmark of Bambara's invitation to radically reimagine collectivity in *The Salt Eaters*; difficulty in *Paradise* is another call to practice.[38]

Morrison herself answers this call with *A Mercy*, which, though not part of the cultural nationalist revision, continues to pursue women's work of inscription. Florens scratches her first-person narrative with the tip of a nail into the floor. Though her words frame the novel, her text remains hidden and unread. Without the aid of a community, she practices her own kind of self-fashioning but achieves none of the freedom of *Paradise*'s Convent women. Insisting, "I am certain the telling will give me the tears I never have. I am wrong," Florens inscribes for the sake of "telling" (158). There is no release of tears and there is no possible reader. She addresses her beloved blacksmith: "You won't read my telling. You read the world but not the letters of talk. You don't know how to. . . . If you never read this, no one will" (160–61). The illiterate addressee of Florens's tale will never read this text. Morrison's reader also faces a kind of denial. The novel's reader is the "no one" who sees this inscription, but the text insists she is not reading it. Morrison closes off the possibility of interpretation by insisting on inscription, by framing the text as not only unread but unreadable.

Turning away from interpretation and toward the entangled work of inscription highlights women's work to build and interrogate collectivity. The struggle of each inscription to reach a reader often fails in *Paradise*, but this is a productive condition. Inscriptions of text and image restore the multiplicity foreclosed by Ruby and the nation-state. This disruption, rather than their short-lived coalescence, is the legacy of the Convent woman.

Women's work in *Paradise* yields not just disruption but other fruits of collaborative labor as well. African American women's inscriptions constantly make and remake a multivalent archive in the novel. In *Paradise* the archive is repeatedly hidden, erased, and obscured. There is no single ledger in the attic as in *Mama Day* or one story of Ibo Landing as in *Praisesong for the Widow*. The archive in *Paradise* is a highly unstable practice. Brent Edwards asserts that his study of international journals during the interwar period "necessitates unearthing and articulating an *archive*, in the sense not so much of a site or mode of preservation of a national, institutional, or individual past, but instead of a 'generative system': in other words, a discursive system that governs the possibilities, forms, appearance, and regularity of particular statements, objects, and practices—or, on the simplest level, that determines what can and what cannot be said" (19). Shange treats the archive as a culinary "discursive system" made up of flexible recipes for practicing geography and identity. Naylor's archive moves toward the practice of a "generative system" that can travel, adding the work of conjure and the names of female ancestors to "what can . . . be said." *Paradise* inherits this use of the archive as generative and practiced; the novel struggles toward "unearthing and articulating" an African American archive precisely by demonstrating the difficulty and ongoing necessity of this struggle. Morrison's archive of inscriptions in *Paradise* necessarily destabilizes any set "national, institutional, or individual past." Unearthing the archive, established in *Mama Day* as a form of women's work crucial to the African American nation, emerges in *Paradise* as a precursor to the parallel women's work of troubling that very archive, of constantly inscribing and even erasing it as a productive site of contestation and conflict.

Raising the possibility that this multivalent work of inscription will continue, the Convent women, including those shot and presumed dead, manage to get away.[39] The story circulated in Ruby proclaims, "The women took other shapes and disappeared into thin air" (296); both Lone DuPres and Reverend Misner think the women have been lifted away through the grace of God. In the final chapter, the surviving women, all past wanderers, are on the road again, going to their former homes, getting whatever they need, and heading out to destinations unknown, in this world or the next. The final lines read, "When the ocean heaves sending rhythms of water ashore, Piedade looks to see what has come. Another ship, perhaps, but different, heading to port, crew and passengers, lost and saved, atremble for they have been disconsolate for some time. Now they will rest before shouldering the endless work they were created to do down here in paradise" (318). Piedade is a diasporic maternal figure named for an island known as the Brazilian Eden. Her appearance in the final lines of the novel suggests that new possibilities for community may lie geographically only outside U.S. borders. In paradise, the space of the novel, at home and abroad, women are, even in their most amazing of labors, beasts of burden shouldering "endless work." While many texts I have considered are interested in both the process and products of women's work, *Paradise* ends on the work for its own sake, emphasizing the hardship of knowing that there is no rest in sight. "Another ship," crossing oceans literal and figurative, is always struggling to find a "port." Remembering and revising the history of the Middle Passage and slavery, "endless work" in this "new world" is collaborative. Those saved and lost, the crew and their passengers, share responsibility for a communal path. There is no such thing as going along for the ride; being a passenger promises as much labor as being a crewmember. Paradise is neither the racially isolated town of Ruby held together by violence and will nor the female family in the Convent forged in the face of danger. This new world, wide and integrated, is a place of work toward an unknown future, a figure for the United States after the civil rights and black power eras.

A decade and a half before *Paradise* was published, Morrison contemplated the losses and limits created by the end of racial segregation: "In a community, black people felt safe, you know, fairly happy. The real pain came—even though it was progress—during the movement toward integration. Black people were thrown into contact with well-meaning white people, but also faced the ire and anger of those who were hostile to integration. . . . I understood exactly what was important about [integration], but I always thought that the fruits of that labor were going to carry, perhaps, a little poison, as well" (R. Lester 50–51). *Paradise* bites into this poison fruit, making earth after the fall of integration decidedly anti-Edenic. The eroding racial and gender segregation that define Ruby and the Convent, respectively, becomes unsustainable. Women's work of inscription foments, records, and shapes this decline. Having achieved the sovereignty sought in a number of contemporary African American women's novels, *Paradise* closes the twentieth century illustrating the dangers of that goal. Through women's work of inscription, the novel depicts the possibilities and risks of defining community as a closed circle.[40] The women of *Paradise* inscribe their identities in text and image, but not as a means of fashioning and entering a broader community.[41] The simultaneous creation of self and community practiced in Bambara's organizing, Shange's cooking, Marshall's dancing, and Naylor's mapping dissolves in *Paradise*; the individual and the community, the neighborhood and its pariahs, are no longer mutually constitutive. At novel's end, the women are in the world beyond the Convent. "Now they will rest before shouldering the endless work they were created to do down here in paradise"; the space of the title is right here on earth, in local sites of struggle as well as home, of labor at least as much as of belonging. *Paradise* insists we not only see but also value that struggle, that labor, that women's work to make, and unmake, community.

# Conclusion

In the last two decades of the twentieth century, a group of African American women's novels reclaimed and revised cultural nationalism. Women's work—organizing, cooking, dancing, mapping, inscribing, archiving, mothering, and writing—constantly produces a cultural nation. When Minnie Ransom heals Velma Henry in *The Salt Eaters*; when Shange's Indigo creates dolls made of foodstuffs from across the African diaspora; when Avey Johnson performs the Big Drum Dance in *Praisesong for the Widow*; when Cocoa celebrates Candle Walk in *Mama Day*; and when the Convent women paint themselves on a cellar floor in *Paradise*, these are rituals for fashioning self and community.

These forms of women's work, all simultaneously ordinary and extraordinary, both depend on the black arts tenet that literature should do work in the world and offer a feminist critique of BAM. Novels of the cultural nationalist revision expand the genre, gender, and geography of BAM and break with its realist bent. Authors in this constellation turn away from strict realism, using magic, conjure, and the extrareal to claim cultural nationalism as process and practice. Madhu Dubey writes that "conjuring and orality combine to produce an emphatically antimodern, anti-urban, and antitextual model of community" in some contemporary African American novels (*Signs* 170). This is problematic for Dubey because "certain racial minority groups become the bearers of sheer, untranslatable difference" (23). The literary moment I have charted in the preceding chapters refuses to make black women "bearers of sheer, untranslatable difference" by rendering women's work specific, visible, and local. The novels examined in *Women's Work* transmit information through text and performance, traverse both rural and urban spaces, and look to the past primarily to inform a future-oriented stance. They insist on marrying the meta and material to give specificity to practices of community rather than allowing African American women characters to become "bearers of sheer, untranslatable difference."

Women's work in these novels is a theoretical intervention; these novels define identity and revise cultural nationalism through the specific and local work of organizing, cooking, dancing, mapping, and inscribing. In this vein, I hope to have taken up here the call that Deborah McDowell issues in the closing chapter of *The Changing Same*, for scholars to "bring 'theory' and 'practice' into a productive tension that would force a re-evaluation on each side" (167). A complex, sometimes uneasy entanglement of theory and practice characterizes the novels of the cultural nationalist revision. Each act of organizing, cooking, mapping, dancing, and inscribing in these novels insists on the simultaneity of theorizing and practicing nation and other communities. I am particularly concerned with the stakes that McDowell describes: "When the writings of black women and other critics of color are excluded from the category of theory, it must be partly because theory has been reduced to a very particular practice" (169). This matters for the study of African American literature, to be sure, but for literary study more generally as well. The implicit hierarchical model of theory and practice depends not only on a false binary but also on raced and gendered assumptions about what constitutes intellectual work. Accepting this dichotomy and locating practice but not theory in African American women's writings both marginalizes the study of these works and impoverishes the humanities.

Bambara, Shange, Naylor, Marshall, and Morrison break down divisions between theory and practice and resist an oral/written binary. They claim all of it as women's work and depict that work in their fiction. The relationship of theory and practice as mutually constitutive in these novels helps to account for their continuing reliance on cultural nationalism long after nation has fallen out of fashion in academic discourse. The "antitextual model" that Dubey describes, one that includes Naylor and Morrison in her reading, promises a seductive "community of cultural insiders engaged in harmonious, crisis-free, acts of knowing, speaking, and listening" (*Signs* 170). In fact, tension, dissent, and conflict saturate the practice of nation in a literary moment that begins with *The Salt Eaters* and ends with *Paradise*. I hope to have illuminated this, in part, by reading the contemporary cultural nationalist revision through the writings of Bambara, who, as Dubey cedes, takes up "issues of ancestry, conjuring, oral tradition, or the South in the city" without "offer[ing] readers the fix of tribal values or aestheticized racial difference" (237). As Dubey's diction suggests, a romanticized African American community is elusive and inviting; it provides a kind of "fix" for the reader yearning for solid cultural ground. The polyvocality, instability, and future-oriented stance of *The Salt Eaters*, however, reveals that Bambara began a conversation among fictional works that offer a less rigid vision of community. My reading of *Mama Day*, for example, demonstrates that Willow Springs is not the closed, culturally static, nostalgic community that scholars suggest.

The cultural nation of these novels has a shifting, often metaphorical terrain. Though this community depends on imagining the African diaspora, it is practiced in a uniquely U.S. context. All the novels I have considered are concerned, like David Walker's "Appeal" a century and a half earlier, with the "Colored People of the World, but in particular, and very expressly, those of The United States of America." Novels of the cultural nationalist revision push readers to grapple with African American exceptionalism by asserting that U.S. black cultural nationalism has continued relevance even amid the current move toward global, diasporic, and transnational perspectives in the humanities. The conversation among these novels suggests that scholars too must reclaim and reinvent nationalism, or at least cope with its enduring legacy.

Paul Gilroy's important work has moved African American studies away from nation and toward the "Black Atlantic" as a geography of identity. Gilroy calls for "a more refined language for dealing with these crucial issues of identity, kinship and affiliation" ("It ain't where you're from" 122). One incarnation of this language had been at work in novels by African American women for at least two decades before Gilroy's lament. Gilroy turns to music and explicitly discards the discourse of nationalism to find such a language. The novels I have discussed redefine cultural nationalism not as the rigid collective bent on authenticity that Gilroy disparages but as the ongoing practice of various women's work. African American women novelists negotiate a position between the absolutism Gilroy attributes to cultural nationalism and a pluralism that he critiques as too diffuse to be sufficiently alert to racial dynamics (123). For Gilroy, "the artist" and "the community" are separate entities, and "work" and "artistic expression" are mutually exclusive (138). The strain of African American literature I examine in this study binds together cultural nationalism and pluralism, uniting "the artist" and "artistic expression" of the former with "the community" and "work" of the latter. These relatively widely read works of literary fiction are not removed, not above the fray of cultural work. These novelists and their characters are not theorizing their communities from outside; rather, the worker and the intellectual reside in the same body. As *The Salt Eaters* depicts, the health of the individual and of the communal body is inseparable. There is no version in these novels of Gilroy's lofty, isolated artist; the women in these texts perform everyday work that is artistic expression.

In *The Black Atlantic*, Gilroy's interest in the infinite multiplicity of identity leads him to reject any kind of unity other than "the Atlantic as one single, complex unit of analysis" (15). He treats nationalism as a homogeneous, undertheorized political stance. He elevates the "difficult" (2) and insists that no form of nationalism quite lives up to his standard of difficulty. He treats "global, coalitional politics" and "African-American exceptionalism" as mutually exclusive, the latter a product of "merely national" thinking (4). The absence of women as primary figures in all but the last section of *The Black Atlantic* points to the danger of erasing or minimizing the value of women's labors. Black feminism appears in Gilroy's volume as the site of the kind of difficult theorizing he values, but the particulars, the practice of this work, never quite surface in his writings. The feminisms of my chosen authors perform just the complicated negotiation of identity that Gilroy imagines, but do so through identification with the cultural nation that he would discard. The cultural nationalism in these texts provides neither Gilroy's homogeneous nationalist community nor Dubey's "harmonious" "community of cultural insiders," but rather ways of practicing a mutable, diverse African American collective. Women's work, though difficult and fraught with obstacles, fashions and celebrates individual and communal identity in daily, local practice. Gloria Naylor defines cultural nationalism as a decision "to be militant about your being . . . to celebrate voraciously that which is yours" (Bellinelli 107). It is this mode of cultural nationalism as "voraciously" claiming and celebrating self and community, with all its scars and complexity, that these novels put forth.

Naylor's mode of cultural nationalism finds full expression in African American women's novels of the 1980s and 1990s. Cheryl Wall writes in 1989, "Over the last two decades, Afro-American women have written themselves into the national consciousness." Wall calls 1970 a moment when a "community of black women writing" emerged (Introduction 1). The publication of Bambara's *The Black Woman*, the reprinting of Zora Neale Hurston's *Mules and Men*, and the appearance of first novels by

Toni Morrison and Alice Walker make 1970 a turning point. Ten years after this rise to literary visibility, and at the dawn of the two decades considered in this study, we see a move away from the self-fashioning of Hurston's Janie Crawford and Morrison's Sula Peace. A particular group of novels, beginning with *The Salt Eaters*, treats women's work as the simultaneous creation of community and self. Barbara Christian notes this movement toward theorizing community: "The particular community in each work has its own unique style, legends, and rituals, although it also contains basic elements that it shares with other black communities. . . . The result of this approach is that we arrive at an understanding of the larger configuration, black culture, by focusing on the particular, and, at the same time, we do not lose the richness that variations have to offer" (*Black Women* 240). The 1980s and 1990s bear out Christian's assertions. Use of the "particular" and local "unique styles, legends, and rituals" became, in the years following Christian's *Black Women Novelists* (1980), a key route to "the larger configuration, black culture." Works by Bambara, Shange, Marshall, Naylor, and Morrison use local practices, difference within unity, and the particular to claim "the larger configuration, black culture." With their emphasis on individual, particular practices of nation, these novelists reveal the tension and dissent that both constitutes and threatens the collective.

Christian, Mary Helen Washington, Mari Evans, Eleanor Traylor, and others studied the increasingly visible literary productions of African American women in the 1980s and 1990s. As scholars, anthologists, and teachers, these women identify and celebrate an African American women's literary tradition. Twenty years after a necessary struggle with pressure to automatically affirm an increasingly visible body of African American women's writings, scholars have some new freedoms. Since 1990 Morrison has won the Nobel Prize for Literature and Oprah Winfrey's audience has gamely tackled *Paradise* in a televised discussion; Henry Louis Gates Jr. has brought works of nineteenth-century African American women to print in a Schomburg Library series; new scholarly articles and books on all the authors considered here have appeared; and high school and college students have staged *for colored girls* in ways that are meaningful in their contemporary moment. The chorus of students, teachers, and readers of these women's writings continues to grow, voicing many opinions from many corners. It would have been hard twenty years ago to do anything but celebrate that a version of *for colored girls* had reached movie viewers everywhere, but the work of filmmakers like Kasi Lemmons, Camille Billops, and Julie Dash gives scholars the vocabulary and authority to voice concerns about "Medea" creator Tyler Perry's interpretation of Shange's choreopoem.

The popularity of this literary fiction seemed tenuous while it was happening (Morrison comments on how difficult it was to get African American writers published during her years as an editor at Random House), but from the vantage point of the twenty-first century, it looks undeniable. This means not only that scholars can give these texts the kind of attention that they deserve but also that there is room to identify specific strands and trends within contemporary African American literature. Like the writings of any place and period, it is not monolithic. Nor is it a matter of books that are contemporary narratives of slavery and books that are not. In the 1980s and 1990s alone, lots of different things were happening in texts written by African Americans, from the growing science fiction and detective genres (think Octavia Butler and Walter Mosley) to a group of novels that revisit Ellison's *Invisible Man* (Yam Man in Mat Johnson's *Drop* and Lila Mae's journey in Colson Whitehead's *The Intuitionist*). This study is about one important literary practice in these decades: the reclamation and revision of African American cultural nationalism as everyday and extraordinary women's work to fashion self and community.[1]

The close of the twentieth century marks a shift as important as the turn toward community that Christian notes in 1980: African American women's novels depict an increasingly limited horizon of possibility. Bambara's *The Black Woman* promises nearly infinite modes of coalition. Shange, Marshall, Naylor, and Morrison seize on this multivalent notion of the black woman to portray African American women as makers of an alternative cultural nation. Economic factors, cultural tourism, gender difference, heterosexism, and the impossibility of translation across diasporic boundaries are all obstacles to collectivity. Across these authors' works, failures of female coalescence increasingly hinder the practice of an African American nation. By the late 1990s, in Morrison's *Paradise*, women's work has a limited reach and fails to sustain the individual within the context of community. The concentric circles of healing promised by *The Salt Eaters* fail to materialize in *Paradise*; the object of any future-oriented gaze remains unclear. What lies just beyond the apocalyptic storm at the end of *The Salt Eaters* is a group of novels by Shange, Marshall, Naylor, and Morrison that imagine a cultural nation created by many forms of women's work. What lies just beyond the horizon of those books is the twenty-first century and Morrison's ambiguous "work down here in paradise."

Male authors are part of the "work down here in paradise." One male writer important for novels of the cultural nationalist revision writes much earlier in the twentieth century. Jean Toomer is a crucial male predecessor for contemporary African American women's literature. *Cane* (1923) is a model for Bambara's formal experimentation and depicts the South as a site of culture and crisis necessary for any representation of African American identity. Toomer is the only male "mother" cited in Alice Walker's essay "In Search of Our Mother's Garden's," and he appears as a guiding spirit in the last paragraph of Shange's *If I Can Cook*. Toomer's influence on contemporary African American women novelists suggests that modernism, perhaps more than postmodernism, remains an important force in African American literature.

Contemporary African American male novelists also take up the concerns of the texts considered here, from Ishmael Reed's experiments with novelistic form to David Bradley's exploration of the African American archive. Colson Whitehead's Lila Mae is close kin to the women characters I have considered in the preceding chapters. Whitehead's *The Intuitionist* (1999) indicates that male authors have a crucial role to play in grappling with the complex inheritance of twenty-first-century African American writers. Whitehead's protagonist Lila Mae uses the second sight of Indigo, Mama Day, Minnie Ransom, and Velma Henry in her work as a city elevator inspector in the New York City of Whitehead's satiric, fond imagining. Dubey notes, "What is most unusual about Whitehead's novel is that it presents intuition as a medium of futurity, a way of extending rather than recoiling from the project of urban modernity" (*Signs* 240). This is not so "unusual" in contemporary African American fiction. Rather, Whitehead builds on the "future-oriented stance" of Bambara's *The Salt Eaters*, on the shifting possibilities for life in the city in Naylor's *Mama Day*, and on the magical real in Morrison's *Paradise*.

These women authors utilize strategies of African American modernism, anthologies, nationalism, and the black arts movement. It remains largely to be seen how their descendants will navigate a legacy of practice, women's work, and difference within unity in the twenty-first century. The textual shape of Morrison's "work down here in paradise" offers a moment of possibility. This work, however, is left largely to the reader. In writing stories that redefine home, community, and nation, these authors offer models for collectivity in the world outside the text. Morrison says of her novels, "I don't want to close it, to stop the imagination of the reader, but to engage it in such a way that he fulfills the book in a way that I don't" (Raus 108). What might it mean for the reader to "fulfill the book" in the cases I have considered here? Though perhaps unsatisfying, the absence of precise instruction gives readers in the twenty-first century the same sort of wide field of possibility promised by *The Black Woman* in 1970. The process of making a changed future is indeterminate. These novels end ambiguously: Avey's return to Tatem in *Praisesong* is promised but not completed, the question of what comes after Velma Henry's healing and the novel's concluding storm in *The Salt Eaters* remains unanswered, and the final pages of *Mama Day* see the title character lighting out for unknown territory. The continuing work of radically imagining and practicing the future lies beyond the text, like Shange's recipes waiting to be performed in readers' kitchens. This is an ongoing legacy of the black arts movement. The work of revising and reclaiming cultural nationalism may be on the wane, but the texts that do this work leave a lasting call for practices of community in the world. Like recipes performed again and again with variations, this labor never ends. As Audre Lorde writes, "Revolution is not a one-time event" ("Learning" 140).

The novels I have considered here offer practices for taking up Morrison's "endless work" to fashion self and community, whether or not nation remains relevant. They insist on the importance of women's work of organizing, cooking, dancing, mapping, and inscribing, to be sure, but also the women's work of reading and writing texts. They demand readerly labor as material and detailed as the work in the novels; they offer performance possibilities to men and women outside the text. The "endless work" for readers is not the gray future that concludes Morrison's *Paradise*. Rather, the work ahead lies in Bambara's "neighborhoods—bookstores, communal gardens, think tanks, arts-and-crafts programs, community-organizer training, photography workshops" ("Deep Sight" 174); Shange's cooking; Marshall's sacred and secular dances; and Naylor's mapping. If the time for practicing community has come to a close in novels, it may be on the rise in the world beyond the text.

The cultural nationalist revision happened after the Moynihan Report laid the groundwork for neoliberal racism. These were post–civil rights era years, when racial injustice took forms that were less obvious but as oppressive as Jim Crow segregation. Ronald Reagan's policies increased economic disparities along racial lines and his coded language endorsed racism from the Oval Office; redlining limited housing and financial services available to residents of black neighborhoods, even after the practice was made illegal; the beating of Rodney King and the subsequent verdict exonerating the police amounted to state endorsement of racial profiling and police brutality; Affirmative Action came under attack; and George H. W. Bush's successful manipulation of racialized fear in the Willie Horton ads helped him win a presidential election. The revised and revitalized nationalism in the novels I have discussed in *Women's Work* is, in part, a reaction to these particular conditions of racial injustice. These events, though perhaps more subtle or pernicious than legal segregation, continue to forcefully shape American society. As Shange writes to her deceased father in 2011, "Ronald Reagan . . . has Alzheimer's now, so he can't feel guilt or remorse for the plight of sick people anymore. If he had his whole brain he still wasn't capable of experiencing compassion. Daddy, the era of politics Reagan ushered in has outlived you and more poor & black people are dying, suffering, homeless, violent, desperate for a vision of a world for us like you had" (*Lost* 97). The current recession and housing crisis, unemployment and incarceration rates for African American men, attacks on women's reproductive rights, and dangerous claims that the United States became postracial with the election of Barack Obama all create a climate that suggests the ongoing need for communities of resistance. This may not be an enclave of cultural preservation on a Georgia Sea Island or a community of wild women living in a former convent, but it will take shape in the world, perhaps through some of the practices learned from these women's works. The "vision of the world" that Shange evokes is the radically imagined alternative space at the center of novels of the cultural nationalist revision. These novels remake cultural nationalism to sound the alarm, to insist that the 1980s and 1990s were years of racial crisis, even though that crisis may be complex or hard to see. Resistance too remains central to these writers, even when that resistance is less visible than a civil rights march or a Black Panther patrol.

The stakes of the cultural nationalist revision in black women's novels of the 1980s and 1990s are thus political as well as literary. In their close attention to particular and local practices of identity, these authors resist impulses toward universalism, postracialism, or color blindness, dangerous neoliberal trends that, as Nikhil Pal Singh demonstrates in *Black Is a Country*, function to erase "any positive particularities that may have accrued to black cultural and communal practices over time" (40). In their close focus on women's work, on such "positive particularities" in "black cultural practices," the authors I have considered work against the danger of a so-called color-blind politics that Singh describes thus: "This stance . . . ironically perpetuates a situation in which blacks remain the group in the United States denied ethnic honor (the honor of having 'ethnicity') and in which whiteness remains the (unstated) cultural norm" (40). African American women's work in these novels follows black cultural nationalism's rejection of whiteness as an "(unstated) cultural norm" and claims "ethnic [or racial] honor" and particularity. My chosen authors rewrite the incomplete narrative that "the mid-1960s were the moment when black people emerged (at long last) as individual subjects of capitalist-liberalism and as formal participants in democratic-nationalism" (214). These texts insist that work to dismantle ongoing white supremacy and patriarchy in this country is necessary; they depict that work in kitchens, on dance floors, on the page, and in the archive.

Turning back to the texts, however, we are left with a less optimistic view. In the face of failure and dissolution of various forms of African American coalescence, Morrison greets the twenty-first century refuting the future-oriented stance of the novels considered in this study. In an attempt to decouple community and nation-state, A Mercy looks back to the 1680s, a prenational moment. She sets her novel in "the period before there was a United States, before there was even an idea of America, just a name of a continent . . . fluid," when "there was nothing going on that couldn't possibly change."[2] Following the turn of the century and decades of women's work to reclaim, redefine, and practice cultural nationalism, Morrison can find the same broad horizon of possibility and "change" promised in The Black Woman only by looking back to a moment "before slavery and black became married."[3] Possibility for Morrison lies not in claims of a postracial era that have been so prominent in the media of recent years, but in looking backward to a preracial and prenational period, a time before historical conditions demanded a cultural nationalism defined by African American exceptionalism, indeed before African Americanness quite existed. Efforts to "celebrate voraciously" a self and community that claims every aspect of African Americanness is left to those "down here in paradise," in the world beyond the text. African American women's novels of the 1980s and 1990s have given us guidance and invited us to take up this women's work.

# Notes

## Introduction

1. Jacqueline Jones writes, "Wives and mothers of all ages served as ardent supporters of and investors in Marcus Garvey's Universal Negro Improvement Association, but with the notable exception of Henrietta Vinton Davis, no women held high leadership positions in this influential organization" (193).

2. See J. Jones; Giddings; Davis; White; Bryan. Also see *African American Review*, special issue on Anna Julia Cooper, 43.1 (2009).

3. See the program for Bambara's funeral (Dec. 17, 1995) in the Hatch-Billops Collection, New York City. Morrison was also involved in the SEEK Program. See "In Depth with Toni Morrison," CSPAN, 2001, http://www.c-spanvideo.org/program/ToniM (accessed Nov. 28, 2012).

4. The Association of Artists for Freedom formed in response to the 1963 Birmingham, Alabama church bombing that killed four African American girls: Denise McNair, Addie Mae Collins, Carole Robertson, and Cynthia Wesley.

5. See Rambsy on the artist-critic-activist in BAM, especially chapter 5, "The Poets, Critics, and Theorists Are One."

6. The novel did sometimes serve as a means of critiquing, complicating, and satirizing black power politics in the 1960s and 1970s. See Fran Ross's *Oreo* (1974). Rolland Murray writes, "The relatively peripheral place of fiction with both the ideology of nationalist aesthetics and the material production of texts made it possible for the novel to become a more likely vehicle for dissent" (8). In the 1980s and 1990s African American women's novels moved from a "relatively peripheral place" in the literary marketplace but held on to the possibility of dissent in the novel as a vehicle for cultural critique.

7. Shockley defines *polyvocality* in poetry as "the extent to which its language, tone, diction, form and other stylistic choices generate the effect of multiplicity in a single speaker's voice or create a space for a number of different speakers" such that "works

might be heard differently by different listeners" (*Renegade Poetics* 17–18). I use *polyvo-cality* here primarily in the sense that contemporary women novelists make "stylistic choices" to "create a space for a number of different speakers" and points of view. Shockley's reading of Gwendolyn Brooks is particularly illuminating regarding the functions of polyvocality in black women's writing (27–54).

8. Tension, dissent, and this "turbulence of change" are part of African American freedom movements from their beginnings. See Singh for his useful study of the "long civil rights era" (8, 214) in this vein.

9. Also see Singh 46.

10. Houston Baker, among others, has demonstrated this in each of his scholarly monographs. See especially *Blues, Ideology and Afro-American Literature*. Also see Albert Murray's *The Hero and the Blues*.

11. This debate has been important to African American literary studies at least since 1988, when Henry Louis Gates Jr. offered the productive figure of the "speakerly" text in *The Signifyin' Monkey*. Many literary scholars have questioned the usefulness of sharp divisions between spoken and written literature. Marcellus Blount, for example, uses *performance* to describe "a range of cultural and literary phenomena" (583). For ideas on the place of oral traditions, vernacular forms, and related discourses of authenticity, see *New Essays on the African American Novel*, edited by Lovalerie King and Linda Selzer. Dubey adds useful nuance to this conversation by teasing out the complex relationship in literature and criticism of the 1980s between print and vernacular forms in what she calls "the postmodern moment." Particularly useful is her attention to the "print-literary medium through which oral communities are constructed" in works by Naylor and Morrison (*Signs* 171–72).

12. Alice Walker's essay "In Search of Our Mother's Gardens," short story "Everyday Use," and novel *Meridian* are important intertexts for the cultural nationalist revision. For Walker, the productions of women's hands, particularly quilts and gardens, are almost always located in the South and have a kind of romantic, magical quality. The novels I consider move away from Walker's romantic vision of southern folkways to expand the literal and metaphorical geography of a cultural nation.

13. See Mel Watkins, "Sexism, Racism and Black Women Writers," *New York Times*, June 15, 1986, for an example of such criticism. As with most such attacks, Watkins's most egregious misreading is the assumption that works by Morrison, Walker, Gayl Jones, Bambara, and Naylor are primarily about men. Deborah McDowell's July 20, 1986, letter to the editor of the *Times* offers a productive rebuttal to Watkins, especially in terms of refuting his limited notion of the African American literary tradition as one that does not "air dirty laundry," a phrase used by Ishmael Reed and others in these debates about black women's writing. Also see McDowell, chapter 7, "Reading Family Matters," in *The Changing Same*.

14. Qtd. in Hilton Als, "Ghost in the House," *The New Yorker*, Oct. 27, 2003, 64.

15. One hallmark of Reed's novel that significantly complicates this dynamic is the author's intimate, often fond familiarity with the works of Shange, Walker, Bambara, Morrison, and Marshall, all of whom appear directly or obliquely in *Reckless Eyeballing*.

16. For more on this transition in genre, see Cheryl Clarke, who notes that women poets of the black arts movement "opened a wider field for black women fiction writers who came to prominence in the 1970s, among them, Toni Cade Bambara, Alice Walker, Toni Morrison, and Gayl Jones" (3). Also see Rambsy 156–57.

17. Or, as Saidiya Hartman asks in *Lose Your Mother*, "What connection had endured after four centuries of dispossession? The question of *before* was no less vexed since there was no collective of Pan-African identity that preexisted the disaster of the slave trade. Were desire and imagination enough to bridge the rift of the Atlantic?" (29).

18. As Smethurst suggests, black radical imagining of alternative homelands in the black arts era has roots in the U.S. Communist Party, particularly the Party's "Black Belt thesis" that "African Americans in the rural South constituted an oppressed nation with the right to political and economic control" (16–19, 24–25). Although the Black Belt thesis was problematic, the CPUSA officially abandoned it in the 1950s, and members of black power groups disavowed earlier connections to the CPUSA, Smethurst reveals the significant influence of both the CPUSA and the Old Left on black arts–era intellectual and organizers. The centrality of vernacular or folk culture in defining a "Black Belt republic" seems to have been a lasting legacy of the CPUSA's thesis.

19. For an exploration of one woman's difficulty incorporating both the history of slavery and life in the real African country of Ghana (rather than an imagined African continent) into what I am calling an African American nation of shared affect and experience, see Hartman.

20. See Courtney Thorsson, "James Baldwin and Black Women Novelists," *African American Review*, forthcoming.

21. Deborah McDowell argues that these single-name novel titles are deceiving and do not necessarily connote a traditional protagonist or signal a coherent and knowable self. See chapter 6, "Boundaries," in *The Changing Same*. She also explores the importance of proper names as a way of centering female subjectivity in the titles of contemporary narratives of slavery (143).

22. Dubey includes Morrison's *The Bluest Eye* (1970) and *Sula* (1973) in this group, which confirms my reading of Morrison's earlier works as less a cultural nationalist revision of self and community than part of the 1970s work of novels to articulate and define a diverse African American female self.

23. A number of African American women authors in and around this period write novels that revisit slavery; these works stand outside the literary moment that is the subject of this study. Margaret Walker's *Jubilee* (1966), Octavia Butler's *Kindred* (1979), Sherley Anne Williams's *Dessa Rose* (1986), and Morrison's *Beloved* (1987) all explicitly explore slavery and its legacies. These are examples of contemporary African American literary fiction by women, but none of them focuses on women's work as a future-oriented practice of cultural nationalism. *Women's Work* identifies a group of texts that are more interested in envisioning the future than in looking to the past. The Middle Passage, for example, becomes not an actual memory as in contemporary narratives of slavery but a way to layer meaning onto water crossings in Marshall's *Praisesong*, Naylor's *Mama Day*, and Morrison's *Paradise*. Contemporary novels of slavery are concerned to varying degrees with Americanness in ways that resonate with the nationalist project of the texts under consideration. Margaret Walker's chapter "Fourth of July Celebration" in *Jubilee* describes a public hanging of two women on that holiday to demonstrate that the national identity of the United States is deeply entangled with racial violence. bell hooks makes a similar claim, positioning *Mama Day* and *Praisesong for the Widow* as part of a literary strain distinct from contemporary narratives

of slavery. hooks makes the distinction in terms of "healing": "While novels like *Dessa Rose* or *Beloved* evoke the passion of trauma during slavery as it carries over into black life when that institution is long gone, these works don't necessarily chart a healing journey that is immediately applicable to black life" (*Yearning* 226).

24. Addison Gayle asserts in his introduction to *The Black Aesthetic* that W. E. B. Du Bois, by moving to Ghana in 1961, had chosen the only viable option: "de-Americanization" (xxii). Du Bois is a model in Gayle's view; he rejected Americanness as African American men were beginning to do in increasing numbers, particularly as the Vietnam War continued to demand the ultimate sacrifice from them in a conflict many Americans did not support.

25. For an analysis of the role of anthologies in establishing the presence and aesthetics of the black arts movement, see Rambsy, especially chapter 2, "Platforms for Black Verse: The Roles of Anthologies."

26. See J. Jones 312–3.

27. See Christian, "Naylor's Geography" 118; Dubey, *Black Women* 18; Jenkins.

28. The Combahee River Collective responds to male-dominated black liberation movements in their "Black Feminist Statement": "Black feminist politics also have an obvious connection to movements for Black liberation, particularly those of the 1960s and 1970s. Many of us were active in those movements (civil rights, Black nationalism, the Black Panthers), and all of our lives were greatly affected and changed by their ideology, their goals, and the tactics used to achieve their goals. It was our experience and disillusionment within these liberation movements, as well as experience on the periphery of the white male left, that led to the need to develop a politics that was antiracist, unlike those of white women, and antisexist, unlike those of white men" (14).

29. For more on the work of prefaces, particularly in terms of the necessity to read African American literature on formal terms, see Gates, "Preface to Blackness."

30. Rolland Murray usefully analyzes the ways African American male novelists "tracked the unevenness, political incoherence, and anxiety that beset nationalisms tethered to masculinist identity politics" during the "heyday of Black Power" (2). His work, like Harper's, cautions us against reading literary politics as homogeneous, even during the height of the black power and black arts movements.

31. See White for more on consciousness-raising sessions (243). Credit for this inclusion belongs, in part, to Nina Finkelstein, Signet's editor for the 1970 edition of *The Black Woman*. Shortly after editing *The Black Woman*, Finkelstein became a founding editor of *Ms* magazine.

32. See Edwards's reading of James Weldon Johnson's preface to *The Book of American Negro Poetry* in "Variations on a Preface" in *The Practice of Diaspora*.

33. Two anthologies published after *The Black Woman* illustrate its singularity and legacy, respectively. Amiri Baraka and Amina Baraka's *Confirmation: An Anthology of African American Women* is in implicit conversation with *The Black Woman* but takes a different approach. Amiri Baraka writes, "The purpose of this volume is to draw attention to the existence and excellence of black women writers" (15). Though Baraka insists in his introduction (written only by him, though Amina Baraka coedits the volume) that the book is not "a line of demarcation," it privileges literary genres. *Confirmation* includes mostly poetry and short fiction, with first-person narratives by Faith Ringgold and Vertamae Grosvenor as well as one piece of literary criticism by Eleanor Traylor. Further "demarcations" include Baraka disparaging "Phyllis

Wheately [sic]–Jupiter Hammon slavemaster-sanctioned house-negro writing" (23) and calling out Ntozake Shange and Julia Field for not contributing (25).

The Black Woman also cleared space that Michael Harper and Robert Stepto would inhabit with their anthology *Chant of Saints: A Gathering of Afro-American Literature, Art, and Scholarship*. More diverse in genre and geography than *Confirmation*, *Chant of Saints* contains poetry, fiction, scholarship, visual arts, and interviews, including work by Chinua Achebe and Derek Walcott. This "gathering" includes Africans and West Indians in its definition of Afro-American. Harper and Stepto do not explicitly claim to work in the tradition of *The Black Woman*, but *Chant of Saints* does capitalize on the ways Bambara redefines the African American anthology. They name their text for collaboration in the world outside the page ("a gathering") and suggesting that "Afro-American" is a designation unbound by geography. The sonic connotations of "chant" are both a collective vocalization (as in religious ritual) and music (*Chant* xv). Here we see performance, intertextuality, and exchange among multiple art forms and genres, all legacies of the black arts movement and *The Black Woman*. *Chant of Saints* depends on the dual legacy of Amiri Baraka performing "Wailers" and "Bud Walked In" with horn players and of Bambara insisting that Paule Marshall's and Alice Walker's short stories help readers "get basic with each other" in a nationalist project. *Chant* treats literary scholarship as an important aspect of the African American tradition and reads that scholarship as the anthology's "conversings" (xv). While *Confirmation* explicitly seeks to highlight women's writings, the method of *Chant of Saints* makes it closer kin to *The Black Woman*.

34. This is partly a legacy of BAM. Smethurst acknowledges the masculinist ideology of both groups but also notes, "The Black Arts and Black Power movements were among the few intellectual spaces in the United States in the 1960s where it was comparatively easy to raise the issue of male supremacy" (86). Rambsy makes a similar claim: "Critiques of sexism in the [black arts] movement reveal that not all participants accepted the oppressive practices operating in African American discourse communities" (26). Rambsy attends especially to Nikki Giovanni's public "concerns about the relegation of black women to less important roles in the movement in the interest of advancing black men" (27).

35. I borrow the phrase *female coalescence* from Awkward (98). Also see Griffin, "Conflict and Chorus."

36. See especially Davies, "Mothering and Healing"; Hirsch on "a daughterly tradition in relation to a complicated maternal past" in contemporary African American women's novels (261); hooks, "Feminism."

37. Albert Murray mentions the "getting place" several times in *Train Whistle Guitar*. Sterling Brown uses the term *folk storehouse* in his "Folk Literature" essay of 1941 and elsewhere.

38. These novels are part of the critical mass of black women's fiction that gained increased visibility beginning in the 1970s, such that, in 1990 Hernton writes, "Collectively, it is the *mass presence* of literature written by black women that is unprecedented. In the past one had to search for black-women-authored literature. Today the literature seeks you out" (203). In his preface to *Toni Morrison: Critical Perspectives Past and Present*, Gates writes, "It is an important feature of today's literary culture, however, that Toni Morrison, along with her contemporaries, Black woman novelists Alice Walker, Jamaica Kincaid, and Terry McMillan, are read more widely and by a

broader cross section of the American reading public that any other Black writers have ever been in this country" (x). I use the term *visible* here to suggest that reports of the economic and critical success of African American women's novels in these decades are often exaggerated. Morrison notes that *The Bluest Eye* was rejected by "12 or 14" publishers before finding a home at Knopf and that she always hoped for, but rarely saw, books by African American women garner the broad readership that those currently featured by Oprah's book club do ("In Depth with Toni Morrison," CSPAN). The nonacademic readership of these works has been perhaps more invested in nationalism than their academic audience. Smethurst writes, "This fascination with the BPP and other Black Power and Black Arts activists [in literature aimed at a popular audience] serves as a reminder that outside academia the Black Power, Black Arts, Chicano, Nuyorican, and Asian American movements never really disappeared" (2). Smethurst argues that Morrison and others "continued to embrace what was essentially a nationalist stance in their work long after 1975" (3).

39. My approach is indebted to McDowell (36); Davies (*Black Women* 19); and Valerie Smith (xviii). Also see Ann Ducille's *Skin Trade* (1996) for a critique of Baker's *Workings of the Spirit*.

40. This resistance to a binary between theory and practice is a defining feature of black feminist scholarship. See Valerie Smith's introduction to *Not Just Race, Not Just Gender* and McDowell's chapter "Transference" in *The Changing Same*.

41. Dubey's reading of Susan Willis's scholarship is instructive in this vein (*Black Women* 5–7). Dubey is rightly keen to historicize and locate vernacular forms of culture rather than use them as a metric of racial authenticity.

## 1 / Organizing Her Nation

1. bell hooks makes a similar connection in *Sisters of the Yam*, asserting that her volume is a "radical departure" because it insists on "the link between self-recovery and political resistance" (xii). This intervention is the reason that *Sisters of the Yam* opens with a dedication to Bambara and an epigraph from *The Salt Eaters*. Also see K. Brown 189, 191.

2. While many visible leaders in the civil rights movement were men, "the number of women who carried the Movement is much larger than that of the men," as literacy activist Ella Baker asserts (qtd. in Bryan 60).

3. Carmichael reportedly made this comment about women of SNCC in response to a paper by Ruby Doris Smith Robinson in 1964 titled "The Position of Women in SNCC." See J. Jones 283. Also see Wallace *Black Macho and the Myth of the Superwoman*, especially the introduction and last two paragraphs.

4. For more on Bambara's "future-oriented" stance, see Gordon.

5. Scholars are currently complicating the narrative of the Black Panthers in useful ways. See, for example, Singh 196–97.

6. The time span of the novel is ambiguous. Houston Baker reads it as half an hour, and Cheryl Wall suggests that Velma's healing takes no more than ten minutes. Reading the events as simultaneous to Velma's recovery, I imagine the action of the novel's present to occur in a period of about two hours.

7. Griffin attends especially to Sherley Anne Williams's *Dessa Rose*, but I am more concerned here with the usefulness of her concept of "textual healing" for novels contemporary to Williams's that are *not* narratives of slavery, a move Griffin models in her analysis of Michelle Cliff's *Abeng*.

8. Examples include Angela Davis and June Jordan's *Body and Soul* and bell hooks's *Sisters of the Yam.*

9. Wideman makes this point, noting that Bambara "makes us understand that what is at stake in Velma Henry's journey back to health is not only one woman's life but the survival of the planet." John Wideman, "The Healing of Velma Henry," *New York Times,* June 1, 1980.

10. While *organizing* is my key gerund for reading Bambara's work, people who knew her often use *gathering* to describe her labors. My use of *organizing* builds on Traylor's reading of Bambara "gathering" self, material, and people ("Re Calling the Black Woman" xvi–xvii). Morrison says *The Salt Eaters* is about "'gathering' women . . . women who know medicine and roots, root-workers who are not hunting perhaps—maybe they are—, but they have to know a poison-leaf from a non-poison leaf. Ajax's mother [in *Sula*] is like that. That kind of wisdom which is discredited in almost every corner of the civilized world" (Koenen 219).

11. Erna Brodber takes up this concern in *Louisiana,* where the women's work of second sight is revealed as a "black nationalist" (148) asset. In the history uncovered by the title character as she channels three deceased people, "Mammy was a Garvey organiser and a psychic" (148). The story of Sue Ann Grant-King, who passes on but continues to communicate through the protagonist Louisiana, culminates in the revelation that "she continued her political work intertwining it with her psychic work, a combination which served to make her a legend" (153).

12. Jacqueline Trescot, "Black Writers in the '70s," *Washington Post,* May 6, 1977.

13. See S. Jones on the ways *Those Bones* strategically overwhelms the reader and the characters (264–65).

14. Bertha of "Broken Field Running" speaks the phrases "we salt eaters" and "eat our own history" (Bambara, *Sea Birds* 55–56).

15. Jamel Brinkley suggests a similar argument in terms of the dedication of *The Salt Eaters*, with its attention to women's work on the page: "The reminder that the manuscript was assembled, edited, and typed (by Loretta Hardge, a female laborer) indicates where the novel's allegiances lie" (9).

16. Suzanne Jones argues that the lesson of Gaines's novels is to reimagine black masculinity (146).

17. On parenting in Bambara's work, see Willis *Specifying*; Alwes.

18. Ishmael Reed similarly experiments with form to mirror the reliance on many ways of knowing so crucial to his worldview. Like *The Salt Eaters*, *Mumbo Jumbo* layers many source texts and discourses across multiple time periods to inform the portrayal of a particular moment without dissolving into pastiche.

19. Old Wife instructs Minnie to "rip them fancy clothes off" as part of this work, suggesting that at least temporary abandonment of the trappings of the middle class are crucial to women's work toward identification of self and community. Marshall's *Praisesong for the Widow* shares and complicates this stance, as I discuss in chapter 3.

20. See Chandler. In this interview, Bambara asserts, "I know that we must reclaim those bones in the Atlantic Ocean" (348). Marshall's Avey Johnson makes a similar journey, a Middle Passage through individual and collective history to see her way to cultural nationalism. These are not tellings of the historical Middle Passage as in contemporary narratives of slavery but figurative uses of that harrowing journey as a

means of understanding the present and future. Hartman writes, "The Middle Passage was the birth canal that spawned the tribe" (103).

21. Willis's implied critique of Hurston's romantic South, leveled in the phrase "with just enough reference to migrant agricultural workers to give it credibility," does not quite pertain to Bambara's novel, which is less invested than Hurston's work in ideas of racial authenticity.

22. Bambara suggests that an atavistic connection to many forms of knowledge is especially available to a collective of women of color. In her foreword to *This Bridge Called My Back*, she writes of a time "before the breaking of the land mass when we mothers of the yam, of the rice, of the plantain sat together in a circle, staring into the camp fire, the answers in our laps, knowing how to focus" (viii). She uses "sister of the yam," "rice," and "plantain" to refer to African American, Asian American, and Jamaican American members of the Seven Sisters, respectively, in *The Salt Eaters*.

23. Campbell, a reporter and waiter at the diner where some of the Seven Sisters sit during the novel's present, also exemplifies this multiplicity of modes of knowledge. Campbell recalls when he "knew in a glowing moment that all the systems were the same at base—voodoo, thermodynamics, I Ching, astrology, numerology, alchemy, metaphysics, everybody's ancient myths—they were all interchangeable, not at all separate much less conflicting" (210).

24. See M. Kelley for one example.

25. As Dubey points out, *womanish* is a "black folk word" that informs Alice Walker's black feminist designation "womanist" (*Black Women* 111).

26. Meadows's transformation and reentry into community appears in his interaction with three men in Claybourne: M1/Emwahn, Hull, and Thurston (189). In their eyes, Meadows changes from being an outsider in terms of class, geography, and race to being a fellow African American man trying to escape the coming storm with his new friends and a drink. Black masculinity appears fairly rigid in this interaction, undoing some of the complexity granted to men in Bambara's portrayal of Campbell, Obie, and the masseur Ahiro.

27. Mathes examines the workings of this sonic boom and other sounds in *The Salt Eaters* ("Imagine").

28. Gordon writes, "At the end of *The Salt Eaters*, environmental racism and corporate pollution have not been eliminated, the bus driver Fred Holt's friend Porter is still dead from exposure to state-sponsored radioactivity, police brutality remains a hazard of an active protest life, the enraging and exhausting gendered division of the labor within grassroots movements lingers, intimacy and love is still a difficult achievement" (263–64).

29. Holloway reads the conclusion of *The Salt Eaters* as a hopeful, but not simple, reentry into community: "The most significant meditation occurs in the final pages of *The Salt Eaters*. Here the reader learns of Velma's membership in the ancestral line of spiritual women that Minnie and Old Wife have incarnated in the text. . . . Velma's nexus is now part of a community that is simultaneously past and present, temporal and detemporalized. The collective at the end of the book is a spiritual one" (119).

## 2 / Cooking Up a Nation

1. McDowell's words about *The Color Purple* apply here: "The novel elevates the folk forms of rural and southern blacks to the status of art. In a similar fashion, it elevates

the tradition of letters and diaries, commonly considered a 'female' tradition (and therefore inferior), from the category of 'non-art' to art" (49).

2. Fran Ross is an important predecessor to Shange in this practice. Her 1974 novel *Oreo* uses a menu, in addition to equations, a multiple-choice quiz, and math and logic problems to push against novelistic form. Ross's "La Carte du Diner d'Helene" (68–72) conveys overlapping routes of identity (Jewish, American, Italian, and French among them) through its wildly varied and extensive menu.

3. Shange terms her theater works *choreopoems*, which Neal Lester describes as, "a series of poems, with occasional music and dance, that when put together become one statement or voice" (*Ntozake Shange* 11).

4. Olaniyan's reading of Shange's "anticonventional" textual strategies as embedded in a Fanonian stance of "combat breathing" is a useful examination of Shange's distinct punctuation, capitalization, and spelling (120–28). Also see Shange, *Lost* 20.

5. Julie Dash's work also makes use of the recipe form to insist on a life beyond print. Her book *Daughters of the Dust: The Making of an African American Woman's Film* includes recipes for "Aunt Gertie's Red Rice" and "Mommy Dash's Gumbo" (viii–vix). Like Shange's recipes, these are both attributed and emblematic of a familial inheritance. In *Daughters of the Dust: A Novel*, Dash includes recipes for "Home Sweetener" (23), "Peace Bath" (308), and "Joy Cream" (310).

6. Sassafrass evokes African American cooking; she is named for the plant that, when dried, yields the filé used in making gumbo, particularly in Louisiana. Like her sisters, she is also named for one source of the natural dyes her family uses in coloring their hand-woven fabrics.

7. Shange's name change suggests her allegiance to BAM, as many black arts poets adopted Africanized names. Amiri Baraka, formerly Leroi Jones, and Haki Madhubuti, formerly Don Lee, are two examples. Shange changed her birth name, Paulette Williams, to the Zulu name Ntozake, "one who comes with her own things," and Shange, "one who walks like a lion" (Lester, *Ntozake Shange* 10). Even as she critiques BAM, Shange writes, "Neither am I saying that the black arts movement had no substantial effect on me. I must confess to a certain hero worship of Toomer, Baraka & Reed" (*Lost* xiv), surprisingly suggesting that Toomer might be read as a black arts poet despite the much earlier publication dates of his works.

8. This mode of argument made through radical formal experimentation in novels also appears in Ishmael Reed's fiction. *Mumbo Jumbo* includes narrative, dialogue unmarked by quotation marks, a photograph, and quotations from Louis Armstrong and *The American Heritage Dictionary* in its front matter. Reed's novel also uses stage directions to frame characters. His portrayal of Charlotte as a figure in a staged plantation drama in *Mumbo Jumbo* (43–44) might be read as a move akin to Shange's portrayal of Sassafrass, formally drawing attention to the ways women are conscripted. Reed, as Shange's relationship to his work suggests, cannot be dismissed as simply a misogynist. His complex portrayal of Charlotte, Isis, and Earline in *Mumbo Jumbo* offers one place to start a more nuanced reading of the gender politics of his work.

9. This earlier version has less standard punctuation and spelling than Shange's later novel, so it reads as a long prose poem. This is one example of a typical move by Shange of publishing versions and variations of her work, sometimes with small presses, thus exemplifying the improvisation, versioning, and repetition so important to her publishing practice.

10. Witt's psychoanalytic, cultural, and historical reading takes "soul food," in all its complex incarnations, as a framework to examine the construction of American identity around ideas about African American women. Demonstrating its close kinship to my project, Witt's *Black Hunger* began as a study of literature. Witt explains, "Food struck me as pivotal in the work of many contemporary African American women writers" (8).

11. For further discussion of Geechee, Gullah, and the Sea Islands, see chapter 4.

12. The call for African Americans to lay claim to southern land, even to make a reverse migration as Sassafrass did, is evident in Hilda Effania's lament in a letter to Sassafrass: "Did you know that one Geechee after another is selling little parcels of land right off those islands? . . . If you must come back to the South, why don't you stay here? Charleston is as lovely as ever " (131–32). On the other hand, Sassafrass is surrounded by female guidance wherever she is geographically. Holloway writes, "Characters like Gwendolyn Brooks' Maud Martha and Shange's Sassafrass see themselves surrounded by a tradition of women like them"; she calls the deceased blues women who visit Sassafrass "her spirit informants" (58). For Shange, even when her female characters are seemingly alone, a women's community is there in the presence of ancestors.

13. Blue Sunday and Indigo are two shades of the same color. That color is both a marker of blues music and the blue of the ocean from which Blue Sunday emerges. Indigo, like the dye, colors the world both literally (with her presence) and figuratively (with her artistry). Both women's names evoke the term *blue-black*, used to describe very dark skin tones. Louis Armstrong's "What Did I Do (to Be So Black and Blue?)," emphasized by its appearance in the prologue to Ellison's *Invisible Man*, meditates on *blue-black* as a designation for skin tone that always evokes the black and blue of a bruise. Toni Morrison riffs on *blue-black* with the coal-mine-derived designation of dark skin tone "8-rock" in *Paradise*.

14. See the diverse visions of mothering Shange presents in her novel *Betsey Brown*. Betsey's mother, Jane, her grandmother Vida, and her women caretakers and guides (Maureen, Regina, and Carrie) each have a different vision of what Betsey needs on her journey toward womanhood. Varied in terms of class, work, background, and ideologies, these women teach Betsey a variety of lessons. *Daddy Says*, Shange's novel for young readers, considers parenting from the perspective of two young girls with an emphasis on their father's evolving parenting strategies in the wake of their mother's death.

15. In a 1986 interview with Neal Lester, Shange describes her work as a set of guides especially for young women, noting, "Langston Hughes cannot help a fifteen-year-old adolescent girl come to terms with being fifteen years old. There are certain things that happen in a woman's life—like having her first period or getting pregnant—that are surprises. . . . Now there are novels, short stories, poems, and plays that deal with things I had no idea about" ("At the Heart" 719–20).

16. See Witt's appendix of African American cookbooks; Prettyman's selected list of cookbooks by African American authors; and the online catalogue of the David Walker Lupton African American Cookbook Collection at the University of Alabama Library (http://www.lib.ua.edu/lupton/luptonlist.htm).

17. Grosvenor and Shange were in a women's writing group together in New York in the 1970s. Grosvenor wrote the foreword for *If I Can Cook*.

18. Ellison's protagonist consuming a baked yam in Harlem in *Invisible Man* articulates the migratory possibilities in food consumption. Dixon writes, "Take, for example, the scene in Ellison's *Invisible Man* when the nameless protagonist eats a yam purchased from a Harlem street vendor. He, of course, asserts his birthright in the delirium of his joy when he exclaims 'I yam what I am.' Most critics have reflected upon the affirmation of identity and cultural punning that occurs here. But further investigation reveals that with one delicious bite the protagonist is projected back to the South of his cultural condition and source of his present rebellion" ("Memory" 21). The possibility of travel that lies in every bite is not always liberation. The yam serves as a reminder of the oppression that drives Ellison's protagonist north. Ellison's yams are kin to Baraka's "sweet potato pies" that "taste more like memory, if you're not uptown" ("Soul Food" 102). The yam transports the Invisible Man from Harlem to the American South, and the sweet potato pie carries Baraka to Harlem just a decade later. Morrison too turns to food as a means of articulating connections across migrations: "Black people take their culture wherever they go. If I wrote about Maine, the black people in Maine would be very much like the black people in Ohio. You can change the plate but the menu would still be the same. . . . They cook a little bit differently, but I know what the language will be like" (Tate 119). If music is the paradigmatic form for masculine articulations of black collectivity in the twentieth century (as it is for Ellison, Baraka, and Paul Gilroy, among others), then perhaps culinary terms take on this role in the writings of African American women. Morrison's statement suggests this is the case as she imagines "the menu" as a kind of "language" of "black people," here defined as African Americans with a geographic range from Maine to Ohio. Edwards's nuanced reading of Claude McKay's *Banjo*'s "relation to music" more closely resembles my sense of the relation between cooking and Shange's writings, particularly in terms of how these other forms of artistry help us read texts that are productively difficult to pin down in terms of genre. See Edwards, "Vagabond Internationalism," in *The Practice of Diaspora*.

## 3 / Dancing Up a Nation

1. For more on Avey's journey to wholeness, see Christian, "Ritualistic Process"; Waxman; Pettis, *Toward Wholeness*; Rogers.

2. In one example of the dense intertextuality with both written and oral texts that pervades *Praisesong*, the first section is titled for Robert Hayden's poem "Runagate, Runagate." This provocatively suggests a parallel between the runaway slave of Hayden's verse and Avey running from a Caribbean cruise.

3. See Waxman 96; Busia 200.

4. Wall adds that *avatara*, "derived from the Sanskrit, carries the meaning of passing down or passing over" (*Worrying* 187).

5. McDaniel, acknowledging the diasporic reach of this story, makes it a framing device for her anthropological book *The Big Drum Ritual of Carriacou* (57). Bambara notes that Julie Dash uses Ibo Landing for the Peazant family picnic to "commandeer the space to create a danger-free zone" ("Reading the Signs" 94). According to Bambara, Dash and Marshall reinscribe the landing while acknowledging its violent history: "The Ibos' deep vision becomes an injunction to Avey. She must learn to see, to name, to reconnect" (112).

6. Abena Busia calls *Praisesong* a journey toward "diasporic literacy," a term for

comprehension and cultural exchange that she draws from Veve Clark's writings on Maryse Condé. Busia sees the novel as a lesson in cultural literacy for Marshall's readers (197). This is perhaps the reading of *Praisesong* most in line with my understanding of the novel's didactic function. I concur wholly with Busia's assertion that "the widow's narrative becomes a map," but I am less convinced than Busia that the "journey's end is Africa" (199).

7. Toomer's *Cane* appears as an intertext in many novels by contemporary African American women, sometimes in their depictions of the South, as in Naylor's *Mama Day*, and sometimes as echoes of Toomer's Avey, an artist without a medium. We see one such echo in Morrison's title character *Sula*, who, "had she paints, or clay, or knew the discipline of dance, or strings; had she anything to engage her tremendous curiosity and her gift for metaphor, she might have exchanged restlessness and preoccupation with whim for an activity that provided her with all she yearned for. And like any artist with no art form, she became dangerous" (121). Avey Johnson's name in *Praisesong* references Toomer's title character of the short story "Avey" in *Cane*. Joyce Pettis cites a 1989 lecture in which Marshall says that she had Toomer in mind when naming her protagonist (*Toward Wholeness* 159n11). Toomer's narrator imagines Avey as a woman who has no place in the world because "an art that would open the way for women the likes of her has yet to be born" (*Cane* 46). Marshall makes Avey the agent of her tale, restoring the narrative power denied Toomer's Avey.

8. Jacqueline Jones notes that during the Civil War, the Sea Islands were an important site of African American collaborative communities, particularly for women. She gives the example of "several hundred women form the Combahee River region of South Carolina" who "made up a small colony unto themselves in a Sea Island settlement. They prided themselves on their special handicrafts" (51).

9. For more on Marshall's understanding of Africa, see J. Williams.

10. The novelist John Killens highlights the cultural tourism of Marshall's novel in his review of *Praisesong for the Widow*. He writes that Carriacou is Avey Johnson's "Africa in the West Indies" and "her Caribbean Africa" (49), suggesting a shift from literary uses of African roots to articulate black identity in the United States to a focus on New World islands shaped by African cultural influences. Killens's ultimately laudatory review sees Avey as fully integrated into her "tribe (or nation)" in a kind of wholly positive unification of "the Southern experiences with that of the Caribbean, both as an African experience" (49–50).

11. Olmsted makes this point, noting that Bournehills shares this proximity to Africa with Marshall's native Barbados (251).

12. See, for example, Alice Walker's "The Black Writer and the Southern Experience." Sterling Brown anticipates this need to figure African American cultural resources in rural and agricultural terms with his phrase *folk storehouse*, which appears in his 1950 essay "Negro Folk Expression" and throughout his essays on black cultural production. Jazz musicians' notion of the "woodshed" as a metaphor for the place where inspiration and material are gathered is a similar metaphor for a repository of useful African American culture imagined in rural terms. For more on how the trend of reverse migration among African Americans has shaped contemporary southern Literature, see S. Jones, *Race Mixing*, especially the introduction, "Writing Race Relations."

13. Wall makes a similar point about Carriacou as it appears in Audre Lorde's *Zami*:

*A New Spelling of My Name*. Wall writes of Lorde's not finding Carriacou on any map, "Being unable to fix its location and thus being free of its history of colonization, the young Audre is able to use Carriacou for her own purposes" (*Worrying* 45, 182).

14. Christian refers here both to Avey's mental wanderings and to Avey's great-grandmother, from whom the name Avatara comes. Marshall writes of the elder Avey, "Her body she always usta say might be in Tatem but her mind, her mind was long gone with the Ibos" (39). Marshall draws on this construction in her memoir *Triangular Road*, when she describes "the runaway part of [her] mind" traveling down the James River in Virginia (56).

15. Mary Helen Washington asserts that the major query of all Marshall's fiction is "How do we remember the past so as to transform it and make it usable?" ("Afterword" 319). As I discuss in chapter 1, this is almost verbatim the question Bambara claims as her motivation for writing.

16. Denniston calls the "threads" of connection in *Praisesong* an "umbilical cord," suggesting the nurturing and uniquely female aspects of this physicality (139). Hoefel claims that the loss of the Johnsons' "breathtaking and ritualized lovemaking" is the "most lamentable" of the many losses attendant on the shift in Avey and Jay's marriage toward constant striving for material gain (141).

17. Dubey notes similar "literal rather than metaphorical explanations of magic" in Naylor's *Mama Day* and Morrison's *Song of Solomon* (*Signs* 179).

18. Marshall's memoir *Triangular Road* takes Hughes's "The Negro Speaks of Rivers" as a framing device. It opens with her recollection of traveling with Hughes on a State Department tour and proceeds in three sections, titled "I've Know Rivers: The James River," "I've Known Seas: The Caribbean Sea," and "I've Known Oceans: The Atlantic."

19. In an interview with Joyce Pettis, Marshall acknowledges the importance of Gwendolyn Brooks as an influence in this vein: "I did find that Gwendolyn Brooks' *Maud Martha* was extremely helpful to me, when I started thinking about *Brown Girl*, especially with its characters, because in *Maud Martha* for the first time, you had the interior life of a black woman dealt with in great depth" (127). Like Shange, Naylor, and Morrison, Marshall asserts in interviews that part of her motivation to write stems from the need for texts in which black women see themselves. Each of these authors addresses this need by writing books that depict "the interior life of a black woman" as inextricably tied to definitions of home, community, and nation. Often, as with Brooks's *Maud Martha* and Marshall's "wordshop of the kitchen," this interior life takes place in domestic spaces that are unexpected bases of power.

20. In 1994 Marshall said that she writes and travels to "bring about a connection, a linkage, between the, as I put it, scattered tribes of the diaspora, you know, from Brazil to Brooklyn." *Lanahan Literary Video Series*, vol. 39: *Paule Marshall*, dir. Dan Griggs, interviewer Michael Silverblatt, videocassette, Lanahan Foundation, 1994.

21. Marshall uses a selection from Baraka's poem "Leroy," which includes this phrase, as an epigraph to section 1 of *Praisesong* (8).

22. The title of this section evokes Johann Sebastian Bach's 1731 cantata commonly called "Sleepers, Wake" or "Sleepers, Awake." Bach's piece is a Lutheran hymn inspired by the book of Matthew.

23. Washington calls Avey's bath on Carriacou "part of the ritual baptism into a new state of consciousness" (*Black-Eyed Susans* 158). This island cleansing process

occurs in Naylor's *Mama Day* as well, when Ophelia begins every visit to the Sea Island of Willow Springs with a bath and purging to get rid of "them nasty city germs," as her great aunt says (48).

24. Each of the African nations *Praisesong* mentions is determined more by language use than by maps, though they are all West African. The Cromanti are, however, associated specifically with Carriacou.

25. Marshall refers to *Shadow and Act* more or less explicitly in almost every interview she gives. She calls Ellison's collection of essays her "literary bible." See James Kaufmann, "Author's Afro-American View of Reality," *Los Angeles Times*, May 23, 1983.

26. As Davies warns, "The Caribbean is too easily identified as the place of playful world traveling for us to engage that formulation [of travel to the Caribbean] without caution" (*Black Women* 23). The reviewer Christopher Lehmann-Haupt implicitly makes this point when he refers to the residents of Grenada in *Praisesong* as "festive natives" ("Books of the Times," *New York Times*, Feb. 1, 1983). In her review of *Praisesong*, the novelist Anne Tyler makes this point as well, asking whether readers will "willingly accompany [Avey] on her journey backward to find her own 'tribe'" ("A Widow's Tale," *New York Times*, Feb. 20, 1983).

27. See also Bonetti, "Marshall," in which the author says, "My heroines are always, at the end of the stories or the novels, moving off, in a sort of continuing search for self, coming into consciousness, which makes the continuing search necessary." She says that her novels emphasize "the continuing need to define self," especially for black women.

## 4 / Mapping and Moving Nation

1. Unmapped spaces regularly appear in Naylor's fiction. The setting of *The Women of Brewster Place* is a building in an unspecified urban, northern neighborhood just outside a large city. Recalling the South, Ben, the building's superintendent, describes Richland Plantation in Tennessee and asserts, "No point in looking for it on a map 'cause Richland only existed in the map of our minds" (11).

2. See, for example, Alice Walker's *Meridian* and Morrison's *Song of Solomon*.

3. James Baldwin makes a similar claim: "I am, in all but technical fact, a Southerner. My father was born in the South—my mother was born in the South, and if they had waited two more seconds I might have been born in the South. But that means I was raised by families whose roots were essentially southern rural" (qtd. in Wall, *Women* 22).

4. I refer to Cocoa by her "pet name," given because of her light skin color. Cocoa often tries to darken her skin with tanning and makeup, reversing the common narrative of color hierarchy that appears in Morrison's *The Bluest Eye* and Gwendolyn Brooks's *Maud Martha*, in which the community privileges lighter-skinned women. Cocoa's birth name, Ophelia, comes from her great-grandmother who, like her Shakespearean namesake, sought respite from life by drowning. By surviving and breaking a family cycle of women dying as men tried too hard to hold on to them, Cocoa breaks with the legacy of her birth name, so I choose not to call her Ophelia here. Her great-aunt Mama Day and maternal grandmother, Abigail, also call her by the "crib name" "Baby Girl" or "the Baby Girl," the latter signifying that she's the last of the Day family line.

5. In this sense, Naylor works in relationship to the function of the map that Dubey describes in novels by Sapphire, John Edgar Wideman, and Octavia Butler. For Dubey, mapping is "a form of critical literacy that can disclose the concealed structural logic of postmodern cities" (*Signs* 62), but she reads *Mama Day* as an example of "the southern folk aesthetic" rather than part of this kind of mapping. See chapter 4 of *Signs*.

6. Naylor's portrait of this ethnographer may signify on Zora Neale Hurston's ethnographic research, often done with a tape recorder, in the U.S. South.

7. Lamothe rightly reads the ethnographer "as a cautionary figure for individuals like Cocoa and George, who also want to reclaim and reconstruct their origins" (162).

8. Dubey makes a related claim that the novel presents "a participatory model of communication based not on a literal but a figurative return to the oral storytelling situation: read this book *as if* you were an insider listening to the members of a closed community speaking among themselves" (*Signs* 176).

9. Naylor reclaims and revises the Sapphire stereotype. Patricia Bell Scott writes, "The term 'Sapphire' is frequently used to describe an age-old image of Black women. The caricature of dominating, emasculating Black woman is one which historically has saturated both the popular and scholarly literature" (85). In choosing to name the key ancestor Sapphira, Naylor takes on this "caricature" and gives it real, human, powerful dimensions. Crucially, this is the ancestor of a culture that creates a homeland for men as well as women. Perhaps this revision is Naylor's impetus for changing of the name, or perhaps "Sapphira" is chosen for its feminine declination.

10. This works like performance, which Taylor notes "belongs to the strong as well as the weak" and "underwrites de Certeau's 'strategies' as well as 'tactics'" (22). Taylor usefully remarks, "If, as de Certeau suggests, 'space is a practiced place,' then there is no such thing as place for no place is free of history and social practice" (29).

11. Though Naylor's cluster of items in the front matter of *Mama Day* is unusual, the use of a map to initiate the reader is not so uncommon. William Faulkner's *Absalom! Absalom!* concludes with a genealogy, a chronology, and a map of Yoknapatawpha County, all meant as guides for the reader hoping to navigate the complex novel. Colson Whitehead's *Sag Harbor* opens with a map of "Benji's Sag Harbor" that includes streets, landmarks, events, and places that are important in the story. Whitehead's map points, for example, to "The Rock," creating a readerly curiosity satisfied some forty pages later, when that "powerful psychological meridian" reappears as the landmark that marks the boundary between white and black beaches (36–37). Whitehead's social map is one of several narrative tactics in his work that suggest contemporary male authors are inheritors of the women's work charted in this study. Protagonist Benji asserts in *Sag Harbor*, "You truly live in a place when you don't bother with chump stuff like street names, because the names of streets are irrelevant. The Big Red Barn, the Burned-Out House, the second left, these were inarguable coordinates and all the map you needed" (143). These words aptly express the view of Naylor's Miranda Day and many of Morrison's characters. In Whitehead's novel, they appear in the distinct voice of an African American teenage boy learning to inhabit his complex raced, classed, and culturally layered identity.

12. Brett Williams investigates the presence of southern communities among northern urban migrants in Washington, D.C. and Champaign-Urbana. She notes, "Southern residents import the South, yet these same southerners often feel they have left the South behind" (30). Williams examines neighborhoods where residents

"embrace or modify Southernness as a shared identity" (30) in black migrant communities of Washington.

13. Gayl Jones imagines a metaphorical South, which she terms Kentucky. In her essay "About My Work," she writes, "I like the idea of Kentucky in my work, though I don't always place my stories there. But it's like a 'magic word.' Often in works that take place somewhere else, I'll make references to Kentucky or have some of the characters be from there. . . . I think there'll always be references to Kentucky as place/as home even when the characters are somewhere else" (234). Naylor's South, like Jones's Kentucky, is more "idea" than literal "place." "Even when the characters are somewhere else," an idea of the South shapes both women's writings.

14. Lamothe calls this "a radical, activist politics of nostalgia" (156).

15. In Naylor's fiction, the American Dream is always a false hope, especially for black men. One of Naylor's concerns is that striving for economic advancement almost always re-creates the patriarchy of white America. Naylor's second novel, *Linden Hills*, uses Dante's circles of hell to describe a black middle-class neighborhood. This extends the conflict between cultural nationalism and capitalism that appears with Jay in Marshall's *Praisesong*. For an insightful analysis on authenticity and class in film, see Valerie Smith's chapter "Authenticity in Narratives" in *Not Just Race, Not Just Gender*.

16. In addition to being a Day family ancestor, Sapphira is also an ancestor for the novel in that she came to Naylor long before *Mama Day*. Naylor says Sapphira "had been guiding" her through the writing of her first four novels: "Sapphira Wade has been with me since way back although she was never mentioned until *Mama Day*" (Loris 255–56).

17. Lamothe, on the other hand, argues that George's "death signifies his failure as a castaway because his differences can't be erased or assimilated into that collective's values." She adds, "George's death also signifies the defeat of his Western, masculinized rationality to the African-derived matriarchy that rules over the island." Lamothe builds on this reading to argue that George's "lack of history" might be a valuable state worth preserving (167).

18. This is a more optimistic reading than Dubey's: "Even as the southern folk aesthetic appears to be resolving the difficulties of constituting a knowable community in postmodern times, this resolution cannot work because it remains irresolute about whether the southern folk community is imaginary or real, literary fabrication or literal reflection" (*Signs* 181). I have argued that *Mama Day* presents Willow Springs as a useful "literary fabrication" meant to serve as a model for a community that is both "knowable" and less rigid or static than Dubey's vision of a "southern folk community."

19. Speaking at the Yari Yari Pembari Conference at New York University in 2004, Naylor read a passage from *Mama Day* about the ordinariness of storms on Willow Springs and asserted that she used a hurricane in the novel because such storms usually follow the route of the Middle Passage. See the documentary of the conference, "Yari Yari Pembari: Black Women Writers Dissenting Globalization," dir. Jayne Cortez, produced by Manthia Diawara, Third World Newsreel, 2007.

20. See Witt's useful reading of Evelyn Creton Nedeed as the "insatiable appetite of the book as a whole" and a "disruptive" "belowground plot" essential to understanding *Linden Hills* (207).

21. Also see Ernest Gaines's *The Autobiography of Miss Jane Pittman*, in which a

fictional account of a woman's life is framed as a collective, oral, African American archive. Even in the tale told in a woman's voice, *Miss Jane Pittman* privileges men as leaders of the race, relegating women to mostly supporting roles. Naylor's mention of both Bradley and Gaines as authors of "classics in the making" in her essay "Love and Sex in the Afro-American Novel" suggests that these novels were on her mind around the time she completed *Mama Day* (30).

## 5 / Inscribing Community

1. See McKoy, "Paratext" and "Race" on paratext in relationship to African American literature and race.

2. This is not to say that slavery doesn't matter for reading *Paradise*. The founding fathers of the novel's two all-black towns went west after Emancipation to settle on homesteading land. Their experience (and that of their descendants) is unquestionably shaped by a slave past.

3. In Morrison's novel *Love*, 1976 marks the end and failure of "the Revolution" (82). Neither the militancy of a "fake military jacket" and "Che-style beret" nor "an authentic position and a powerful statement" survived integration and nationalism (97). *Love* critiques the black power movement through Christine, who recalls many abuses she suffered at the hands of men in that movement. She is a victim of the systemic rape that is part of the black power group she belongs to (163–65). The novel suggests that Christine and Heed's particular generation of women suffered, like Bambara's Velma Henry, from a virulent strain of sexism in black liberation movements.

4. For more on the complexity of this dynamic, see Spillers on a postintegration "new 'New South,'" which depends on a "cosmopolitan and multicultural ambition" and erases racial and geographic specificity (154–55). One loss wrought by integration is nuanced "public discourse" (161) in a contemporary climate where "racial and gender identity, for example, is simultaneously muted *and* expressed today, depending on the stakes" (168).

5. Hilton Als's *New Yorker* profile of Morrison has her describing a moment that blurs the gendered distinction between motto and inscription so rigid in *Paradise*. Inscription meets metalwork in the labors of Morrison's father: "I remember my daddy taking me aside—this was when he worked as a welder—and telling me that he welded a perfect seam that day, and that after welding the perfect seam he put his initials on it. . . . I said, 'Daddy, no one will ever see that.' Sheets and sheets of siding would go over that, you know? And he said, 'Yes. But I'll know it's there'" ("Ghost in the House," *The New Yorker*, Oct. 27, 2003, 64).

6. See Page "Furrowing" 638; Gauthier 399.

7. Inscription is women's work across Morrison's canon. Her two novels with male protagonists, *Song of Solomon* and *Home*, do not have clear scenes of characters inscribing text or image. *Home* complicates this a bit with protagonist Frank Money's commands to the author to "write" and "describe" (40–41, 103) aspects of his story. If there is women's work of inscription in *Home*, these imperative moments of direct address indicate that any inscription in this novel falls to Morrison rather than her characters. Also see *Home* 133–34.

8. *Paradise* offers some terrifying visions of motherhood. In the most extreme example, Mavis kills her twins by leaving them in a hot car. For Mavis, marriage and motherhood are a prison that she can escape only by sneaking out, in whatever clothes are at hand, and stealing her husband's car. She even fears her eleven-year-old

daughter, Sally, is out to murder her and will trap her if she wakes as Mavis escapes. In the last chapter of *Paradise*, Mavis departs after a short surprise visit to Sally, restaging the earlier abandonment. *Paradise* refuses to reconcile these women, suggesting the novel's general rejection of maternity.

9. The novel is thus directly in dialogue with the "sense of loss" after integration that Suzanne Jones reads in contemporary southern literature by African Americans (15) and obliquely in dialogue with a dynamic Dubey describes: "Nostalgic notions of segregated southern communities or the golden days of the ghetto are doing really dangerous kinds of political work, being used as sticks with which to beat the black urban poor" (*Signs* 238).

10. This work is necessarily retrospective. As Spillers notes of her own pre-integration childhood community, the "bonds" that held it together "were not then even understood as *sympathetic*, as well as coerced" (177). Morrison's novel explores this duality of community forged with love in the face of segregation and racial danger, a group bound by both sympathy and necessity.

11. *Paradise* is the third novel in Morrison's trilogy about excessive love. *Beloved* explores love between mother and child, *Jazz* treats excessive romantic love, and *Paradise* charts the dangers and possibilities of a more abstract love of collective identity. Scholars characterize this historical trilogy in various ways, sometimes asserting that *Paradise* is about love of God (Sweeney 42). Shockley reads the novels as "focusing on the relationship between excessive love and violence" (Review 718). Davidson writes, "Morrison's trilogy is concerned with 're-membering' the historical past for herself, for African Americans, and for America as a whole" (355). Morrison says, "When I wrote *Beloved*, I had in mind three stories of the same theme of variations of human love. Love of a mother for children, romantic love, and spiritual love. And I call the whole thing *Beloved*. . . . Parental love, romantic love, and love of God." See "In Depth with Toni Morrison," CSPAN, 2001, http://www.c-spanvideo.org/program/ToniM (accessed Nov. 29, 2012).

12. See Willis on the neighborhood in Morrison's fiction ("Eruptions" 37).

13. In "City Limits, Village Values," Morrison argues that this can be an urban phenomenon: "The affection of Black writers (whenever displayed) for the city seems to be for the village within it: the neighborhoods and the population of those neighborhoods" (37).

14. These losses are, in part, the subject of *Love*, which Morrison prefaces with the words "Beneath (rather, hand-in-hand with) the surface story of the successful revolt against a common enemy in the struggle for integration (in this case, white power) lies another one: the story of disintegration—of a radical change in conventional relationships and class allegiances that signals both liberation and estrangement" (xi).

15. This act, and the subsequent expansion of its legislation in 1909, depended on forcing Native Americans off their lands and selling off reservation property. Native American displacement was especially devastating in Oklahoma, where *Paradise* occurs.

16. The distinction here is that many critics (see Gauthier and Romero for two examples) are concerned with the ways *Paradise* is distinctly American and the ways African Americans use American Exceptionalism. I am concerned, on the other hand, with the novel's practices regarding an African American cultural nation separate from the United States. In other words, Morrison's critique of black nationalism is

more central to my reading that her critique of the United States. As Jenkins asserts, *Paradise* is less a "commentary on white American exceptionalism and the Puritan roots of the American republic" than a narrative focused on "the perceived boundaries of black identity and community" (123).

17. This is, in part, because Ruby follows the U.S. model Singh describes: "The reiteration of American universalism has long been central to the making of Americans at both individual and collective levels. This story of nationhood must be told over and over, because there is nothing natural about the nation or the fashioning of its predominant civic identities" (19).

18. During the Bataan Death March in 1942, Japanese soldiers forced 75,000 Americans and Filipino prisoners of war to walk sixty miles to prison camps. Like those prisoners, the founding families of Ruby walk for days without food. While Japan was later tried for war crimes, those who refused sanctuary, food, and water to migrating African American families never faced consequences. Guam, captured in 1944, remains a territory of the United States. Like the denizens of *Paradise*, residents of Guam are officially U.S. citizens but have a culture apart. Guam remains dependent economically on U.S. defense installations on the island but does not pay taxes to the U.S. government. This territory, like Ruby and Haven, is both part of and distinct from the United States.

19. During World War II, African American newspapers participated in the "double victory" campaign, for victory against the Axis powers abroad and against segregation at home. The FBI punished papers for running the double victory symbols and slogans, suggesting that notions of victory held by the nation-state and by its African American citizens were incompatible. See J. Jones 233.

20. Morrison's original title for the novel was *War*.

21. One of the two insightful readers for the University of Virginia Press suggests that Seneca has actually read the letter so many times over the years that the lipstick text has been blurred into illegibility. In other words, Seneca knows the text, but Morrison's reader does not.

22. The men attacking the Convent are, predictably, offended by ambiguity. Unable to know the contents of the letter, they misread it as "a letter written in blood so smeary its satanic message cannot be deciphered" (7).

23. Seneca's cuts also record communal suffering: she marks the assassinations of Martin Luther King Jr. and Robert Kennedy by cancelling her baby-sitting job and staying home to mourn by cutting "short streets, lanes, alleys into her arms" (261).

24. Her surname, mentioned only once in *Paradise*, evokes both Pecola Breedlove of Morrison's *The Bluest Eye* and Trueblood of Ellison's *Invisible Man*.

25. Also see Wall on Morrison's role in editing the multigenre collective archive *The Black Book* (*Worrying* 88–96).

26. And might she be the same Sorrow who appears in Morrison's later novel *A Mercy*?

27. Gauthier 400; Page, "Furrowing" 640.

28. Morrison makes a similar move in her foreword to the 2005 reprint of *Love*, where she discusses "rules of composition" and "narrative voice" (x–xi). Given her completion of a master's degree in literature at Cornell in 1955, during the height of New Criticism, this is perhaps not so surprising. See "In Depth with Toni Morrison," CSPAN, 2001, http://www.c-spanvideo.org/program/ToniM (accessed Nov. 29, 2012).

29. This is distinct from the archive in Gayl Jones's novel *Corregidora*, which Morrison edited while working at Random House. Jones's women follow the imperative to "make generations" by procreating, storytelling, and singing in order to "leave evidence" of a history of slavery and sexual abuse in the face of an archive destroyed by the Portuguese slaveholder Corregidora (10, 14).

30. As Gauthier points out, the Convent reminds us of the "suppressed history" of the "the removals and forced assimilation of American Indians" (397). Morrison depicts an all-girls school as anything but a safe place in her short story "Recitatif."

31. Morrison repeatedly uses the metaphor of removing cataracts (along with opening a door) to describe the goals of her writing. See Neustadt for an example (86).

32. Dreaming in *Paradise* is collective, unlike dreams in Morrison's *Tar Baby*, in which, as Willis describes, "with every dreamer dreaming a separate dream, there are no bridges to the past and no possibility of sharing an individual experience as part of a group's social history. . . . A dream, as Son finds out, cannot be pressed into another dreamer's head" ("Eruptions" 36). Connie's ritual of "loud dreaming," on the other hand, does just that, pressing each woman's past "into another dreamer's head." This echoes the narration in *Beloved*, which Wall describes: "The voices blend into each other; readers cannot differentiate among the characters' thoughts" (*Worrying* 107). Morrison employs a similar narrative strategy in *A Mercy*, using both first person and free indirect discourse to narrate from the points of view of Florens, Lina, Rebekka, and Sorrow, who penetrate one another's thoughts to varying degrees.

33. Many readers of *Paradise* take up Morrison's use of *white* as a floating or ambiguous signifier. See Sweeney 45; Krumholz 28. Contra Sweeney and others, I do not take this move to mean that Morrison's vision of collectivity in the novel "renders conceivable a community in which race no longer sharply delimits possibilities for human interaction" (Sweeney 46). Rather, more in line with Jenkins, I read *Paradise* as concerned with the possibilities and limits of imagining a community defined by its African Americanness.

34. Jenkins argues, "Consolata's character simultaneously represents the concept of the African diaspora and of a specifically 'black' multiraciality in this text" (147). Morrison aims in *Paradise* "to see whether or not race-specific, race-free language is both possible and meaningful in narration" ("Home" 9). Notice that race continues to matter here and that language is simultaneously "race-specific" and "race-free" such that "white" exists in *Paradise*, but does not necessarily connote the bodies, privileges, obstacles, or meanings one might assume.

35. The term *throwaway people* appears repeatedly in Morrison's prose. In *Beloved* it refers to Sethe and the white woman Amy who helps deliver Denver (100). One labor of Morrison's novels is the recovery of "throwaway" people and their stories.

36. See Romero 415; Schur 292; Krumholz 25; McKee 205, 208.

37. Morrison compared her own "layering" to that of the collage artist Romare Bearden in a 2004 lecture at Columbia University as part of the Center for Jazz Studies conference on Bearden.

38. For a useful reading of how Morrison's "Rootedness" and "City Limits" "[betray] the extreme difficulty of sustaining folk cultural claims to racial representation in the medium of print literature" see Dubey's afterword to *Signs* (236). As my reading of Morrison should suggest, I am not convinced that her novels are about "sustaining

folk cultural claims to racial representation," but Dubey's writing on postmodern African American novels does important work around this claim.

39. The novel's conclusion is prefigured by the epigraph to *Paradise*, the final stanza of "The Thunder, the Perfect Mind," a poem in a female voice from the Gnostic manuscripts. The epigraph reads:

> For many are the pleasant forms which exist
> in numerous sins
> and incontinencies
> and disgraceful passions
> and fleeting pleasures,
> which (men) embrace until they become
> sober
> and go up to their resting place.
> And they will find me there,
> and they will live,
> and they will not die again.

The Convent in *Paradise* is the place of "disgraceful passions" and "fleeting pleasures," especially for Deek Morgan, who comes there to court Consolata. The female "me" of this stanza promises to disappear to the "there" of a final "resting place," suggesting that some of the disappeared women may be in a place of eternal life where neither the women of the Convent nor the "(men)" who have depended on it for everything from hot peppers to social order will ever "die again." For the full translated poem, see "The Thunder, Perfect Mind," trans. George W. MacRae, *Frontline*, PBS, http://www.pbs.org/wgbh/pages/frontline/shows/religion/maps/primary/thunder .html.

40. Morrison says her childhood neighborhood in Lorain, Ohio, was made up of a group of people: "There was this kind of circle around them—we lived within 23 blocks—which they could not break" (Stepto, "Intimate Things" 12). While this "circle" is cause for celebration, even nostalgia, in Stepto's 1976 interview with Morrison, the danger and limits suggested by "could not break" come to the fore in *Paradise* two decades later.

41. Spillers describes in political and historical terms what Morrison depicts in a novel: "In the apparent collapse of 'movement,' what we are witnessing now is the absence of a 'joining thing,' in which case youth and their elders have devised no common language of engagement and critique" (171).

## Conclusion

1. As this cultural nationalist revision comes to a close, Naylor, Marshall, and Shange turn to another genre: memoir. Naylor's *1996* offers a fictionalized account of her year of harassment at the hands of U.S. government. Marshall's *Triangular Road: A Memoir* developed from a series of talks at Harvard on the theme "bodies of water." Shange's *If I Can Cook / You Know God Can*, which I address briefly in chapter 4, contextualizes the author's international travels with historical information and theorizes diaspora through a group of recipes. Naylor's turn to memoir is intensely individual, while Marshall's is staunchly public. Neither Naylor's intimate recollections of paranoia, justified or not, nor Marshall's lectures, which render personal experience as if

from a vast distance, negotiate a practiced relationship between individual and community. These later works are thus not part of the cultural nationalist revision.

2. "Toni Morrison Interview," *New York Times*, Nov. 28, 2008, podcast, www
.nytimes.com.

3. "Toni Morrison Interview," *New York Times*, Nov. 28, 2008, podcast, www
.nytimes.com.

# Bibliography

Alwes, Derek. "The Burden of Liberty: Choice in Toni Morrison's *Jazz* and Toni Cade Bambara's *The Salt Eaters*." *African American Review* 30.3 (1996): 353–65.

Anderson, Benedict. *Imagined Communities*. New York: Verso, 1983.

Andrews, Larry R. "Black Sisterhood in Naylor's Novels." In *Gloria Naylor: Critical Perspectives Past and Present*, edited by Henry Louis Gates Jr. and Kwame Anthony Appiah. New York: Amistad, 1993. 285–301.

Ashford, Tomeiko R. "Gloria Naylor on Black Spirituality: An Interview." *MELUS* 30.4 (2005): 73–87.

Awkward, Michael. *Inspiriting Influences*. New York: Columbia University Press, 1989.

Baker, Houston. *Blues, Ideology and Afro-American Literature: A Vernacular Theory*. Chicago: University of Chicago Press, 1987.

———. *Workings of the Spirit: The Poetics of Afro-American Women's Writing*. Chicago: University of Chicago Press, 1991.

Bambara, Toni Cade, ed. *The Black Woman: An Anthology*. 1970. New York: Washington Square Press, 2005.

———. "Deep Sight and Rescue Missions." In *Deep Sightings and Rescue Missions*. New York: Random House, 1996. 146–78.

———. Foreword to *This Bridge Called My Back: Radical Writings by Women of Color*. Watertown, MA: Persephone Press, 1981. vii–viii.

———. "How She Came By Her Name." In *Deep Sightings and Rescue Missions*. New York: Random House, 1996. 201–45.

———. "On the Issue of Roles." In *The Black Woman: An Anthology*. 1970. New York: Washington Square Press, 2005. 123–35.

———. "Reading the Signs, Empowering the Eye." In *Deep Sightings and Rescue Missions*. New York: Random House, 1996. 89–138.

————. *The Salt Eaters*. New York: Random House, 1980.

————. *The Sea Birds Are Still Alive*. 1974. New York: Random House, 1982.

————, ed. *Tales and Stories for Black Folks*. New York: Zenith Books, 1971.

————. *Those Bones Are Not My Child*. 1999. New York: Random House, 2000.

Baraka, Amiri (Leroi Jones). "'Black' Is a Country." In *Home*. New York: William Morrow, 1966. 82–86.

————. Foreword to *Black Fire*, edited by Amiri Baraka and Larry Neal. New York: William Morrow, 1968. xvii–xviii.

————. "Soul Food." In *Home*. New York: William Morrow, 1966. 101–4.

Baraka, Amiri, and Amina Baraka, eds. *Confirmation: An Anthology of African American Women*. New York: William Morrow, 1983.

Beale, Frances. "Double Jeopardy: To Be Black and Female." In *The Black Woman: An Anthology*, edited by Toni Cade Bambara. 1970. New York: Washington Square Press, 2005. 109–22.

Bellinelli, Matteo. "A Conversation with Gloria Naylor." In *Conversations with Gloria Naylor*, edited by Maxine Lavon Montgomery. Jackson: University Press of Mississippi, 2004. 105–10.

Blackwell, Henry. "An Interview with Ntozake Shange." *Black American Literature Forum* 13.4 (1979): 134–38.

Blount, Marcellus. "The Preacherly Text: African American Poetry and Vernacular Performance." *PMLA* 107.3 (1992): 582–93.

Bonetti, Kay. Interview. "Toni Cade Bambara." American Audio Prose Library. KOPN Radio, Columbia, Missouri. Feb. 1982.

————. Interview. "Paule Marshall." American Audio Prose Library. KOPN Radio, Columbia, Missouri. Mar. 1984.

————. "An Interview with Gloria Naylor." In *Conversations with Gloria Naylor*, edited by Maxine Lavon Montgomery. Jackson: University Press of Mississippi, 2004. 39–64.

Bradley, David. *The Chaneysville Incident*. New York: Harper & Row, 1981.

Brinkley, Jamel. "Finding a Bridge Language: The Poetics of Dedication in *The Salt Eaters*." Unpublished essay, Columbia University, 2005.

Bröck, Sabine. "'Talk as a Form of Action': An Interview with Paule Marshall, September 1982." In *History and Tradition in Afro-American Culture*, edited by Günter H. Lenz. New York: Campus Verlag, 1984. 194–206.

Brodber, Erna. *Louisiana*. Jackson: University Press of Mississippi, 1994.

Brown, Kimberley Nichele. *Writing the Black Revolutionary Diva: Women's Subjectivity and the Decolonizing Text*. Bloomington: Indiana University Press, 2010.

Brown, Sterling. *A Son's Return: Selected Essays of Sterling A. Brown*. Boston: Northeastern University Press, 1996.

Bryan, Dianetta Gail. "Her-Story Unsilences: Black Female Activists in the Civil Rights Movement." *Sage* 5.2 (1988): 60–64.

Busia, Abena P. A. "What Is Your Nation? Reconnecting Africa and Her

Diaspora through Paule Marshall's *Praisesong for the Widow*." In *Changing Our Own Words: Essays on Criticism, Theory, and Writing by Black Women*, edited by Cheryl A. Wall. New Brunswick, NJ: Rutgers University Press, 1989. 196–211.

Chandler, Zala. "Voices beyond the Veil: An Interview with Toni Cade Bambara and Sonia Sanchez." In *Wild Women in the Whirlwind: Afra-American Culture and the Contemporary Literary Renaissance*, edited by Joanne M. Braxton and Andrée Nicola McLaughlin. New Brunswick, NJ: Rutgers University Press, 1990. 342–62.

Christian, Barbara. *Black Women Novelists: The Development of a Tradition, 1892–1976*. Westport, CT: Greenwood Press, 1980.

———. "Naylor's Geography: Community, Class and Patriarchy in *The Women of Brewster Place* and *Linden Hills*." In *Gloria Naylor: Critical Perspectives Past and Present*, edited by Henry Louis Gates Jr. and K. A. Appiah. New York: Amistad, 1993. 106–25.

———. "Ritualistic Process and the Structure of Paule Marshall's *Praisesong for the Widow*." *Callaloo*, no. 18 (Spring–Summer 1983): 74–84.

Christol, Hélène. "Reconstructing American History: Land and Genealogy in Gloria Naylor's *Mama Day*." In *The Critical Response to Gloria Naylor*, edited by Sharon Felton and Michelle C. Loris. Westport, CT: Greenwood Press, 1997. 159–65.

Clark, Joanna. "Motherhood." In *The Black Woman: An Anthology*, edited by Toni Cade Bambara. 1970. New York: Washington Square Press, 2005. 75-86.

Clark, Patricia E. "Archiving Epistemologies and the Narrativity of Recipes in Ntozake Shange's *Sassafrass, Cypress & Indigo*." *Callaloo* 30.1 (2007): 150–62.

Clarke, Cheryl. *"After Mecca": Women Poets and the Black Arts Movement*. New Brunswick, NJ: Rutgers University Press, 2006.

Cohen, Robin. *Global Diasporas: An Introduction*. Seattle: University of Washington Press, 1997.

Collier, Eugenia. "The Closing of the Circle: Movement from Division to Wholeness in Paule Marshall's Fiction." In *Black Women Writers (1950–1980)*, edited by Mari Evans. New York: Anchor Books, 1984. 295–315.

The Combahee River Collective. "A Black Feminist Statement." In *All the Women Are White, All the Blacks Are Men, But Some of Us Are Brave: Black Women's Studies*, edited by Gloria T. Hull, Patricia Bell Scott, and Barbara Smith. New York: Feminist Press at the City University of New York, 1982. 13–22.

Dash, Julie, writer and director. *Daughters of the Dust*. Kino Video, 1991.

———. *Daughters of the Dust: The Making of an African American Woman's Film*, with Toni Cade Bambara and bell hooks. New York: New Press, 1992.

———. *Daughters of the Dust: A Novel*. 1997. New York: Plume, 1999.

Davidson, Rob. "Racial Stock and 8-Rocks: Communal Historiography in Toni Morrison's *Paradise*." *Twentieth-Century Literature* 47.3 (2001): 355–73.

Davies, Carole Boyce. *Black Women, Writing, and Identity: Migrations of the Subject.* New York: Routledge, 1994.

———. "Mothering and Healing in Recent Black Women's Fiction." *Sage* 3.1 (1985): 41–43.

Davis, Angela Y. *Women, Race and Class.* 1981. New York: Vintage, 1983.

de Certeau, Michel. *The Practice of Everyday Life.* Translated by Stephen Randall. Berkeley: University of California Press, 1984.

Denniston, Dorothy Hamer. *The Fiction of Paule Marshall: Reconstructions of History, Culture, and Gender.* Knoxville: University of Tennessee Press, 1995.

Dixon, Melvin. "The Black Writer's Use of Memory." In *History and Memory in African American Culture,* edited by Geneviève Fabre and Robert O'Meally. New York: Oxford University Press, 1994. 18–27.

———. *Ride Out the Wilderness: Geography and Identity in Afro-American Literature.* Chicago: University of Illinois Press, 1987.

Dubey, Madhu. *Black Women Novelists and the Nationalist Aesthetic.* Indianapolis: Indiana University Press, 1994.

———. *Signs and Cities: Black Literary Postmodernism.* Chicago: University of Chicago Press, 2003.

Edwards, Brent. *The Practice of Diaspora: Literature, Translation, and the Rise of Black Internationalism.* Cambridge, MA: Harvard University Press, 2003.

Ellison, Ralph. "Richard Wright's Blues." 1945. In *The Collected Essays of Ralph Ellison,* edited by John F. Callahan. New York: Modern Library, 2003. 128–44.

———. "Society, Morality and the Novel." 1957. In *The Collected Essays of Ralph Ellison,* edited by John F. Callahan. New York: Modern Library, 2003. 698–729.

———. "Some Questions and Some Answers." In *Shadow and Act.* 1953. New York: Vintage Books, 1995. 261–72.

Gaines, Ernest. *The Autobiography of Miss Jane Pittman.* 1971. New York: Bantam, 1972.

Gates, Henry-Louis. "Preface to Blackness: Text and Pretext." In *Afro-American Literature: The Reconstruction of Instruction,* edited by Dexter Fisher and Robert B. Stepto. New York: MLA, 1978. 44–69.

———. Preface to *Toni Morrison: Critical Perspectives Past and Present,* edited by Henry Louis Gates Jr. and Kwame A. Appiah. New York: Amistad, 1993. ix–xiii.

Gauthier, Marni. "The Other Side of *Paradise*: Toni Morrison's (Un)Making of Mythic History." *African American Review* 39.9 (2005): 395–414.

Gayle, Addison, Jr. Introduction to *The Black Aesthetic,* edited by Addison Gayle Jr. New York: Doubleday, 1971. xv–xxiv.

Genette, Gerard. *Paratexts: Thresholds of Interpretation,* edited by Jane E. Lewin. New York: Cambridge University Press, 1997.

Giddings, Paula. *When and Where I Enter: The Impact of Black Women on Race and Sex in America.* 1984. New York: Harper Collins, 2001.

Gilroy, Paul. *The Black Atlantic: Modernity and Double Consciousness*. Cambridge, MA: Harvard University Press, 1993.

———. "It ain't where you're from, it's where you're at." In *Small Acts*. London: Serpent's Tail, 1993. 120–45.

Gomez, Jewelle. "Belles Lettres Interview: Ntozake Shange." *Belles Lettres* 1.1 (1985): 9.

Gordon, Avery F. "something more powerful than skepticism." In *Savoring the Salt: The Legacy of Toni Cade Bambara*, edited by Linda Janet Holmes and Cheryl A. Wall. Philadelphia: Temple University Press, 2008. 256–72.

Griffin, Farah Jasmine. "Conflict and Chorus: Reconsidering Toni Cade's *The Black Woman: An Anthology*." In *Is It Nation Time? Contemporary Essays on Black Power and Black Nationalism*, edited by Eddie Glaude. Chicago: University of Chicago Press, 2001. 113–29.

———. "Textual Healing: Claiming Women's Bodies, the Erotic and Resistance in Contemporary Novels of Slavery." *Callaloo* 19.2 (1996): 519–36.

———. *"Who Set You Flowin'?" The African-American Migration Narrative*. New York: Oxford University Press, 1995.

Grosvenor, Vertamae Smart. Foreword to *If I Can Cook / You Know God Can*. Boston: Beacon Press, 1998. xi–xiv.

———. "The Kitchen Crisis." In *The Black Woman: An Anthology*, edited by Toni Cade Bambara. 1970. New York: Washington Square Press, 2005. 149–54.

———. *Vibration Cooking or the Travel Notes of a Geechee Girl*. 1970. New York: Ballantine Books, 1992.

Guy-Sheftall, Beverly. "Commitment: Toni Cade Bambara Speaks." In *Sturdy Black Bridges: Visions of Black Women in Literature*, edited by Roseann P. Bell, Bettye J. Parker, and Beverly Guy-Sheftall. New York: Anchor Books, 1979. 230–49.

Hahn, Steven. *A Nation under Our Feet: Black Political Struggles in the Rural South from Slavery to the Great Migration*. Cambridge, MA: Harvard University Press, 2003.

Harper, Michael S., and Robert B. Stepto, eds. *Chant of Saints: A Gathering of Afro-American Literature, Art, Scholarship*. Chicago: University of Illinois Press, 1979.

Harper, Phillip Brian. "Nationalism and Social Division in Black Arts Poetry of the 1960s." *Critical Inquiry* 19 (Winter 1993): 234–55.

Hartman, Saidiya. *Lose Your Mother: A Journey along the Atlantic Slave Route*. New York: Farrar, Straus and Giroux, 2007.

Hatch, James, and Camille Billops. "Toni Morrison." Interview. Owen Dodson Oral History Project. Hatch-Billops Collection, New York City, Apr. 3, 1986.

Hernton, Calvin. "The Sexual Mountain and Black Women Writers." In *Wild Women in the Whirlwind: Afra-American Culture and the Contemporary Literary Renaissance*, edited by Joanne M. Braxton and Andrée Nicola McLaughlin. New Brunswick, NJ: Rutgers University Press, 1990. 195–212.

Hilfrich, Carola. "Anti-Exodus: Countermemory, Gender, Race, and Everyday Life in Toni Morrison's *Paradise.*" *Modern Fiction Studies* 52.2 (2006): 321–49.

Hirsch, Marianne. "Maternal Narratives: 'Cruel Enough to Stop the Blood.'" In *Toni Morrison: Critical Perspectives Past and Present*, edited by Henry Louis Gates Jr. and Kwame A. Appiah. New York: Amistad, 1993. 261–73.

Hoefel, Roseanne. "Praisesong for Paule Marshall: Music and Dance as Redemptive Metaphor in *Brown Girl, Brownstones* and *Praisesong for the Widow.*" *MaComère* 1 (1998): 134–44.

Holloway, Karla. *Moorings and Metaphors: Figures of Culture and Gender in Black Women's Literature.* New Brunswick, NJ: Rutgers University Press, 1992.

Holmes, Linda Janet, and Cheryl Wall. "An Introduction." In *Savoring the Salt: The Legacy of Toni Cade Bambara*, edited by Linda Janet Holmes and Cheryl A. Wall. Philadelphia: Temple University Press, 2008. 3–6.

hooks, bell. "Feminism as a Persistent Critique of History: What's Love Got to Do with It?" In *The Fact of Blackness: Frantz Fanon and Visual Representation*, edited by Alan Reed. Seattle: Bay Press, 1996. 76–85.

———. *Sisters of the Yam.* Cambridge, MA: South End Press, 2005.

———. *Yearning: Race, Gender, and Cultural Politics.* Boston: South End Press, 1990.

Hull, Gloria T. "'What It Is I Think She's Doing Anyhow': A Reading of Toni Cade Bambara's *The Salt Eaters.*" In *Conjuring: Black Women, Fiction, and Literary Tradition*, edited by Marjorie Pryse and Hortense J. Spillers. Bloomington: Indiana University Press, 1985. 216–32.

Hurston, Zora Neale. *Mules and Men.* 1935. New York: Harper Collins, 1990.

———. *Tell My Horse.* 1938. New York: Harper & Row, 1990.

———. *Their Eyes Were Watching God.* 1937. New York: Harper & Row, 1990.

Jenkins, Candice M. *Private Lives, Proper Relations: Regulating Black Intimacy.* Minneapolis: University of Minnesota Press, 2007.

Jones, Gayl. "About My Work." In *Black Women Writers (1950–1980)*, edited by Mari Evans. New York: Anchor Books, 1984. 233–35.

———. *Corregidora.* 1975. Boston: Beacon Press, 1986.

Jones, Jacqueline. *Labor of Love, Labor of Sorrow: Black Women, Work and the Family, from Slavery to the Present.* 1985. New York: Vintage, 1995.

Jones, Suzanne. *Race Mixing: Southern Fiction since the Sixties.* Baltimore: Johns Hopkins University Press, 2004.

Karenga, Ron. "Black Cultural Nationalism." In *The Black Aesthetic*, edited by Addison Gayle Jr. New York: Doubleday, 1971. 32–38.

Kelley, Margot Anne. "'Damballah Is the First Law of Thermodynamics': Modes of Access to Toni Cade Bambara's *The Salt Eaters.*" *African American Review* 27.30 (1993): 479–93.

Kelley, Robin. *Freedom Dreams: The Black Radical Imagination.* Boston: Beacon Press, 2002.

Killens, John O. Review of *Praisesong for the Widow*. *Crisis* 90.7 (1983): 49–50.

King, Lovalerie, and Linda Selzer, eds. *New Essays on the African American Novel*. New York: Palgrave Macmillan, 2008.

King, Woodie, Jr. "The Black Book." *Black World,* July 1974. 71–72.

Koenen, Anne. "'Women out of Sequence': An Interview with Toni Morrison." In *History and Tradition in Afro-American Culture*. New York: Campus Verlag, 1984. 207–21.

Krumholz, Linda J. "Reading and Insight in Toni Morrison's *Paradise*." *African American Review* 36.1 (2002): 21–34.

Kubitschek, Missy Dehn. "Paule Marshall's Women on Quest." *Black American Literature Forum* 21.1–2 (1987): 43–60.

Lamothe, Daphne. "Gloria Naylor's *Mama Day*: Bridging Roots and Routes." *African American Review* 39.1–2 (2005): 155–69.

LeClair, Thomas. "The Language Must Not Sweat: A Conversation with Toni Morrison." 1981. In *Conversations with Toni Morrison*, edited by Danille Taylor-Guthrie. Jackson: University Press of Mississippi, 1994. 119–28.

Lester, Neal A. "At the Heart of Shange's Feminism: An Interview." *Black American Literature Forum* 24.4 (1990): 717–30.

———. *Ntozake Shange: A Critical Study of the Plays*. New York: Garland, 1995.

Lester, Rosemarie K. "An Interview with Toni Morrison, Hessian Radio Network, Frankfurt, West Germany." 1983. In *Critical Essays on Toni Morrison*, edited by Nellie Y. McKay. Boston: G. K. Hall, 1988. 47–54.

Lindsey, Kay. "The Black Woman as Woman." In *The Black Woman: An Anthology*, edited by Toni Cade Bambara. 1970. New York: Washington Square Press, 2005. 103–8.

Lorde, Audre. "Learning from the 60s." 1982. In *Sister Outsider*. Berkeley: Crossing Press, 1984. 134–44.

———. "Uses of the Erotic." In *Sister Outsider*. Berkeley: Crossing Press, 1984. 53–59.

Loris, Michelle C. "Interview: 'The Human Spirit Is a Kick-Ass Thing.'" In *The Critical Response to Gloria Naylor*. Westport, CT: Greenwood Press, 1997. 253–63.

Lubiano, Wahneema. "Black Nationalism and Black Common Sense: Policing Ourselves and Others." In *The House That Race Built*, edited by Wahneema Lubiano. New York: Random House, 1997. 232–52.

Marshall, Paule. *Brown Girl, Brownstones*. 1959. New York: Feminist Press at the City University of New York, 1981.

———. *The Chosen Place, the Timeless People*. 1969. New York: Vintage, 1992.

———. *Daughters*. 1991. New York: Penguin, 1992.

———. "From the Poets in the Kitchen." *Callaloo* 18 (Spring–Summer 1983): 22–30.

———. *Praisesong for the Widow*. New York: Penguin, 1983.

———. "Shaping the World of My Art." *New Letters* 40.1 (1973): 97–112.

———. *Triangular Road: A Memoir.* New York: Perseus Books, 2009.

Mason, Theodore O. "The African-American Anthology: Mapping the Territory, Taking the National Census, Building the Museum." *American Literary History* 10.1 (1998): 185–98.

Massey, Doreen. *Space, Place, and Gender.* Minneapolis: University of Minnesota Press, 1994.

Mathes, Carter Alexander. "Imagine the Sound: Modalities of Resistance and Liberation in Post–Civil Rights Black Literature." Ph.D. dissertation, University of California, Berkeley, 2005.

———. "Scratching the Threshold: Textual Sound and Political Form in Toni Cade Bambara's *The Salt Eaters.*" *Contemporary Literature* 50.2 (2009): 363–96.

McDaniel, Lorna. *The Big Drum Ritual of Carriacou: Praisesongs in Rememory of Flight.* Gainesville: University Press of Florida, 1998.

McDowell, Deborah E. *"The Changing Same": Black Women's Literature, Criticism, and Theory.* Indianapolis: Indiana University Press, 1995.

McKay, Nellie Y. "The Journals of Charlotte L. Forten-Grimké: *Les Lieux de Mémoire* in African-American Women's Autobiography." In *History and Memory in African American Culture,* edited by Geneviève Fabre and Robert O'Meally. New York: Oxford University Press, 1994. 261–71.

McKee, Patricia. "Geographies of *Paradise.*" *CR: The New Centennial Review* 3.1 (2003): 197–223.

McKoy, Beth. "Paratext, Citation, and Academic Desire in Ishmael Reed's 'Mumbo Jumbo.'" *Contemporary Literature* 46.4 (2005): 604–35.

———. "Race and the (Para)textual Condition." *PMLA* 121.1 (2006): 156–69.

Montgomery, Maxine Lavon. "Good Housekeeping: Domestic Ritual in Gloria Naylor's Fiction." In *Gloria Naylor's Early Novels,* edited by Margot Anne Kelley. Gainesville: University Press of Florida, 1999. 55–69.

Moretti, Franco. *Atlas of the European Novel 1800–1900.* New York: Verso, 1998.

Morrison, Toni. *Beloved.* 1987. New York: Vintage, 2004.

———. "City Limits, Village Values: Concepts of the Neighborhood in Black Fiction." In *Literature and the Urban Experience,* edited by Michael C. Jaye and Ann Chalmers Watts. New Brunswick, NJ: Rutgers University Press, 1981. 35–43.

———. "Home." In *The House That Race Built,* edited by Wahneema Lubiano. New York: Random House, 1997. 3–12.

———. *Home.* New York: Knopf, 2012.

———. *Love.* 2003. New York: Random House, 2005.

———. *A Mercy.* New York: Knopf, 2008.

———. *The Nobel Lecture in Literature, 1993.* New York: Knopf, 2006.

———. *Paradise.* 1997. New York: Penguin, 1999.

———. "Rootedness: The Ancestor as Foundation." In *Black Women Writers (1950–1980),* edited by Mari Evans. New York: Anchor Books, 1984. 339–45.

———. *Song of Solomon.* 1977. New York: Vintage, 2004.

———. *Sula.* 1973. New York: Penguin, 1982.

Murray, Albert. *The Hero and the Blues.* 1973. New York: Vintage, 1996.

———. *Train Whistle Guitar.* 1974. New York: Vintage, 1998.

Murray, Rolland. *Our Living Manhood: Literature, Black Power, and Masculine Ideology.* Philadelphia: University of Pennsylvania Press, 2007.

Naylor, Gloria. *Bailey's Cafe.* 1992. New York: Vintage, 1993.

———. *Linden Hills.* 1985. New York: Penguin: 1986.

———. "Love and Sex in the Afro-American Novel." *Yale Review* 78.1 (1989): 19–31.

———. *Mama Day.* New York: Vintage, 1988.

———. *The Men of Brewster Place.* New York: Hyperion, 1998.

———. *1996.* Chicago: Third World Press, 2005.

———. *The Women of Brewster Place.* 1982. New York: Penguin Books, 1983.

Naylor, Gloria, Maryse Condé, Barbara Reynolds, Tina McElroy, et al. "Finding Our Voice." *Essence* 26.1 (1995): 193–200, 256.

Neal, Larry. "An Afterword / And Shine Swam On." In *Black Fire*, edited by Amiri Baraka and Larry Neal. New York, William Morrow, 1968. 638–56.

———. "The Black Arts Movement." In *The Black Aesthetic*, edited by Addison Gayle Jr. New York: Doubleday, 1971. 272–90.

Neustadt, Kathy. "The Visits of the Writers Toni Morrison and Eudora Welty." 1980. In *Conversations with Toni Morrison*, edited by Danille Taylor-Guthrie. Jackson: University Press of Mississippi, 1994. 84–92.

Olaniyan, Tejumola. *Scars of Conquest / Masks of Resistance: The Invention of Cultural Identities in African, African-American, and Caribbean Drama.* New York: Oxford University Press, 1995.

Olmstead, Jane. "The Pull to Memory and the Language of Place in Paule Marshall's *The Chosen Place, The Timeless People* and *Praisesong for the Widow.*" *African American Review* 31.2 (1997): 249–67.

O'Neal, John. "Black Arts: Notebook." In *The Black Aesthetic*, edited by Addison Gayle Jr. New York: Doubleday, 1971. 47–58.

Page, Phillip. "Furrowing All the Brows: Interpretation and the Transcendent in Toni Morrison's *Paradise.*" *African American Review* 35.4 (2001): 637–49.

———. *Reclaiming Community in African American Fiction.* Jackson: University Press of Mississippi, 1999.

Pettis, Joyce. "A MELUS Interview: Paule Marshall." *MELUS* 17.49 (1991–92): 117–29.

———. *Toward Wholeness in Paule Marshall's Fiction.* Charlottesville: University of Virginia Press, 1995.

Prettyman, Quandra. "Come Eat at My Table: Lives with Recipes." *Southern Quarterly* 30.2–3 (1992): 131–40.

Rambsy, Howard, II. *The Black Arts Enterprise and the Production of African American Poetry.* Ann Arbor: University of Michigan Press, 2011.

Raus, Charles. "Toni Morrison." 1981. In *Conversations with Toni Morrison*, edited by Danille Taylor-Guthrie. Jackson: University Press of Mississippi, 1994. 93–118.

Reed, Ishmael. *Mumbo Jumbo*. 1972. New York: Scribner, 1996.

———. *Reckless Eyeballing*. 1986. Champaign, IL: Dalkey Archive Press, 2000.

Rich, Adrienne. "Notes toward a Politics of Location." In *Blood, Bread, and Poetry: Selected Prose 1979–1985*. New York: Norton, 1986. 210–31.

Robolin, Stéphane. "Loose Memory in Toni Morrison's *Paradise* and Zoë Wicombs' *David's Story*." *Modern Fiction Studies* 52.2 (2006): 297–320.

Rogers, Susan. "Embodying Cultural Memory in Paule Marshall's *Praisesong for the Widow*." *African American Review* 34.1 (2000): 77–93.

Romero, Channette. "Creating the Beloved Community: Religion, Race, and Nation in Toni Morrison's *Paradise*." *African American Review* 39.3 (2005): 415–30.

Ross, Fran. *Oreo*. 1974. Boston: Northeastern University Press, 2000.

Rowell, Charles H., and Farah Jasmine Griffin. "An Interview with Farah Jasmine Griffin." *Callaloo* 22.4 (1999): 872–92.

Rushdy, Ashraf. *Remembering Generations: Race and Family in Contemporary African American Fiction*. Chapel Hill: University of North Carolina Press, 2001.

Salaam, Kalamu ya. "Searching for the Mother Tongue: An Interview with Toni Cade Bambara." In *Savoring the Salt: The Legacy of Toni Cade Bambara*, edited by Linda Janet Holmes and Cheryl A. Wall. Philadelphia: Temple University Press, 2008. 56–69.

Sanders, Fran. "Dear Black Man." In *The Black Woman: An Anthology*, edited by Toni Cade Bambara. 1970. New York: Washington Square Press, 2005. 87–94.

Schur, Richard. "Locating 'Paradise' in the Post–Civil Rights Era: Toni Morrison and Critical Race Theory." *Contemporary Literature* 45.2 (2004): 276–99.

Scott, Patricia Bell. "Debunking Sapphire: Toward a Non-Racist and Non-Sexist Social Science." In *All the Women Are White, All the Blacks Are Men, But Some of Us Are Brave: Black Women's Studies*, edited by Gloria T. Hull, Patricia Bell Scott, and Barbara Smith. New York: Feminist Press at the City University of New York, 1982. 85–92.

Shange, Ntozake. *Betsey Brown*. New York: St. Martin's Press, 1985.

———. *Daddy Says*. New York: Simon and Schuster, 2003.

———. *A Daughter's Geography*. New York: St. Martin's Press, 1983.

———. *for colored girls who have considered suicide / when the rainbow is enuf*. New York: Macmillan, 1975.

———. *From Okra to Greens*. St. Paul, MN: Coffee House, 1984.

———. *If I Can Cook / You Know God Can*. Boston: Beacon Press, 1998.

———. *Lecture and Conversation with Angela Davis*. San Francisco State University Poetry Center, 1989.

———. *Lost in Language and Sound, Or How I Found My Way to the Arts: Essays.* New York: St. Martin's Press, 2011.

———. *Nappy Edges.* 1972. New York: St, Martin's Press, 1991.

———. *Ridin' the Moon in Texas.* New York: St. Martin's Press, 1987.

———. *Sassafrass, Cypress & Indigo.* New York: St, Martin's Press, 1982.

Shange, Ntozake, and Romare Bearden. *I Live in Music.* Singapore: Stewart, Tabori & Chang, 1994.

Shange, Ntozake, Renée Green, Lyle Ashton Harris, Marc Latamie, Homi K. Bhabha, Stuart Hall, Gilanes Tawadros, and members of the audience. "Artists' Dialogue." In *The Fact of Blackness: Frantz Fanon and Visual Representation,* edited by Alan Reed. Seattle: Bay Press, 1996. 144–65.

Shockley, Evie. *Renegade Poetics: Black Aesthetics and Formal Innovation in African American Poetry.* Iowa City: University of Iowa Press, 2011.

———. Review of *Paradise. African American Review* 33.4 (1999): 718–19.

Singh, Nikhil Pal. *Black Is a Country: Race and the Unfinished Struggle for Democracy.* Cambridge, MA: Harvard University Press, 2004.

Smethurst, James. *The Black Arts Movement: Literary Nationalism in the 1960s and 1970s.* Chapel Hill: University of North Carolina Press, 2005.

Smith, Barbara. "The Truth That Never Hurts: Black Lesbians in Fiction in the 1980s." In *Wild Women in the Whirlwind: Afra-American Culture and the Contemporary Literary Renaissance,* edited by Joanne M. Braxton and Andrée Nicola McLaughlin. New Brunswick, NJ: Rutgers University Press, 1990. 213–45.

Smith, Ethel Morgan, and Gloria Naylor. "An Interview with Gloria Naylor." *Callaloo* 23.4 (2000): 1430–39.

Smith, Valerie. *Not Just Race, Not Just Gender: Black Feminist Readings.* New York: Routledge, 1998.

Spillers, Hortense J. "'Long Time': Lost Daughters and the New 'New South.'" *boundary 2* 36.1 (2009): 149–82.

Stepto, Robert. *From Behind the Veil: A Study of Afro-American Narrative.* 2nd edition. Chicago: University of Illinois Press, 1991.

———. "Intimate Things in Place: A Conversation with Toni Morrison." 1976. In *Conversations with Toni Morrison,* edited by Danille Taylor-Guthrie. Jackson: University Press of Mississippi, 1994. 10–29.

Straight, Susan. *I Been in Sorrow's Kitchen and Licked Out All the Pots.* New York: Anchor, 1993.

Sweeney, Megan. "Racial House, Big House, Home: Contemporary Abolitionism in Toni Morrison's *Paradise.*" *Meridians* 4.2 (2004): 40–67.

Tate, Claudia. *Black Women Writers at Work.* New York: Continuum, 1983.

Taylor, Diana. *The Archive and the Repertoire: Performing Cultural Memory in the Americas.* Durham, NC: Duke University Press, 2003.

Taylor-Guthrie, Danille. Introduction to *Conversations with Toni Morrison,* edited by Danille Taylor-Guthrie. Jackson: University Press of Mississippi, 1994. vii–xiv.

Toomer, Jean. *Cane*. New York: Liveright, 1923.

Traylor, Eleanor W. "Music as Theme: The Jazz Mode in the Works of Toni Cade Bambara." In *Black Women Writers (1950–1980)*, edited by Mari Evans. New York: Anchor Books, 1984. 59–69.

———. "Re Calling the Black Woman." In *The Black Woman*, edited by Toni Cade Bambara. New York: Washington Square Press, 2005. ix–xvii.

U.S. Department of Labor, Office of Policy Planning and Research. *The Negro Family: The Case for National Action*. 1965. Ann Arbor: UMI Books on Demand, 2001.

Walker, Alice. "The Black Writer and the Southern Experience." In *In Search of Our Mothers' Gardens*. New York: Harcourt, 1983. 15–21.

———. *The Color Purple*. 1982. New York: Harcourt, 2003.

———. *Meridian*. New York: Harcourt, 1976.

———. *The Third Life of Grange Copeland*. 1970. New York: Harcourt, 2003.

Walker, David. *Appeal, in Four Articles; Together with a Preamble, to The Coloured Citizens of the World, but in Particular and Very Expressly, to Those of The United States of America*. 1829. New York: Hill and Wang, 1965.

Walkowitz, Rebecca L. "Shakespeare in Harlem: *The Norton Anthology*, 'Propaganda,' Langston Hughes." *Modern Language Quarterly* 60.4 (1999): 495–519.

Wall, Cheryl A. Introduction to *Changing Our Own Words: Essays on Criticism, Theory, and Writing by Black Women*, edited by Cheryl Wall. New Brunswick, NJ: Rutgers University Press, 1989.

———. "Toni's Obligato: Bambara and the African American Literary Tradition." In *Savoring the Salt: The Legacy of Toni Cade Bambara*, edited by Linda Janet Holmes and Cheryl A. Wall. Philadelphia: Temple University Press, 2008. 27–42.

———. *Women of the Harlem Renaissance*. Indianapolis: Indiana University Press, 1995.

———. *Worrying the Line: Black Women Writers, Lineage, and Literary Tradition*. Chapel Hill: University of North Carolina Press, 2006.

Wallace, Michelle. *Black Macho and the Myth of the Superwoman*. New York: Verso, 1990.

———. "How I Saw It Then, How I See It Now." In *Black Macho and the Myth of the Superwoman*. New York: Verso, 1990. xv–xxxviii.

Washington, Mary Helen. Afterword to *Brown Girl, Brownstones*. New York: Feminist Press at the City University of New York, 1981. 311–24.

———, ed. *Black-Eyed Susans / Midnight Birds: Stories by and about Black Women*. 1975. New York: Anchor Books, 1989.

———. "New Lives and New Letters: Black Women Writers at the End of the Seventies." *College English*. 43.1 (1981): 1–11.

Waxman, Barbara Frey. "The Widow's Journey to Self and Roots: Aging and Society in Paule Marshall's *Praisesong for the Widow*." *Frontiers: A Journal of Women Studies* 9.3 (1987): 94–99.

White, Deborah Gray. *Too Heavy a Load: Black Women in Defense of Themselves 1894–1994*. New York: Norton, 1999.

Whitehead, Colson. *The Intuitionist*. New York: Random House, 1999.

———. *Sag Harbor*. New York: Doubleday, 2009.

Wilentz, Gay. *Binding Cultures: Black Women Writers in Africa and the Diaspora*. Bloomington: Indiana University Press, 1992.

Williams, Brett. "The South in the City." *Journal of Popular Culture* 16.3 (1982): 30–41.

Williams, John, trans. "Return of a Native Daughter: An Interview with Paule Marshall and Maryse Condé." *Sage* 3:2 (1986): 52–53.

Willis, Susan. "Eruptions of Funk: Historicizing Toni Morrison." *Black American Literature Forum* 16.1 (1982): 34–42.

———. *Specifying: Black Women Writing the American Experience*. Madison: University of Wisconsin Press, 1987.

Witt, Doris. *Black Hunger: Food and the Politics of U.S. Identity*. New York: Oxford University Press, 1999.

# Index

Achebe, Chinua, 187n33
African American cultural nationalism:
1960s contours of, 8; African diaspora
literature, 4, 11; archiving as practice
of, 132–39; bicentennial and, 144,
199n3; color-blind politics and, 181–82;
common ties, 12–13; Communist Party
and, 185n18; cookbooks and, 82–85;
diaspora and, 11–12, 90, 96, 98–99,
101–2, 104; explorations of alternative
homelands, 120, 185n18; folktales, 5, 6;
geography, space and, 10–11, 23, 53–55,
67, 108, 110, 112–18, 149–54, 171–72,
175–76; homophobia and, 14; inner
nation and, 44, 45, 60, 134–35; literary
anthologies and, 4, 10, 16–24, 186–
87n33; literary genres and, 5; mapping
and, 112–13; masculinist ideology of,
5, 14–16, 34–36, 39–41, 71–76; Naylor's
definition of, 112; portability of, 111,
114, 121–22, 123–31; possibilities and
dangers of, 13, 182; in post-civil rights
years, 180–81; segregated communities
and, 148, 149–54, 171–72, 200–201n16;
self-governance concept and, 12; as
set of practices or rituals, 31, 43–44,
55–56, 67, 84–85, 90, 98–105, 107–8, 112,
118–19, 137–38, 170, 173, 174; South as
homeland concept, 53–54, 76–82, 90–96,
113–31, 128–30, 192n12, 194n12; theory
vs. practice, 174; twenty-first century

visions of, 178–79, 181–82; women's
revisions to, 1, 5–7, 14–24, 176–77;
women's work as key to, 173, 180–82
African American Exceptionalism,
concept of, 175, 176, 182
African American literature: increasing
acceptance of, 177–78; literacy
narratives in, 143–44; male writers'
influences on women's works, 179;
marginality of same-sex relationships
in, 14; masculinist ideology in, 5,
14–16; memoir genre in, 203–4n1;
novels as theory, 29–32, 174; oral/
written binary in, 8–9, 174, 184n11,
193n2, 197n8; polyvocality in, 5, 9, 15,
17, 23, 161, 183–84n7; readers' work,
179–80; shift in narrative subjects,
14–16; single-name titles in 1970s, 14,
185n21; textual healing process, 37–38,
41; women's revisions to narrative,
174–76, 187–88n38
African American women: collectives
and, 2–3, 22, 134–35, 137–38, 194n8;
feminism and, 1–2, 9–10, 17–18,
20, 173; inscribing of stories about,
141–44; matriarchal structure and, 18;
necessity of women-centered ritual
and community for, 118–19; work of,
2, 180–82
Als, Hilton: *New Yorker* profile of
Morrison, 199n5

Middle Passage, references to: as layer of meaning, 185n23, 189–90n20; in *Mama Day*, 131; in Morrison's *Beloved*, 29; in *Paradise*, 171; in *Praisesong for the Widow*, 97–98, 104; in *The Salt Eaters*, 46, 53; in *Sassafrass, Cypress & Indigo*, 72, 77–78

Montgomery, Maxine Lavon, 135

Moretti, Franco: *Atlas of the European Novel 1800–1900*, 6–7

Morrison, Toni: appearance in Reed's *Reckless Eyeballing*, 184n15; *Beloved*, 9–10, 29, 142, 161, 185n23, 186n23, 200n11, 202n35; binary divisions resisted by, 174; *The Bluest Eye*, 160–61, 163–64, 185n22, 188n38, 196n4; on childhood in Lorain, Ohio, 203n40; "City Limits, Village Values," 200n13, 202n38; dissent and complexity in works of, 22; as editor for Bambara's *Those Bones Are Not My Child*, 45; Gates's views on, 187–88n38; *Home*, 199n7; importance of, 177; individuality in novels of, 16; inscription as theme in works by, 199n7; *Jazz*, 200n11; local practices/rituals portrayed by, 24, 177; *Love*, 199n3, 200n14, 201n28; male criticism of, 9–10; *A Mercy*, 145, 161, 168, 170, 182; on narration's importance to nation, 6, 7; neighborhoods viewed by, 149; *New Yorker* profile of, 199n5; Nobel Prize one by, 177; novel as active force for, 169; polyvocality in novels of, 161; as Random House editor, 4, 178; "Recitatif," 202n31; "Rootedness," 169, 202n38; SEEK Program and, 183n3; on sexism in black power movement, 151; *Song of Solomon*, 45, 120, 128, 149, 161, 195n17, 199n7; *Sula*, 20, 26–27, 148, 149, 150–51, 161, 185n22, 194n7; *Tar Baby*, 202n32; as theorist of identity, 4. *See also Paradise* (Morrison)

Mosley, Walter, 178

mothering as women's work, 26–27; African American men's views of, 48–49; Bambara's portrayal of, 48–50; Morrison's portrayal of, 199–200n8; Naylor's portrayal of, 135; Shange's portrayals of, 80–82, 192n14

Moynihan, Daniel, congressional report (1965), 17–18, 180

Murray, Albert, 27; *Train Whistle Guitar*, 187n37

Murray, Rolland: *Our Living Manhood*, 5, 22, 183n6, 186n30

nation: African Americans' creation of, 10–11, 12–13, 90; African Americans' movement away from, 175–76; anthologies and, 21; in Bambara's *The Salt Eaters*, 35, 43–50; collaboration between, 106–7; inner nation distinguished from, 7, 44; neighborhood and, 149–54; novel's importance in defining, 6–7; as term, 3, 13, 83–84

National Association for the Advancement of Colored People (NAACP), 2, 3

National Association of Colored Women, 41, 134–35

Naylor, Gloria: *1996*, 91–92, 203–4n1; *Bailey's Cafe*, 129–30; binary divisions resisted by, 174; Civil Rights movement viewed by, 4; cultural nationalism defined by, 176–77; dissent and complexity in works of, 22; "Finding Our Voice," 114; individuality in novels of, 16; *Linden Hills*, 27–28, 82, 132–33, 137, 198n15; local practices/rituals portrayed by, 24, 177, 180; "Love and Sex in the Afro-American Novel," 199n21; novels of, 1; Sea Islands in works of, 91, 113–18, 130–31; as theorist of identity, 4; *The Women of Brewster Place*, 14, 137, 196n1. *See also Mama Day* (Naylor)

Neal, Larry, 3; "The Black Arts Movement," 16; *Black Fire* (with Baraka), 8, 17

*Negro Family, The: The Case for National Action* (Moynihan congressional report), 17–18, 180

*Norton Anthology of African American Literature*, 10, 21

Nugent, Richard Bruce, 5

Obama, Barack, election of, 181

Olaniyan, Tejumola, 70, 191n4

Olmsted, Jane, 99–100, 194n11

organizing as women's work, 8, 180; Bambara's portrayal of, 8, 23, 24, 33,

Smith, Valerie, 188n39
Spillers, Hortense J., 200n10, 203n41
Stepto, Robert: *From Behind the Veil,* 143;
    *Chant of Saints* (with Harper), 187n33;
    "Intimate Things in Place," 149
storytelling as women's work, 78, 87–88,
    110–11, 125
Student Nonviolent Coordinating
    Committee (SNCC), 2, 3, 188n3

*Tales and Stories for Black Folk* (anthology
    edited by Bambara), 4
Tate, Claudia: *Black Women Writers at
    Work,* 44, 69, 81
Taylor, Diana: *The Archive and the
    Repertoire,* 28
Taylor-Guthrie, Danille, 159
Terrell, Mary Church, 3, 41
textual healing process, 37–38, 41, 188n7
Toomer, Jean: "Avey," 9; *Cane,* 53, 85, 91,
    179, 194n7; literary style of, 5
Traylor, Eleanor, 177, 186n33; "Music as
    Theme," 45, 46; "Re Calling the Black
    Woman," 189n10

Universal Negro Improvement
    Association, 183n1

Walcott, Derek, 187n33
Walker, Alice: appearance in Reed's *Reckless
    Eyeballing,* 184n15; "The Black Writer
    and the Southern Experience," 53, 92,
    194n12; *The Color Purple,* 9; "Everyday
    Use," 184n12; fiction by, 16, 187n33;
    Gates's views on, 187–88n38; importance
    of, 177; *Meridian,* 20, 184n12; novels of,
    15; recipes viewed by, 65; *In Search of Our
    Mothers' Gardens,* 179, 184n12; *The Third
    Life of Grange Copeland,* 20
Walker, David, 3, 13; *Appeal, in Four
    Articles,* 113–14, 175; ideology of, 19

Walker, Margaret: *Jubilee,* 185n23
Wall, Cheryl A., 10, 188n6; introduction
    to *Changing Our Own Words,* 176–77;
    *Savoring the Salt* (with Holmes), 43;
    "Toni's Obligato," 60; *Worrying the
    Line,* 103, 106, 110–11, 117, 118, 119,
    131–32, 193n4, 194–95n13
Washington, Mary Helen, 87, 177, 195n15;
    *Black-Eyed Susans,* 195–96n23
Watkins, Mel: "Sexism, Racism and Black
    Women Writers," 184n13
Waxman, Barbara, 96
Wells, Ida B., 3
Wheatley, Phillis, 3, 186–87n33
White, Deborah Gray, 35, 41, 134–35; *Too
    Heavy a Load,* 138
Whitehead, Colson: *The Intuitionist,* 178,
    179; *John Henry Days,* 10; *Sag Harbor,*
    197n11
Wideman, John Edgar, 197n5; "The
    Healing of Velma Henry," 189n9
Wilentz, Gay, 92
Williams, Brett, 197–98n12
Williams, Sherley Anne, 16; *Dessa Rose,*
    185–86n23, 188n7
Willis, Susan, 188n41; "Eruptions of
    Funk," 161; *Specifying,* 38, 42, 53, 87,
    190n21
Winfrey, Oprah, 177
Witt, Doris, 70, 73, 80–81; *Black Hunger,*
    192n10
women's work: of African Americans,
    2, 8–9, 23, 24–29, 30; civil rights
    movement and, 34–35, 41–42, 134–35,
    188n2; as enhancement, 31–32; as term,
    1–2
"woodshedding" metaphor, 194n12
Wright, Richard, 3; *Black Boy,* 46; realism
    of, 5
writing as women's work, 30–31, 44–45,
    180